TERROR ON THE AIR!

TERROR ON THE AIR!
Horror Radio in America, 1931–1952

RICHARD J. HAND

WITH A FOREWORD BY DAVID KOGAN

McFarland & Company, Inc., Publishers
Jefferson, North Carolina, and London

The present work is a reprint of the illustrated case bound edition of Terror on the Air! Horror Radio in America, 1931–1952, *first published in 2006 by McFarland.*

LIBRARY OF CONGRESS CATALOGUING-IN-PUBLICATION DATA

Hand, Richard J.
Terror on the air! : horror radio in America, 1931–1952 /
Richard J. Hand ; with a foreword by David Kogan.
p.   cm.
Includes bibliographical references and index.

ISBN 978-0-7864-6919-2
softcover : acid free paper ∞

1. Horror radio programs—United States—History.   I. Title.
PN1991.8.H66H36   2012   791.44'616409730904 — dc22   2005025351

BRITISH LIBRARY CATALOGUING DATA ARE AVAILABLE

© 2006 Richard J. Hand. All rights reserved

No part of this book may be reproduced or transmitted in any form or by any means, electronic or mechanical, including photocopying or recording, or by any information storage and retrieval system, without permission in writing from the publisher.

On the cover: Agnes Moorehead in the '40s and '50s radio play "Sorry, Wrong Number" (Photofest)

Manufactured in the United States of America

*McFarland & Company, Inc., Publishers
Box 611, Jefferson, North Carolina 28640
www.mcfarlandpub.com*

To Sadiyah, Shara and Danya,
who were always happy to listen with me...

Contents

Acknowledgments viii
Radio and the Power of Imagination: A Foreword by David Kogan 1
Preface 3
Terror on the Air: An Introduction 5

CHAPTER 1. Horror Beyond Horror: Horror Radio in the Golden Age of American Broadcasting 13

CHAPTER 2. Hosts and Music, Sound and Silence: Narrative Techniques and Formal Strategies in Horror Radio 23

CHAPTER 3. The Cult of the Actor: Acting and Genre in Horror Radio of the Golden Age 38

CHAPTER 4. The Grandmother of Horror Radio: Alonzo Deen Cole and *The Witch's Tale* (1931–1938) 69

CHAPTER 5. The Ultimate in Horror: *Lights Out* (1934–1947), Arch Oboler and Horror 83

CHAPTER 6. Exploring Horror Form and Genre: *The Hermit's Cave* (1935–1944) 106

CHAPTER 7. The Paradigm of Horror Radio: Himan Brown and *Inner Sanctum Mysteries* (1941–1952) 118

CHAPTER 8. The Eclectic Horrors of Robert A. Arthur and David Kogan: *The Mysterious Traveler* (1943–1952) 131

CHAPTER 9. The Unsettling Universe of Wyllis Cooper and Ernest Chappell: *Quiet, Please* (1947–1949) 145

CHAPTER 10. Conclusion 162

Bibliography 169
Index 177

Acknowledgments

I would like to thank the Arts and Humanities Research Board for a grant to support the research and completion of this book. A very special thank you is owed to David Kogan, one of the great writers in the history of radio drama, who read through some of my preliminary work with such enthusiasm and wrote the foreword to this book. To have David Kogan's active involvement was a profound honor. This book exists thanks to the kindness and patience of some of the greatest authorities on old-time radio drama. In particular, I would like to thank Martin Grams, Jr., and David S. Siegel for reading through sample chapters and offering enlightening feedback. I would also like to thank some of the academic giants of radio studies: Professor Michele Hilmes (University of Wisconsin–Madison), Dr. Frank Chorba (Washburn University) and Professor Andrew Crisell (University of Sunderland), who all greeted my research topic with advice and encouragement. Thanks, too, are due to old-time radio scholars and enthusiasts, especially Howard Blue and the custodians of the *Quiet, Please* website, who were supportive. A special thank you is owed to Mike and Ernestine Thomas, and to Don Dean, who were extremely generous in their support by providing invaluable information or materials. I would also like to thank Corey Klemow (director of the Sacred Fools Theater Company) and Michael Ross, son of the great Miriam Wolfe, for their helpful insights. I would like to thank Michael Henry and all the staff at the Library of American Broadcasting at the University of Maryland. Mike Henry and his colleagues are organized and knowledgeable and were invaluable in optimizing my time at the archives and instrumental in helping this book find its final shape. At the University of Glamorgan, I would like to thank my colleagues Mary Traynor (who, by the time this book reaches print, will have been a collaborator in the live reconstruction of old-time radio in the GTFM broadcast studios), Professor Mike Wilson, Professor Steve Blandford, Diana Brand, Sam Boardman-Jacobs, Katja Krebs and Daryl Perrins for listening to me get overexcited about old-time radio; Mike Davies and his colleagues at Media Resources at the University of Glamorgan for his invaluable assistance in assembling and processing the photographic images in this book; and my students who reconstructed live radio in the drama studio with such passion. Special thanks go to my mother for raising me to be a natural radio listener, and to Professor Don Rude, who sparked my interest in American old-time radio and steered me in the right direction. As ever and always, my love and gratitude go to Sadiyah, Shara and Danya.—R.J.H.

Radio and the Power of Imagination: A Foreword by David Kogan

While audiences in theaters react to horror films with nervous laughter, tensing of bodies, and closing of eyes, there is always the comfort of the surrounding audience.

To listeners of a gripping radio play, particularly in a darkened room, the imagination can take over — sometimes with dramatic consequences.

This was borne out on the night of October 30, 1938. It was on that memorable night that Orson Welles brought to the air his dramatization of H. G. Wells' *The War of the Worlds*. As the program unfolded, it was interrupted by a series of realistic-sounding news announcements of a landing on Earth by a hostile invasion force of Martians armed with deadly "ray guns." The invaders had landed in Grover's Mill, a small (fictional) New Jersey town, spreading death and destruction. During this broadcast, some of the millions listening panicked, believing they were hearing an actual news account of Martian invaders. Many New Jerseyites fled their homes, bringing about street riots and traffic jams. Phone calls swamped the police. It was mass hysteria. The panic kept spreading until officials of the network went on the air to explain to listeners that "War of the Worlds" was just a radio program.

Never was the power of radio to engage human imagination so evident.

I had been hooked on radio since I spent my savings on a crystal set in 1930. In the years of the Depression, radio was an escape for millions of people, and it magically transported people out of the darkness that surrounded them. "War of the Worlds" transported many listeners from darkness into panic. By that time, I was a freelance writer myself, writing for *The Shadow*, *The Adventures of the Thin Man* and *Bulldog Drummond*.

In 1940 I met Bob Arthur, and our first collaboration was *The Mysterious Traveler*, a series of thirty-minute dramas in the broad genre of mystery. The listeners would hear the eerie whistling of a train, then find themselves in the company of the regular host — a mysterious traveler on a train — who would frame each self-contained story. We successfully pitched the idea to Mutual, who contracted us to write, produce and direct weekly scripts and also provide the cast. For their part, as well as broadcasting the show, Mutual would provide the studio, engineer, soundman, organist and announcer. In the subsequent nine years we produced some 450 scripts exploring genres such as horror, science fiction, suspense and fantasy. Mutual gave us complete freedom as to the themes and contents of our scripts, an almost unique privilege perhaps comparable only with Arch Oboler on *Lights Out*.

Bob and I would spend one day a week developing ideas, with me at a desk with pen and paper and Bob lying on a couch. When we had a complete story outline, either Bob or I would write the dialogue. I was always the director and Bob the producer. On the day of broadcast, the cast and I would gather around a table in the studio. We would read through the script. After this we would have a first-time read through on microphone, with myself and the engineer in the control booth. After this, there would be a second run-through with sound and music, with numerous pauses for level settings, sound balance and directorial notes on interpretation. After a short break, the announcer would arrive and we would do a complete dress rehearsal. Timing was critical at this stage: if the show ran over 29½ minutes I would adjust the script accordingly.

We were always interested in the mail we received from listeners all over the country. We usually received a dozen to thirty letters a week, but some shows brought in hundreds of letters. We would do our best to read them and send off a reply. The letters about *The Mysterious Traveler* ranged from admiration to disbelief. Some inquisitive minds had queries on the plot, and there was considerable fan mail for the man behind the voice of the mysterious traveler, Maurice Tarplin.

I am proud to have made a contribution to the golden age of radio drama and to have personally explored the power of radio to engage the human imagination. Looking back at those times, I cannot imagine any other profession that would have been as interesting.

Frankly, I was a little amazed by Richard Hand's passion for our "horror" broadcasts made decades ago in the United States. Were he a native of this fair land, or had the shows been broadcast in Britain, I could understand. How a thirty-something academic in the valleys of Wales acquired so much knowledge of American old-time radio begins to shape up as the makings of a new *Mysterious Traveler* script...

Preface

Horror has always pervaded popular culture. The first stories we are told as children abound with horror: fairy tales are replete with wicked witches and big bad wolves, and usually explore death and anxiety. Horror is a key genre across many media: the rise of the novel saw Gothic horror fiction emerge as a central genre, and, more recently, the development of the computer game soon witnessed horror games becoming a staple feature. However, in the academic field of horror studies, film has enjoyed a hegemonic position. This has meant that whole fields of study have been comparatively marginalized or ignored: the horror genre in television, theater, comics, carnival rides, board games, computer games and even popular fiction has been just as formative for many people—filmmakers included—and is equally worthy of analysis. Horror radio is the most unjustifiably neglected. Aside from the occasional reference—such as Kim Newman's comment that *The Mercury Theater on the Air*'s adaptation of *Dracula* "remains one of the best adaptations of the novel in any medium" (Newman, 1996, 264)—horror radio has been doomed to silence.

I have a natural sympathy for the underdog, and, although a horror movie fan, in my research I have endeavored to explore the more marginal fields of horror culture. Knowing my interest, an academic friend (who listened to old-time radio first time around) suggested that I should investigate golden age horror and suspense. I dutifully bought a Smithsonian collection of archive recordings, and when I listened to this plundered tomb of horror, I was amazed. It exuded, like nothing else I had ever consumed, the thrill of terror. It brought back memories: I remembered my mother describing the experience of listening to a BBC radio adaptation of Poe's "The Tell-Tale Heart" in the 1930s as the most terrifying experience of her childhood, far more frightening than anything the Second World War put her through. I rapidly became an avid listener and collector.

Giving the recordings a more academic scrutiny, it is clear that it is not just horror radio that has suffered; as a whole, the medium has, as Michele Hilmes remarks, "gone remarkably unstudied" (Hilmes, 2002a, 2), condemned to be an "anachronistic embarrassment, the discarded chrysalis" (Hilmes, 2002a, 8) before the triumph of television and film. Similarly, for John Dunning the era of live radio is a "lost art" (Dunning, 1998, xii).

This has obviously had far-reaching implications for the academic study of radio, although things have improved immeasurably since 1982 when James L. Baughman lamented that works on American broadcasting have been written by "the book world's mass cultural 'schlockmasters'" (Baughman, 1982, 195). Radio studies may still be overwhelmed by the dominance of film and, increasingly, television studies, but it is nonetheless enjoying great advancement as a field, with impressive explorations informed by the theoretical discipline of historical, sociological and communications analysis. The study of radio has also been immeasurably enhanced by technological advancements which have increased access to, and therefore contributed to a growing interest in, golden age radio.

This book is the first full-length study of the broad genre of horror radio in the golden age of American broadcasting. The "golden age" is a term with an unfortunately nostalgic register—rather like the equivalent phrase of "old-time radio"—but is taken to mean, very broadly speaking, the period of American radio from the late 1920s to the mid–1950s, before network radio's demise in the early 1960s. This book focuses on the period from 1931 to 1952 simply because those are key dates in relation to the six case studies included here: from the first broadcast of *The Witch's Tale* (May 28, 1931) to the last broadcast of *Inner Sanctum Mysteries* (October 5, 1952). Readers will find that other radio plays from beyond this cut-off point will be referred to, including works pertaining to the related genres of suspense thrillers, crime dramas and science fiction. Similarly, the six case studies were not the only horror programs on the air in the golden age: *Mystery in the Air*, *The Mollé Mystery Theatre*, *The Weird Circle*, *The Haunting Hour*, *Sleep No More*, *Creeps by Night*, *Nightmare*, *The Hall of Fantasy* and many others are all fine examples of horror radio in their own right, but limited space means that only passing reference can be made to a few of them.

The vast majority of the plays studied in this book are unpublished and exist in recordings that vary in quality. Many of the plays are formulaic and easily classified into categories such as killers on the loose, revenge from before or beyond the grave, Transylvanian monsters, abused science and so on. It is fair to say that most listeners—including the original ones—have recognized the plays' formulaic nature. However, the delivery of these plays is another matter. These were performed by live actors and technicians, and the plays retain all the excitement and fervor of a theatrical performance. As an academic of theater and media drama, my interest is in horror radio as a dramatic form. I will analyze the scripts and the methodology of live radio drama as a form of performance practice. I will also provide details of historical contextualization.

I take this opportunity to apologize for any inaccuracies in this book. The dates inserted after the title of a radio play are, to the best of my knowledge, accurate and refer to the date of first broadcast, as well as, in some cases, revivals. More perilously, old-time radio has, as Jim Harmon says, "the most negligent historical documentation of all popular art forms" (Harmon, 1967, 14). For this reason, it is a territory that abounds with myths and fallacies, and I apologize if this book serves to perpetuate any.

In the cinema experience, the moment when the lights dim to darkness is sometimes the most thrilling moment. Horror radio perpetually inhabits that thrilling darkness, waiting for us to listen. We shall now let the dusty crystal radio sets warm up and bring the long dead voices of golden age horror radio back to life to menace us once more as we tune in to the terrors of the air.

Terror on the Air:
An Introduction

Radio is older than television but younger than cinema. By the time of the introduction of radio in the 1920s and its subsequent phenomenal ascendancy, Hollywood had already established itself as the dream factory of American identity. However, in the domestic environment, the living space of the listener, radio was king. From the 1930s through the 1950s, people lived their lives by the sound of radio. The family crowded around a massive wooden set, and the adolescent alone in the bedroom tuning a home-made crystal set, are potent images of the domestic status of, and personal relationship with, radio. In *Theatre Arts* (May 1952), Harriet van Horne informs us that 43 million out of the 44,779,000 households in America are "radio families."

Radio also infused people's lives beyond their closed doors: as Donna L. Halper reminds us, as early as "1938 over four million cars had radios" (Halper, 2001, 89), and the presence of radio in public space forever changed the auditory and social environment of America. Radio had become the preeminent communication media. Its immediacy and potential for eyewitness testimony "as events occur," and its international outreach, made it essential in news, information and, indeed, propaganda broadcasting. It is often said that Vietnam was the first television war; if so, we should describe the Second World War as the first radio war. The radio broadcasts of news and political statements were the key source of information and played a central role in the definition of the war experience.

When radio was on, it was *live*. This means that radio produced a phenomenal amount of material. Although it was possible to revive a script for rebroadcast, it was rare; Arch Oboler said that no play was repeated unless it was "extraordinarily excellent" (*New York Times*, July 23, 1939). Live broadcasting was a deliberate policy on the part of the major networks. As David Morton explains:

> NBC and CBS actively discouraged a viable technological alternative to the
> live network, the transcription disk recording, and denounced recordings as an
> inferior form of culture. These networks went so far as to adopt antirecording

policies, and virtually banned the use of recording equipment in their own studios [Morton, 2000, 72].

Almost all broadcasting was live, although recordings such as phonograph records had an important role in short announcements and some sound effects. Moreover, transcription recordings had been invaluable for local stations since the early 1930s. For the major networks, prerecorded programs did not increasingly become standard until the postwar period with the introduction of recording tape. As Leonard Maltin reveals, Bing Crosby's *Philco Radio Time* sparked a revolution by being "the first taped program on network radio, in 1946" (Maltin, 2000, 293): Crosby wanted the freedoms that prerecording offered both personally (shows could be recorded at the most convenient time) and aesthetically (the chance to edit). In time, prerecording would become standard practice.

From the beginnings of American radio in the 1920s, the medium quickly created and developed a number of distinctive and original genres. Remarkably, many of these genres and formats were not merely adopted by television in its postwar ascendancy, but remain unchanged in the twenty-first century. Contemporary news and current affairs coverage, political reportage and sports broadcasting continue to use formats that have not changed radically since the pioneering experiments of radio. Similarly, distinct genres of popular entertainment, such as quiz shows, soap operas, situation comedies, crime drama and serialized drama, were all invented by radio. The medium was also instrumental in conveying and creating defining moments of American identity, which the haze of time can make it difficult to understand: *Amos 'n' Andy* (1926–1960) enjoyed massive and sustained popularity the scale of which we struggle to comprehend; Joe Louis' legendary and emblematic defeat of Max Schmeling (June 22, 1938) reached millions through Clem McCarthy's ringside commentary. President Franklin D. Roosevelt's "Fireside Chats" (some thirty broadcasts from 1933 until his death in 1945) were an innovative experiment, the astuteness of which would forever change the nature of political broadcasting, for, as Anthony Slide comments, "all of the president's greatest speeches were on radio" (Slide, 1982, 94). Arguably, these major events are frequently divorced from the medium that gave them their immediacy and impact. Certain indelible "radio moments" still remain in the popular imagination, such as the real life horror of Herbert Morrison's eyewitness account of the Hindenburg airship disaster on May 6, 1937 (although even this has typically become the soundtrack to the newsreel footage). However, the single most famous radio event is the one singled out by David Kogan in his foreword to this volume: *The Mercury Theater on the Air*'s "War of the Worlds" broadcast (October 30, 1938).

The radio adaptation of H. G. Wells' *The War of the Worlds* (1898) was written by John Houseman and Howard Koch, but it made its actor-director, the twenty-one-year-old Orson Welles, an international celebrity and provided him with his ticket to Hollywood. It is a landmark in the history of popular culture and stands as fascinatingly tangible proof of the potential impact of performance. Of course, there are stories of the furor that greeted the plays of Henrik Ibsen, the music of Arnold Schoenberg, and the films of Luis Buñuel, but there is nothing so widespread and potentially insurrectional as the *Mercury Theater*'s H. G. Wells adaptation. Radio had invaded the American home as ruthlessly as the Martians had invaded Earth. Historians calculate that some six million heard the CBS broadcast; 1.7 million believed the events to be true, and 1.2 million were "genuinely frightened" (Dunning, 1998, 454). It is worth noting, however, that this was a comparatively small audience: some thirty million were listening to *The Edgar Bergen and Charlie McCarthy Show* on a rival channel (NBC). Despite the fact that it was clearly announced that the broadcast was an adaptation of H. G. Wells, the damage had been done, and hundreds of thousands took to the streets in panic.

The combined notoriety and success of the "War of the Worlds" broadcast was instantaneous and evident to all at CBS as soon as police officers began to flood the studio twenty minutes into *Mercury Theater*'s one-hour broadcast. The broadcast soon became legendary, partly because of remarkable follow-up broadcasts, such as Orson Welles' meeting and discussion with H. G. Wells on KTSA (October 28, 1940), during which Welles reveals that Adolf Hitler referred to the "War of the Worlds" hysteria in a major speech in Munich as evidence of the decadence and corrupt condition of democracy. In the American press, there were some 12,500 newspaper articles in the first three weeks after "War of the Worlds" was broadcast (Douglas, 1999, 165), and there were frequent references to the broadcast in other radio shows of the period. The responses may have ranged from outrage to hilarity, but the broadcast had important consequences for American radio: after "War of the Worlds," as Susan J. Douglas informs us, "Dramatizations of simulated news bulletins became verboten" (Douglas, 1999, 165), while, according to Gerald Nachman, "many didn't believe the announcement of the attack on Pearl Harbor three years later because of the Martian landing hoax" (Nachman, 1998, 445). The controversy of the broadcast is somewhat ironic when one considers that *The Mercury Theater on the Air* had been commissioned by CBS "to ward off federal investigations into radio's overcommercialization" (Hilmes, 2002a, 104). But the legal impact of the "War of the Worlds" broadcast did not prevent it being imitated, albeit tangentially. A good example is "Twelve to Five" (*Quiet, Please*, April 12, 1948), a radio play in which a disc jockey plays popular tunes and begins to announce imminent crimes and deaths, including, ultimately, his own. The play is a clear example of fantasy, but it did not prevent "the Mutual switchboard [being] jammed by callers requesting their favorite songs" (Dunning, 1998, 559). It is rather amusing that ten years after "War of the Worlds" the *Quiet, Please* audience would seem to have been more anxious to request their personal choice of music than perturbed by the gruesome horror story "realistically" unfurling before them.

There are many reasons why *Mercury Theater*'s "War of the Worlds" was so effective. Orson Welles said the hysteria demonstrated that he had underestimated "the extent of our American lunatic fringe" (quoted in Nachman, 1998, 447). But rather than patronize the past unduly, it is worth remembering that 1938 America was a post-depression nation in a global context that was governed by paranoia: an empire like Japan threatened to expand aggressively, as did the sinister fascist regimes in Germany and Italy, while the values of an old world imperialist such as Britain seemed to jostle with the revolutionary ideology of Stalin's Soviet Union. It was an age of anxiety, in which the idea of invasion from any quarter — even from outer space — would not have seemed surprising.

But "War of the Worlds" is also a triumphant example of radio form. The broadcast exploits the listener's imagination in the way that only radio can: the mixture of anchorman in the studio, reporters and eyewitnesses at the scene of the incidents give the play not merely a technical verisimilitude, but a sense of global crisis in the imagination of the listener. As Jim Harmon writes, Welles' Martians "were certainly more convincing than anything the movies have ever provided" (Harmon, 1967, 12). Similarly, it is the successful exploitation of the listener's fears that lies behind Robert L. Hilliard's claim that contemporary revivals of "War of the Worlds" on radio always result "in numerous complaints from people frightened much as the American population was decades ago" (Hilliard, 1985, 1). John Houseman and Howard Koch's script is a masterpiece of radio scriptwriting in the way that it exploits the authenticity of documentary rhetoric while utilizing the formula of classic horror and suspense narrative. If we listen to the original 1938 broadcast we can hear that Welles and the *Mercury Theater* ensemble use the Houseman and Koch script as a basis from which to deliver intense horror and suspense performances. Houseman himself pays special homage to Welles' performance and directorial decisions:

> The reason that show worked as well as it did was ... nerve ... the slowness of the show in the beginning. Those credible pauses were maintained, and Orson really stretched those. The reason the show works as it does is that the acceleration is very carefully calculated and is quite extraordinary; that is why by the time you are twenty minutes into the show you are moving hours at a time ... and no one even noticed [quoted in Maltin, 2000, 81].

The broadcast also succeeds because of its consistent immediacy: the music, sound effects, silences and hesitations throughout the play are as important as its blatant screams of hysteria and the story itself. For critics such as Erik Barnouw, the achievement of the *Mercury Theater* broadcasts may have reached its controversial apogee in "War of the Worlds," but it is just one episode in a truly revolutionary series:

> While the public remembers the *Mercury Theater on the Air* chiefly because of the Martian invasion, the series was far more important in its general impact on radio writing. Most of the broadcasts were in the first person singular. Welles gave a series of brilliant demonstrations of what could be done with the device—and with narrators in general. He did much to loosen up the whole structure of radio drama [Barnouw, 1945, 2].

Orson Welles himself talks explicitly of the "first person singular" (*New York Times*, August 14, 1938) technique which, James Naremore contends, can be seen as the foundation of the "oral narrative" on radio and a simultaneous acknowledgment that the radio "was an intimate piece of living-room furniture" (Naremore, 1989, 13).

Although ostensibly an example of science fiction, *The Mercury Theater on the Air*'s "War of the Worlds" is a great moment in popular horror. The play was deliberately broadcast, after all, on the eve of Halloween, and while H. G. Wells' original novel is one of the founding works in the "speculative" tradition of science fiction, Orson Welles' broadcast functions as a key example of experiential horror. At the end of the broadcast Welles takes evident pleasure in bringing things literally down to earth: the broadcast has been "*The Mercury Theater*'s own radio version of dressing up in a sheet and jumping out of a bush and saying 'Boo!'" Although it is an innovative and a paradigmatic event in the history of radio, it is important to remember that "War of the Worlds" belongs to a tradition of horror radio. By the time of the "War of the Worlds" broadcast, horror radio was a genre already well established. Over eighteen months before the *Mercury Theater*'s Wells adaptation, *Lights Out* had broadcast "Chicken Heart" (March 10, 1937), a play in which a scientific experiment causes a pulsating chicken heart to grow exponentially until it engulfs the world. Its animation of national emergency and mass panic in a recognizably contemporary context make it an unmistakable precursor to "War of the Worlds."

Radio drama as a whole had started in Britain in the early 1920s with the BBC's full-length radio production of Shakespeare's *Twelfth Night* (May 28, 1923), which the corporation followed with what is usually taken to be the world's first play written specifically for radio, Richard Hughes' *A Comedy of Danger* (January 15, 1924). Hughes' play, a thriller set in a coal mine during a power cut, demonstrates how suspense was not merely a generic choice in radio drama, but it was there from the form's inauguration. As a specific genre, horror radio came into being in America.

There were a few isolated examples of suspense and horror drama in the 1920s, but the first fully fledged horror program was *The Witch's Tale*, which premiered on WOR on May 28, 1931. The program was created by Alonzo Deen Cole and featured a host called Old Nancy, the witch of Salem, as framing narrator. The series was an immediate success, and within a few years a vast number of radio shows followed in the wake of *The Witch's Tale*. Martin Grams, Jr., argues that there was a palpable shift to horror because it became evident that "radio listeners favored spine-chilling terrors over situation comedies" (Grams, 2002, 26). Undoubtedly, radio cashed in on the popular taste for horror with its own take on Transylvania, most familiar in the 1930s Universal Pictures horror movies (another "golden age" of popular horror).

In some ways, film and radio had a symbiotic relationship, sharing and echoing themes—formal constraints permitting—and many of the great horror radio creators would work, at some point in their careers, in Hollywood. As a genre, however, horror radio sustained itself longer. It has often been said that after the golden age of Hollywood horror in the 1930s, a decline set in, a symptom being the prevalence of spoofs, such as the *Abbott and Costello Meets...* movies of the 1940s and early 1950s. Film horror relocated its base in the real and psychological horrors of film noir. Horror radio is also manifest in the medium's equivalent dramatic genres of crime and thriller, but the more fantastical side to horror can also be seen as carrying on undaunted. Old-time radio has its own fair share of horror spoofs, but the more earnest examples of horror radio take the genre to new levels of sophistication, as is to be found in Wyllis Cooper's *Quiet, Please* (1947–49) or Arch Oboler's politically conscious wartime run of *Lights Out* (1942–43).

Once a popular penchant for horror had been demonstrated, American radio listeners of the golden age had a daily choice in specific horror listening, as well as many crime, thriller and suspense programs that occasionally strayed unambiguously into the domain of horror. As Grams states, by the late 1940s, "U.S. radio ... fired at least 80 programs of horror and bloodcurdling adventure at its listeners every week" (Grams, 2002, 34). Many of these programs shared generic traits, but all attempted to put an individual stamp on their broadcasts: whether it was through the use of a host-character indelibly associated with a program or episode-specific character-narrators, or the use of classical music or extemporized dramatic chords, such features of the "packaging" of horror radio had major commercial and aesthetic implications.

Horror as a genre is not as easy to define as one might think. "What is horror?" asks Charles Weigl. "That is a dangerously misleading question. We should ask instead, what isn't" (Weigl, 2002, 717). For the author of this book, the experiential dynamic is important: plays that are uncanny or violent in theme, and unfurl their plots in a way that exploits a variety of the available formal strategies and dramatic techniques of suspense, qualify as horror. All the same, although several thousand horror radio plays were broadcast during the golden age of radio, we could probably sort them all into a handful of categories that adhere to the formulaic conventions of horror or suspense narrative which critics such as Noël Carroll (1990) or Martin Rubin (1999) have endeavored to establish. The heroic, vulnerable or foolhardy protagonists of horror radio drama find themselves pitted against vampires, werewolves and other monsters, as well as the most arcane witches and the most revolutionary mad scientists. But even if there is homogeneity in narrative construction in the horror plays, issues of genre can nonetheless be complicated. As well as belonging to the obvious traditions of popular horror, radio also inhabited the same domain as film noir, and produced some of its greatest horror work in the "radio noir" worlds of *Suspense* and countless other crime, detective and mystery series—tales abounding with escaped lunatics, cold-blooded murderers and brutal, eerie mysteries. Sometimes episodes of *Suspense*—such as its adaptation of H. P. Lovecraft's "The Dunwich Horror" (November 1, 1945)—clearly crossed the line into the realms of more conventional horror, while the superheroic adventures of *The Shadow* were frequently in the world of the monstrous: "The Gibbering Things" (September 26, 1943), an episode scripted by horror radio pioneer Alonzo Deen Cole, presents a Frankenstein-style scientist transplanting human brains into monkeys. Mary Shelley's *Frankenstein* (1818) and the countless reworkings and adaptations of the novel have always fallen into an area somewhere between horror and science fiction, a territory reflected in radio drama. Some of the most terrifying and compelling examples of horror radio are to be found in tales of abused science, future dystopias or alien landscapes. The formulaic and generic features of horror radio were highly distinctive and recognizable, making them a favorite target of spoofs in comedy and variety shows on old-time radio, especially around Halloween.

For the researcher, horror radio in its various guises provides a colossal body of material that exceeds, in quantity, any other area of performance horror. While the written record is perhaps not as complete as one would like—many radio broadcasts were transcribed only by chance, and hardly any scripts were retained, let alone published—we are very fortunate that some programs have a large number of recorded examples. Of some 945 episodes of *Suspense* broadcast over a twenty-year period, well over 900 still exist. Until recently it was popularly believed that there were only a handful of episodes and scripts of *Quiet, Please* in existence, but in recent years 89 recordings and all the scripts of the original 106 programs have now come to light. Less fortunately, shows like the Robert Bloch–penned series for Boris Karloff, *Stay Tuned for Terror* (1944), and most of the Wyllis Cooper period (1934–36) of *Lights Out* have yet to come to light, if recordings still exist.

With extant work, the development of computer technology has had a major and exciting impact on recordings of old-time radio, in terms of quality and quantity. Many recordings of broadcasts have been digitally remastered to near perfect quality, while

MP3 technology enables dozens of programs to be placed on a single CD. It is delightfully ironic that such developments in computer technology have been applied to the lacquer discs and early audio tapes of old-time radio. The process has opened up a monolithic archive of achievement to the listener that compels us to analyze and assess an extraordinary contribution to popular horror culture.

This study will now proceed to explore the mechanism and structure of golden age horror radio in a chapter that further appraises the significance and dynamics of the form. The subsequent chapter will analyze the narrative techniques and formal strategies employed in horror radio. This will be followed by a chapter devoted to issues of acting and genre and the cult of the horror actor. After this groundwork, the volume will present case studies that will provide close readings of six of the most significant horror series on radio: *The Witch's Tale, Lights Out, The Hermit's Cave, Inner Sanctum Mysteries, The Mysterious Traveler* and *Quiet, Please*. Each chapter will provide the reader with a critically and historically informed study of each series. After these case studies, a final chapter will look at the demise of horror radio, but will also offer an appraisal of the influence of horror radio in other forms of popular culture.

1

Horror Beyond Horror: Horror Radio in the Golden Age of American Broadcasting

Radio is sometimes labeled the "blind medium," even by some of its greatest exponents and creators—including Arch Oboler (Oboler, 1945, 308). The term is unfortunate, as it seems to imply that radio is afflicted with some deficiency, as though it were television without the pictures. The attempts to define radio drama are manifold and fascinating. For Vincent Price, the era of live radio was "a wonderful combination of the stage and movies" (Price, 1999, 111): it is like the stage because it was live, while its mass communication outreach enabled it to be accessed, like the movies, by an audience of millions. The CBS announcer who presents *The Mercury Theater on the Air*'s opening broadcast ("Dracula," July 11, 1938) claims that the series heralds Orson Welles' desire to shift from theater in order to reach a greater audience via "the Broadways of the entire United States." For Elwyn Evans, "In radio ... the audience to be aimed at is *an audience of one* (infinitely repeated)" (quoted in Shingler and Wieringa, 1998, 115). Radio drama can be seen as exploring a complex interplay between an individual and isolated listener and a potentially limitless audience: an extraordinary mixture of the personal and the social. In the opening preamble to a broadcast on *Suspense* ("The Waxwork," March 1, 1959), the producer, William M. Robson, offers his own definition of radio drama:

> There is an old definition which describes the theater as a plank on two barrels and a passion. And now we might define radio drama as a microphone, a voice, and a story.

This suggests that, regardless of audience, the form has a focal simplicity and intensity, and that, at its most essential, radio drama is a form that tells a story. As Orson Welles writes:

> Of radio script shows there are many kinds; commercial and sustaining, good, bad and indefensible, and among these there is only one that you will listen to: *the kind you can follow* [Welles, 1938, 122].

Welles emphasizes the importance of clarity and focus—a good story that can command the undivided attention of the listener's mind. While this places a major onus upon the writer, it should not be regarded as an unwelcome burden; as Peter Lehman and William Luhr—in a book about film studies, no less—claim: "Of all the arts (theater) and media (television and film) that contain a performance element, radio is the ultimate writer's medium" (Lehman and Luhr, 2003, 227).

Radio may not be a blind medium, but it is nonetheless characterized by *darkness*. For Jim Harmon, radio drama is unprecedented in its ability to explore and exploit "that purity of darkness, that blank slate of imagination" (Harmon, 1967, 80). For Martin Shingler and Cindy Wieringa, the "stage of radio is darkness and silence, the darkness of the listener's skull" (Shingler and Wieringa, 1998, 90). This utter darkness is, by default, ripe for horror, and is precisely what Stephen King celebrates as the triumphant advantage of radio. We could argue that the paradigm of all experiential horror is the anticipation that something wicked lurks behind the door. King believes that in all other forms of narrative horror, from fiction to film, eventually "You have to open the door and show the audience what's behind it" (King, 1982, 133). King acknowledges that there is a school of horror in which the "door" is never opened at all. The classic example of this is probably *The Haunting* (Robert Wise, 1963), which, despite its extraordinary atmosphere and use of sound, shows nothing of a supernatural nature beyond a scene in which a solid wooden door begins to bulge grotesquely. King implies that it is something of a soft option not to open the door, and in his own work he has always taken the challenge of opening that portal:

> And if the audience screams with laughter rather than terror, if they see the zipper running up the monster's back, then you just gotta go back to the drawing board and try it again [King, 1982, 136].

But in radio such dilemmas and perils are redundant because when "you made the monster in your mind, there was no zipper running down its back; it was a perfect monster" (King, 1982, 140). This was understood even in the earliest days of horror radio. Talking about the specialized genre of *Lights Out*, program creator Wyllis Cooper declared:

> I think that the horror slant is good in radio. On the stage there is little difference between the horrible and the ludicrous. Radio hits ears only. Listeners build their own pictures [*Newsweek*, April 20, 1935].

However, it is worth adding a cautionary note in that poor acting or unconvincing sound effects can be as damaging as the costume "zipper": in a recent stage adaptation of Wyllis Cooper's *Quiet, Please* radio play "The Thing on the Fourble Board" (Sacred Fools Theater Company, Hollywood, 2004), the director (Corey Klemow) created a new, more "emotional and feral" sound for the "Thing," believing the 1940s original "sounds ridiculous" to modern ears (Corey Klemow email to Richard J. Hand, January 2005). Significantly, in adapting the radio play to the stage, Klemow still retained the Thing as a sound-only entity, a decision which vindicates Stephen King's belief in the formidable power of radio. The vital combination of suggestion and inference can make radio drama the ultimate form for horror: like nothing else can, radio can make it "real" (King, 1982, 140).

Lehman and Luhr argue that one of radio's key advantages is its ability "to use dramatic sound locations—places where sounds are exaggerated or omnipresent, or where unusual sounds are foregrounded" (Lehman and Luhr, 2003, 227). This is extremely important in genres like science fiction, and it is frequently exploited in horror, which can take the listener into the weirdest and most terrifying locations. For example, numerous horror plays are set in inhospitable wildernesses, while two classic horror offerings from *Suspense*, "The Hitch-Hiker" (originally written for *The Mercury Theater on the Air* and performed on *Suspense*, September 2, 1942) and "On a Country Road" (November 16, 1950), exploit the agoraphobic terror of the open road. Horror radio also delights in claustrophobia, with protagonists trapped in old dark houses, cells or even coffins. In analyzing a BBC sound effect track entitled "The Premature Burial," Andrew Crisell argues that any attempt to film it would lessen the effect, primarily because of the use of light, but also because to show the event would distance and diminish the impact:

> The slightest attempt by a filmmaker to illuminate the situation would reduce the horror it is meant to impart, for however physical and external the victim's predicament may be, the dramatic stage is really located inside his head. In the theater we would observe his ordeal; in the cinema we would observe it very closely; but on the radio the experience becomes subjective—we share the unseeing, claustrophobic horror of the victim [Crisell, 1994, 157].

The premature burial scenes in films such as *The Vanishing* (George Sluizer, 1988; remade in 1993), *Double Jeopardy* (Bruce Beresford, 1999) or *Kill Bill: Volume 2* (Quentin Tarantino, 2004) may be mortifying, but it is nonetheless easy to concur with Crisell. Radio's ability to metamorphose visual objectivity into subjective experience can make horror radio phenomenally powerful. So close are we to the victim in horror radio, our objective empathy can be transformed into a subjective experience: when we hear the stifled breath and panicked thoughts of a person being buried alive in a coffin, or can clearly hear both the murderer and his intended prey talking on the telephone, we are so close we almost *become* the victim.

The theme of premature burial is a primeval horror which finds cultural representation throughout the ages. It has a very significant place in the history of American horror radio. In Arch Oboler's first broadcast for *Lights Out*, "Burial Services" (June 10, 1936), he presented the inner thoughts of a paralyzed girl as she is buried alive. As Oboler reveals:

> I wrote the script in but a few hours; I had no conception, as the pages streamed from the typewriter, that what I had written was horror beyond horror. For I had taken a believable situation and underwritten it so completely that each listener filled the silences with the terrors of his own soul; when the coffin lid finally closed inexorably on the conscious yet cataleptically paralyzed young girl in my play, the reality of the moment, to thousands upon thousands of listeners who had buried someone close, was such that each had the horrifying thought that perhaps sister, or brother, or mother had also been buried... *alive*... [Oboler, 1945, 22].

Many letters of complaint arrived at NBC in the days following this inaugural broadcast, but rather than threaten the existence of the series, it guaranteed its longevity. In popular culture, controversy is not always a bad thing, as it ensures publicity and an audience. Moreover, at that time *Lights Out* was broadcast on Wednesdays at 11:30 p.m. (and occasionally even later), which meant that Oboler was not subjected to managerial constraint or scrutiny in these live broadcasts (not least because the managers were probably asleep in bed!). As Oboler puts it, "no conventional blue pencil crossed the pages of what I wrote" (Oboler, 1945, 23). Moreover, at this stage of its long run, *Lights Out* did not receive commercial sponsorship, which, when present, could exert enormous artistic pressure and demands on a program.

The controversy over "Burial Services" arose because Oboler denied the listeners a happy ending. Of course, this merely demonstrates that the play belongs to the long tradition of premature burial stories in horror literature, most famously in the works of Edgar Allan Poe (but traceable back to Sophocles' *Antigone*). Poe was similarly pessimistic in some of his stories, but fictional horror is different from performance horror. In film studies, the unhappy ending to *Night of the Living Dead* (George A. Romero, 1968) is often cited as a milestone in horror movies, one having an incalculable influence on the genre. But the horror radio of decades before offers countless examples of unhappy endings. Certainly it is inconceivable that the Hollywood of the period we are looking at could have produced a film as unremittingly cynical as golden age radio at its most bleak. Undoubtedly, censorship is of central importance here. Narrative cinema emerged from the theatrical tradition, and theater was traditionally the most stringently censored art form in western culture before film usurped that dubious privilege. The Production Code Administration (established 1930 onwards, consolidating the 1920s "Hays Code") enforced strict regulations on Hollywood film releases. A fine example in relation to censorship is *Frankenstein* (James Whale, 1931). The scene in which the Creature (Boris Karloff) drowns the little girl in the lake was originally passed without problem by the Production Code Administration but met with demands for cuts or complete deletion by local state and city censors. Ironically, when Universal applied to the Production Code Administration for a reissue seal of approval in 1937, the film company was forced to delete the scene.

Not long after the *Frankenstein* reissue, *Lights Out* broadcast "It Happened" (May 11, 1938), which may not have had a young girl as chosen victim but nonetheless condemned a teenage girl to a very grim fate. A few weeks before, *Lights Out* had presented Boris Karloff in "Valse Triste" (March 30, 1938), in which two young women are tormented by a psychopathic murderer. Although the play avoids the taboo of portraying young children as victims, "Valse Triste" remains an extremely disturbing episode, not least because of its sexual aspect. The terrifying "*gentle* man" Mr. Boyd (played by Karloff) entraps two women and tosses a coin to decide who he will kill and who he will "marry." We hear one victim get her throat slit, but the play ends before the "marriage" takes place. Indeed, "marriage" (and everything that particular euphemism implies) is put to similarly horrifying effect in some of golden age horror radio's finest achievements, including "The Thing on the Fourble Board" (*Quiet, Please*, August 9, 1948) and "Behind the Locked Door" (*The Mysterious Traveler*, May 24, 1949; revived November 6, 1951), works that we will study in-depth in later chapters. Other examples of radio drama employed a blatant exploration of the interplay of Eros and Thanatos, sex and death, as a structuring device. In "New Year Nightmare" (*The Mysterious Traveler*, January 5, 1947) a victim of amnesia demonstrates that he knows who he is by embracing his wife:

> CHRIS: Did this "Mr. Arnold" ever put his arms around you ... like this?
> BLANCHE: Oh, yes, often, ha, ha ... Chris, stop squeezing me so ti— tight ... uh—Chris!
> CHRIS: Sorry, darling.
> BLANCHE (*Quietly and breathless*): Oh ... oh ... you're ... you'll squeeze me again...
> CHRIS: That's so you'll remember that I'm your husband and not "Mr. Arnold."

The tense but erotic sensuality in this encounter finds an ironic echo in the next scene, in which Chris murders Blanche, wrestling her to her death over the edge of a canyon.

Radio allows explicitness: we can hear the horrors that we are *told* we are hearing or, sometimes worse when unspecified, what we *imagine* we are hearing. The hideous sounds of slicing, crushing or splitting are as graphic as we dare imagine them to be, just as desperate physical assaults are as brutal as our minds permit. Visual forms, at least at the time of the golden age, were obliged to find a safer distance. In the British horror movie *Dead of Night* (Cavalcanti et al., 1945) a bus crashes and we see the incident in long shot (a model bus is used, unsurprisingly), and we are informed that all the passengers die. The radio play "Present Tense" (*Escape*, January 31, 1950; revived on *Suspense*, March 3, 1957) opens with a train crash, and we are inside the wreckage, surrounded by the moans of the dying and the injured, and we hear a man (Vincent Price) squeeze out from underneath a mutilated corpse. In "Scoop" (*Lights Out*, December 8, 1942) a corpse rises from the grave, and its petrified victim manages to impart to the listener that the "worms and maggots did their work quickly." The zombie that Arch Oboler creates in his listener's mind is less like the somnambulant creatures of Hollywood's contemporaneous *I Walked with a Zombie* (Val Lewton, 1943) than the explicitly decaying living dead in postwar horror comics or the zombies of the George A. Romero generation of 1968 and beyond.

As well as being able to bring the listener close up to carnage and putrefaction, oldtime radio also explored the power of the listener's imagination in relation to another taboo: sexuality. We have already seen the sex and death link in some examples of horror radio, but isolated examples of the exploration of sexuality can be found across radio drama. After all, as Jim Harmon writes, no one could suggest that a woman wore a costume "that fitted rather too snugly for a boy of your age to observe. You ran the show" (Harmon, 1967, 12). This sense of "running the show" reflects a creative aspect of radio listening in relation to personal fantasy. Although impossible to quantify, the radio clearly served an important function in the fantasies of many listeners and helped fuel the most erotic and salacious possibilities. One thinks of Miss Hannigan (Carol Burnett) in *Annie* (John Huston, 1982) reclining and literally embracing her wireless set as she listens to a romantic drama until the orphans interrupt her erotic daydreams, to her unmitigated fury.

Raymond William Stedman reveals that even favorite family listening, such as Carleton E. Morse's *I Love a Mystery*, could offer a startling erotic playfulness:

> One of Carleton E. Morse's ventures into a kind of titillation rarely heard in radio, particularly in a thriller, was a two-day, on-the-air striptease. It happened when a

pretty assistant of the A-1 team was suspected of having in her possession some small object desired by the other side. A femme fatale forced her to disrobe completely, "dress, shoes, everything," in the presence of detective Terence Burke. ... Not until every listener from coast to coast was well aware that the attractive and thoroughly infuriated damsel was excruciatingly naked did she find shelter in an oversize raincoat [Stedman, 1971, 179].

But as Stedman indicates, this type of eroticism was "rarely heard," a statement which signposts the issue of censorship, an issue we will return to in due course. The treatment of sexuality was not simply violent or playful, but could be centrally and maturely explored in plays with philosophical resonance. In Ernest Kinoy's adaptation of J. T. McIntosh's "Hallucination Orbit" (*X Minus One*, May 15, 1956), Colin Ord, an astronaut alone in orbit around Pluto for six and a half years, has descended into hallucinatory madness or "solitosis." Colin talks to himself in a steady voice of cold irony. He is riddled with self-doubt and is unsure about his grip on reality: "concentrate for about fifteen minutes and you'll be able to walk through the walls of this ship." When a female astronaut arrives, Colin doubts if she is real or an "overblown figment," especially as she looks like someone from the "cover of a magazine." To keep his sanity, Colin drives such hallucinations away. In his exasperation, Colin proclaims:

> I would suddenly like to have enough people around me so that I could be sane. I would like to find women as part of life instead of having them pop up here from the depths of my rather ... pornographic subconscious.

He lets the next female astronaut, Dr. Marilyn Lynn, on board, and in scenes of acute dialogue and monologue Colin wrangles over the impossibility of proving reality.

> LYNN: What do you see when you look at me?
> COLIN: Well, you're strong, sort of quietly beautiful. About my age ... and you don't have a wedding ring. I noticed that.
> LYNN: That's what I thought you saw. I'm real. But not your picture of me... I'm a doctor. And I was a girl once, but that was forty years ago. I'm sixty-six.
> COLIN: You can't be ...
> LYNN: When you see me as I really am, you'll be all right.

"Hallucination Orbit" is an impressively complex study of the nature of reality and sexuality, and as such is a precursor to Stanislaw Lem's novel *Solaris* (1961). Colin lives in a world where steel walls can become fluid and is visited by objects of desire, which he rejects in order to stay sane. By the end of the play Colin understands that "reality is the most important thing to learn."

Some situations that radio drama created would have been too problematic for the contemporary stage and screen because they were too sexually explicit or violently gruesome. These situations became acceptable on the air because even if a situation was described extremely clearly, and reinforced through the labors of the actor and the sound effects technician, everything still seemed to reside in the imagination of the listener. But there were censorial limitations. When golden age couples get in bed together—as in "Organ" (*Lights Out*, June 8, 1943)—they are inevitably married, and barring Freudian slips of the William Conrad (and probably apocryphal) "I'll be up your ass in the morning" variety (Maltin, 2000, 126), obscene and profane language is absent.

Officially, there has never been government censorship of radio in the United States, first and foremost because of the First Amendment. But as Mathew Murray states, the "real history of radio censorship ... has been far less clear-cut than this official situation would suggest" (Sterling and Keith, 2003, 307). As Murray suggests, the ability of the Federal Radio Commission — which became the Federal Communications Commission — from the early 1930s to assess past programming when deciding whether to renew a license can be seen as an indirect form of censorship. It may have been rarely implemented, but it was nonetheless, as Martin Grams, Jr., writes, "a Damoclean sword that had given numerous broadcasters the jitters" (Grams, 2002, 33). More critical is the issue of self-censorship. Murray further divides this into two forces: market censorship and private censorship. The former meant that the "commercial basis of the industry discourages the airing of certain 'unpopular' topics or minority perspectives" (Sterling and Keith, 2003, 307), and allegations of political bias were leveled at network and station owners. Private censorship is defined by Murray as the program and advertising prohibitions implemented by station and networks:

> The most commonly restricted subjects during radio's golden age were labor unrest, socialist politics, pacifism, political "radicalism," birth control advocacy, criticism of advertising, anti–Prohibition speeches, unorthodox medical practices, unorthodox religious opinions, excessive excitement in children's shows, "offensive" words, and suggestive situations [Sterling and Keith, 2003, 307].

This list reveals how political concerns were paramount. Nevertheless, some writers could find their way around such restrictions. Arch Oboler always had a social consciousness, and if one of his most celebrated achievements, "Johnny Got His Gun" (*Arch Oboler's Plays*, March 9, 1940), is not a pacifist play, it is nonetheless virulently anti-militaristic. However, the Second World War saw a close relationship between government and the networks emerge, with plays "rewritten to encourage patriotism, enlistment, and home front support" (Sterling and Keith, 2003, 309). No one was more active in this than Oboler, who penned numerous anti-fascist plays. Even the continuing horror shows of *Lights Out* were given literal or metaphorical wartime significance. In the closing narrative frame of "Scoop" (December 8, 1942), Frank Martin asks, "Do you think that under some circumstances a person might return from the dead?" and rather than discuss supernatural horror, Oboler takes the opportunity to describe *real* horror. Oboler invites the listener to sit with closed eyes and think:

> The Japs, the Nazis, they're here for me. Not for someone in the newspaper or someone in a town halfway across the world or someone I don't even know in this neighborhood or even for my neighbor next door. But for me. For me. Yeah. The smirking little Jap is standing at the door. He's there for you. Not in the headlines, not just an idea but actually there for you. It can happen, you know. Three million dead in Europe attest to that fact.

The fact that horror radio continued unabated during the Second World War (the years that form the hub of the golden age) is interesting in itself; one might have expected that during a period of mass hostilities the last thing an audience at home or in an overseas battlefront would have wanted was a genre that explores death and violence. However, it is possible that for some listeners the grim world of horror radio was in itself cathartic or entirely escapist. After all, horror radio at its best could hook and propel the listener into an adrenaline-charged world divorced from everyday reality; it was escapist but never "sugar coated."

Regardless of horror radio's contribution to the war effort, from its inception until the end of the golden age it was not a stranger to controversy and censorial pressure. This is evident in a radio review in the *Washington Post* (December 14, 1935) which admits that *Lights Out* is "tops" as an example of "showmanship," but laments that it is gravely at "fault in dealing with plot situations and climaxes that are stomach-turning": the ambivalence of the review perhaps reveals the guilty pleasures of horror radio. Other examples of journalism were not so ambiguous. Raymond William Stedman cites numerous headlines—from either side of *Mercury Theater*'s "War of the Worlds"—that capture the anxiety that horror, mystery and suspense "imperiled society" (Stedman, 1971, 180): "Terrorism on radio" (*NEA Journal*, May 1935); "Radio Gore" (*Newsweek*, November 8, 1938); and "Slaughter, Sponsored by..." (*New Republic*, October 6, 1941). In a 1930s guidebook on scriptwriting, Peter Dixon warns the wannabe radio writer:

> Any subject that can't be discussed in the average American living-room with the children listening is not suitable for the air. This rule is strictly enforced [Dixon, 1936, 23].

This reflects a central concern in golden age conservatism: the power of radio to corrupt the young. This is reflected in headlines such as "Mothers Fighting Radio Bogies" (*Literary Digest*, March 18, 1933) and "Radio Horror for Children Only" (*The American Mercury*, July 1938), an article that denounced the content of the 5–6 p.m. drama slot. As Michele Hilmes writes of the thriller dramas of the 1930–40s:

> Though popular—or perhaps because of that popularity—they also attracted a certain amount of social criticism due to their emphasis on violence and horror. Was the emotion evoked by radio's sound-based thrills more powerful than film's ... graphic depictions? Many parents thought so, and some of the first studies of radio centered on the effects of such shows on children, particularly potential disruption of their sleep habits [Hilmes, 2002a, 105].

One of the most significant influences on censorship was the National Association of Broadcasters, a lobbying group established in 1923. In 1939, by which time the National Association of Broadcasters represented some 400 radio stations across the United States, the organization drafted an ethical code for its members. The code was controversial but nonetheless came into effect, thus facilitating a more formalized system of self-censorship that suggested restrictions on certain advertising and dramatic content. Popular broadcasting magazines such as *Radio Stars* (September 1940) broached the subject, describing the type of subjects that listeners would not be hearing on their radios, such as mimicry of President Roosevelt, the mildest of oaths (including "Thank God!"), risqué humor and discussion (including medical) of venereal disease. In 1947, the National Association of Broadcasters—in a move that reflected the rapidly changing times—revised the code and effectively banned, in radio drama, extreme horror in slaying, the kidnapping or beating of children, and third-degree methods used by police (Grams, 2002, 35). Eventually, as we shall see in the concluding chapter to this book, such pressures restricted the range and possibilities of golden age horror radio, and signaled its demise.

If changing ethical standards and regulations compromised horror radio, we may wonder what the genre did with its comparative freedom when it had it. We have already seen how horror radio explored violent and gruesome death. The plays also represent an exploration of social anxieties. "War of the Worlds" and other plays of the late 1930s reflect fears of invasion and a general disquiet about scientific and technological advancement. In discussing the horror film in 1930s Hollywood, Richard H. Pells argues that "the symbolic incarnation of evil is generally a solitary scientist" who, through perilous naiveté or willful megalomania, ignores "the ordinary restrictions of law and morality" (Pells, 1973, 270). The same principle applies to the horror radio of the period, which is full of scientists (and occultists) whose ill-advised experiments cause detriment or devastation. During the Second World War horror radio contributed to the propaganda effort with plays that literally or metaphorically animated and extrapolated the horrors of Nazism. In the postwar period the ideological demolition of fascism was replaced by a fear of communism, which created espionage thrillers such as *I Was a Communist for the FBI* (1952–54) and, as in the movies, found a special place as an underlying metaphor in numerous examples of the science fiction genre. Whether the "monsters" were communist party members or terrorists bent on the destruction of the edifice of "Americanism," or super-intelligent aliens from the far reaches of space with their eye set on Planet Earth, they were all, as John Dunning says of the bad guys in *I Was a Communist for the FBI*, "cold and humorless, with their single goal to enslave the world" (Dunning, 1998, 340).

In less tangential examples of horror radio we also find anxieties about the family and matrimony: warped desires, jealousies and resentments; brutal crimes and pitiless retribution that seem to tear a hole in the sanctity of the family or the romanticism of marriage. This inevitably links to sexuality, and, whether as sexually motivated crime or the battle of the sexes, it remains a disruptive aspect of social anxiety detectable in horror radio. As Allison McCracken notes, the gender issues in shows such as *Suspense* owed a great deal to established film genres such as the "paranoid Gothic" (a term developed by Mary Ann Doane), film noir and the 1940s melodramatic "woman's film" (McCracken, 2002, 186). However, *Suspense*—and I believe this can be applied to many more orthodox "horror shows"—does a great deal to assimilate and develop the films' traits in the creation of a profoundly disturbing and unsettling dramatic world. Although, as McCracken states, paranoid Gothic films are like *Suspense* in that "the man really *is* trying to kill the woman" (McCracken, 2002, 187), radio drama can be seen as surpassing contemporaneous film in its unremitting ruthlessness and grisly inventiveness. These qualities are partly mediated by the temporal economy of the form (quintessentially, the thirty-minute drama), but the genre can also be seen as taking advantage of the form: the broadcasts are live, concise and exploit the mind's eye (which will always, in cultural reception, see more than the literal eye).

If the problematic relationships and conflicts between men and women are observed with a cynical eye in horror radio, the place of the female voice in isolation has a fascinating place in the genre. Allison McCracken, following theories developed by Michele

Hilmes (including Hilmes, 1997, 130–50), writes of the "horror of the disembodied voice" (McCracken, 2002, 184). The presence of the radio actor is almost entirely perceived through vocal utterance, and although this can be comforting, the horror genre frequently exploits this intimacy for its own disturbing ends. In his nationally syndicated radio and television review column (January 1952), John Crosby writes that he has "concluded that most vengeful, vindictive and menacing spirits are not men but women." The female disembodied voice is a particularly powerful tool in the creation of the uncanny. Many of the horror programs under analysis utilize phenomenal examples of disembodied female voices, with the intention to achieve supernatural effect or, conversely, to make a scene of violence ultra-realistic: never was the "scream queen" ability in popular performance horror more compelling and important than on radio.

In horror radio of the American golden age we find an exploration of themes and stories, ranging from the old-fashioned to the original, combined with an extraordinary investigation into the power of the medium: radio drama's formidable combination of the human voice, sound effects and the listener's imagination has limitless potential for horror. An awareness of this potential is evident from the earliest days of the genre. Horror radio, at its best, can play formidable tricks on the imagination of its listeners, or rather can make its listeners play formidable tricks on themselves. Horror radio may give us a mere suggestion, a word, or a sound, and we have the habit of imagining "the most outrageously nasty possibilities" (King, 1982, 152). After all, as Stephen King says, real horror does not "come alive in front of a camera but on the screen of the mind" (King, 1982, 150): what initially seems to be radio's disadvantage—a visionless medium—is really its greatest asset.

2

Hosts and Music, Sound and Silence: Narrative Techniques and Formal Strategies in Horror Radio

Horror drama is, of course, like every other kind of radio program: it belongs in a lineup of programs that must follow a strict schedule. As far as the broadcasting corporations were concerned, the greatest technical skill of a director-producer in the era of entirely "live" radio was the ability to stick to the schedule with discipline and infallible accuracy. For an example of archetypal practice, it is interesting to look at the personal directing scripts of, say, Wyllis Cooper on *Quiet, Please* and see how his marginal notes in red pencil record the passing of each 30 seconds during the dress rehearsal, and offer notes for the performers or even modifications to the script when the action was evidently running a fraction too fast or too slow. The majority of the examples of the horror radio genre adhere to the 30-minute format. The actual "drama time" within this format may be further compromised by the needs for station identification, sponsorship advertising, and other forms of "framing," whether in the form of a presenter, a more consciously "dramatic" host, or a musical signature theme. Furthermore, these aspects of the horror program might also recur at the end of the scheduled slot and, as a rule, at some midpoint in the broadcast. However, it would be a mistake to see the components of a 30-minute slot as somehow at odds with each other, or to feel obliged to divorce the live play from the overall fabric of the complete broadcast. The opening frame of a radio show fulfils two functions: *demarcation* and *access*. The opening frame establishes a clear demarcation of itself within the schedule, and it also creates a point of access into its dramatic universe: in other words, a way into not just the story that the play will tell, but the program's own "take" on the chosen story and a self-reflexive and self-conscious stance on itself as a 30-minute "show" which, as we will see, can range from being deadly earnest to frivolously ironic.

As our own point of access into horror radio's narrative techniques and formal strategies, we will look at the horror radio "host." Old Nancy, the Witch of Salem, was the character-host of *The Witch's Tale*, and her approach to the horror stories she "tells" us is one of deliberate humor. Like all such horror narrators with a comic touch, the possible functions of their narrative are multiple. One is never sure if their comic preamble is a way of establishing the absurdly heightened world of horror that they and their tales frequently inhabit. Alternatively, the conscious juxtaposition of comedy with horror may be like the classic *douche écossaise* (a "hot and cold shower") of the Théâtre du Grand-Guignol, which alternated its short sex comedies and horror plays, with the result that although a comedy might superficially relax the audience, it was also a rather devious strategy that would disarm an audience even more profoundly over the course of the subsequent horror play (in short, make them laugh and then shock them deep). The *douche écossaise* might even be a point of allusion in an episode of *Inner Sanctum Mysteries* where Raymond tells the listeners:

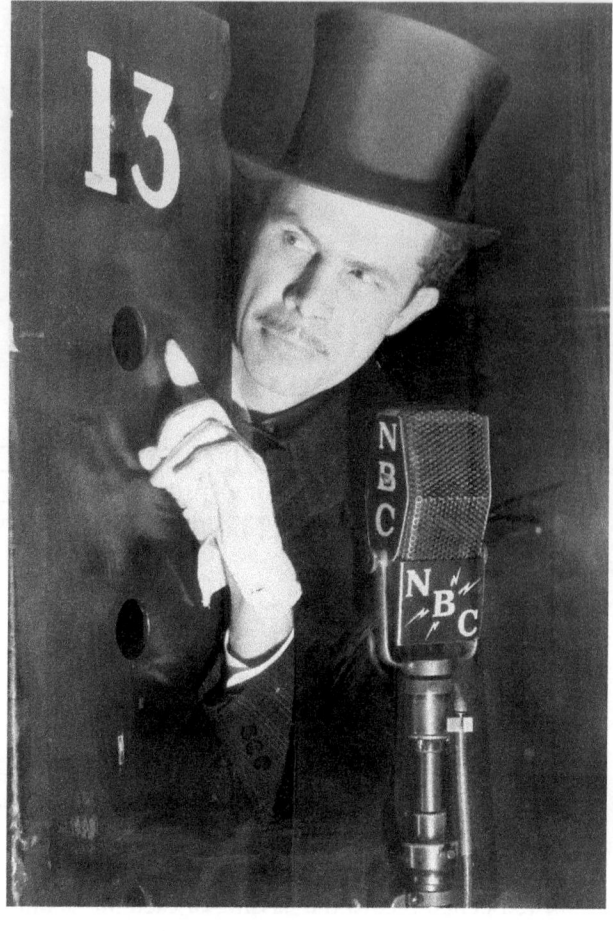

Raymond, host of *Inner Sanctum Mysteries* (Photofest).

> I hope you've all made yourselves comfortable. If it's too warm for you, we'll be glad to chill you a bit. Or if it's too cold we'll be glad to make it hot for you. As a matter of fact, from now on you'll get it both hot and cold ["The Black Seagull," March 7, 1943].

It is also possible that because the character-host's prologues are, by default, concise and colorful, they succeed in hooking our attention extremely efficiently and focus us for what can be a more measured narrative establishment and development in the central play. In *The Witch's Tale*, it was Old Nancy's birthday every week, and her age was never consistent, but at the end of her preamble she would invite us to "gaze deep into the embers" and focus our attention as we entered the uncanny central narratives. Utilizing the grimly comic persona of a host like Old Nancy is also an extremely economical way of creating the program's identity, a major part of which is making the listener establish a close relationship with the host and hence the program as a whole. We will look at Old Nancy in more depth in the chapter on *The Witch's Tale*; I believe that Old Nancy is not simply the grandmother of all horror radio hosts, but, arguably, a figure of major importance to all horror hosts in popular culture.

Having stated the importance of Old Nancy in the establishment of the horror host, it is worth stressing that traditional horror fiction employed framing narrators long before *The Witch's Tale*. The framing device was a standard practice in the nineteenth-century Gothic tale and ghost story, and we may consider H. G. Wells' *The Time Machine* (1895) and several of M. R. James' ghost stories as works that depend on their meaning by employing a framing narrator. It received complex development in fiction like Henry James' *Turn of the Screw* (1898), where the unnamed Governess' account of her "supernatural" experiences are critically framed by a group of men reading her manuscript. Likewise, in Joseph Conrad's *Heart of Darkness* (1899), Marlow's account of his journey up the Congo is necessarily framed by being recounted to the reader by one of Marlow's listeners. In such proto-modernistic fiction, the reader is meant to be acutely aware of *who* is telling us the story, and the use of a framing narrative helps to establish through its multiple layers an objective distanciation for the reader and, no less, for the novelists themselves. The hosts in the golden age of horror radio may seem a far cry from the framing narrators in the groundbreaking fiction of James and Conrad, yet their function is no less complex or essential. The horror radio host is an effective conduit into the impossible or incredible worlds of horror that the characters in the central story will inhabit. While some are earnest in setting the mood and scene, the irony that a character-host such as Old Nancy and Raymond (*Inner Sanctum Mysteries*) employs is consistently playful, and frequently operates with a different performance style than the main story: the framing narrative may use the language of puns and a system of self-irony, while the story proper might be played "sincerely" (albeit with conscious melodrama). This emphasizes how, rather than the conventional framing storytellers of fiction, the horror radio hosts belong, more consciously, to a theatrical tradition.

Examples of framing narrators within plays have existed throughout theater history, from the Chorus in Greek drama and narrators in classical Japanese theater, to the diverse "Prologues" of Elizabethan-Jacobean drama. Although highly unusual in the Grand-Guignol repertoire of plays, Octave Mirbeau's *Les Amants* (1901) includes a "Director" character who, several decades before Thornton Wilder's Stage Manager in *Our Town* (1938), speaks directly to the audience in a narrative frame, setting the scene before the action begins. But all of these are scripted within their respective plays, whereas the prototypical horror host must be separate from the actual play, yet still become a major component in the overall horror show "package." Therefore, a better example of a theatrical precedent to the horror radio host is probably Oscar Méténier, the founder of the Grand-Guignol, who, at the end of the nineteenth century, would famously arrive before performances at his theater, dressed all in black and flanked by two bodyguards, and recount to the audience outside the theater, the gruesome details of horrific crimes (Deák, 1974, 36). The horror radio host is similarly outside of the play, distanced with an almost extemporary style compared to the world of the play, a quality enhanced by the fact that while in every episode the story is completely different, the host remains the same. The host is a trademark of a program, but they also remain a certainty: the listener knows they will be returned to the host at the end of the show and in the following week. This guarantee of security lies in stark contrast to the characters in the story: the adventurers in *I Love a Mystery* will always live to fight another day in the next episode, while the one-off constructions in most horror programs may not survive another day, let alone another week.

Examples of the framing host are more familiar on film: at the beginning of *Frankenstein* (James Whale, 1931) Edward van Sloan emerges from behind a theater curtain as himself—and not in his subsequent on-screen role as Dr. Waldman—to alert the audience to the theme of the film, concluding with, "Well, we've warned you." Such a framing role will be important in many postwar television drama series, and will later characterize programs such as Rod Serling's *The Twilight Zone* and *Night Gallery*. But in large part, the framing host would take on a consciously ironic function, as in the television horror hosts in the Vampira or Ghoulardi style. The simultaneously archaic and humorous quality of the framing horror host has also been lovingly celebrated in the form of Criswell (Jeffrey Jones) emerging from the creaking coffin and talking directly to the viewer in *Ed Wood* (Tim Burton, 1994). Despite these examples, the horror host enjoys its most sustained and essential presence on radio. All the horror hosts had an individual style and all were ironic, even if this quality was more ostentatious in some than in others. The host as framing mechanism gives each horror program its individual stamp, and it is no surprise that several hosts acquired a cult status. Martin Grams, Jr., quotes a fan letter sent to *Inner Sanctum Mysteries* that demonstrates how the status of the host, Raymond, often surpassed the appreciation for the material: "I get such a kick out of Raymond and his squeaking door—more than I do out of the programs themselves" (Grams, 2002, 37).

The horror radio hosts encompass a diverse range of styles in the creation of the signature for their respective shows. At one extreme, the horror host is less a master of ceremonies than a ringmaster. For example, we may consider the gruesome puns of the sardonic Host (Paul McGrath) on *Inner Sanctum Mysteries*:

> THE HOST: Good evening, friends of the Inner Sanctum. This is your host of the squeaking door again. Just, um, slither in and let me dispel your weariness with a bit of eeriness, hmm? Ha, ha, ha, ha, ha... Oh no, no, no, no, no... Please don't sit in that chair... I'm, er, saving it for rigor mortis to set in, ha, ha, ha, ha, ha! [*Inner Sanctum Mysteries*, "The Lonely Sleep," September 25, 1945].

In contrast, a typical opening to *The Weird Circle* functions as a conscious establishment of atmosphere:

> SOUND OF BREAKING WAVES
> FIRST VOICE: The Weird Circle. In this cave by the restless sea we are met to call from out of the past stories, strange and weird. Bell keeper, toll the bell so that all may know that we are gathered again in The Weird Circle.
> CHIMING BELL
> SECOND VOICE: Out of the past, phantoms of a world gone by speak again the immortal tale...

The Hermit's Cave, with its hermit and his baying wolves; *The Hall of Fantasy*, with its echoing footsteps and kettledrum; and the trademark openings of many other horror programs are distinctive yet very similar in their establishing function. *The Sealed Book* is also in the same mold, but it borders on self-parody. There is some variation in its openings, but here is a typical example:

> KEEPER: Ha ha ha ha ha ha ha... The Sealed Book!
> GONG
> ORGAN MUSIC AND GONG
> VOICE: Once again the keeper of the book is ready to unlock the ponderous volume in which is recorded all the secrets and mysteries of mankind through the ages. All the lore and learning of the ancients, all the strange and mystifying stories of the past, the present and the future.
> GONG AND LENGTHY PASSAGE OF ORGAN MUSIC
> VOICE: Keeper of the book, what tale will you tell us this time?
> KEEPER: First I must unlock the great padlock which keeps the sealed book safe from prying eyes. Ha ha ha ha ha ha ha...
> SOUND OF PADLOCK BEING UNLOCKED
> KEEPER: Now, what story shall I tell you? I have here tales of every kind. Tales of murder, of madness, of dark deeds and of events strange beyond all belief... Ha ha ha ha ha... Here...
> SOUNDS OF PAGES TURNING
> KEEPER: Yes... yes... Here's a tale for ya. A dark story of two brothers, one of them killed because he could not help himself, the other was interested in murder too, but in a very different way. The title of the tale is...
> ORGAN STING
> KEEPER: "The Hands of Death"
> GONG
> KEEPER: Here is the tale as it is written in the Sealed Book...
> ["The Hands of Death," March 18, 1945]

This opening takes over three and a half minutes—a significant percentage of the entire broadcast—and is perhaps only rivaled by the length of the opening theme tune in early examples of *The Witch's Tale*.

Perhaps the most austere and consciously unnerving introduction is a comparatively minimalist one: the foreboding voice of Arch Oboler in his *Lights Out* preamble:

> VOICE: Arch Oboler's *Lights Out*... everybody.
> CHIME CHIME CHIME CHIME
> ARCH OBOLER:
> It...CHIME
> Is... CHIME
> Later... CHIME
> Than... CHIME
> You... CHIME
> Think... CHIME CHIME
> This is Arch Oboler bringing you another in our series of stories of the unusual. And once again we caution you: these *Lights Out* stories are definitely not for the timid soul, so we tell you calmly and very sincerely, if you frighten easily turn off your radio now.
> LOUD GONG
> ["The Flame," March 23, 1943]

In terms of minimalism, even this was a considerable expansion of the standard 1930s opening to *Lights Out* as used by Oboler but inaugurated by Wyllis Cooper:

> VOICE: Lights out, everybody!
> SOUND: THIRTEEN CHIME NOTES
> WIND UP ON ELEVENTH
> OUT BEHIND
> GONG

The psychology of the horror event so effectively exploited by Oboler in the 1940s is that if someone warns you that what you are about to experience is truly frightening, the majority of the audience may start to feel nervous, and the rest are at least on guard. If the more humorous hosts are ringmasters or take us for a ride on a rollercoaster in a conscious half hour of escapism, Oboler, as host to his own work, strives to emphasize authenticity. In the closing narrative frame to "Bon Voyage" (November 10, 1942), before promoting war bonds, Oboler takes the opportunity to sum up the *Lights Out* repertoire:

> Some of our stories are based on fact; some are a mixture of scientific fact and fiction; and others are ghost stories founded upon unexplainable but nevertheless apparently real happenings to real people.

Although Oboler acknowledges in the same frame that we have just listened to an "out-of-the-world story," at no point does he admit that any of the *Lights Out* stories are without some basis in fact and reality. What this reveals is that Oboler is aiming for a sense of authenticity in his work, a fear effect that will continue after the broadcast is over. It is an interesting tactic in that it demonstrates that Oboler attempts to place even the wildest fantasy and melodrama of *Lights Out* within the realm of possibility. It is rather ironic that while the *Mercury Theater*'s "War of the Worlds" narrative frame makes it clear that the listener has just heard a Halloween trick, Oboler takes pains to emphasize that anything is possible and everything is based on fact. In contrast, when *Inner Sanctum Mysteries* leaves us to our "pleasant dreams," it signifies that 30 minutes of escapism is over and yet simultaneously acknowledges that the horrors it created will live on to trouble us in the fictional realm of our unconscious.

To return to Oboler and the issue of authenticity, in the 1942-43 season of *Lights Out* he was not working alone. The announcers— including Bob LeMond — who provide the commercial frame outside of Oboler's narrative frame greet the ending of each play with a "Phew," followed by a question to Oboler that reinforces the notion of authenticity and suspends disbelief for a few moments more. At the end of "Poltergeist" (October 20, 1942) the announcer speaks to Oboler in the hesitant, breathless tone of a shocked man:

> ANNOUNCER: Phew... Uh... Um... Mr. Oboler... would you mind telling us—me — whether there are such things as poltergeists?
> ARCH OBOLER: All I can tell you is this. There are authenticated records in existence...

Oboler creates an authenticity of horror within the framing narrative, but this is enhanced by the announcer's convincing state of shock and naiveté, all of which reinforces Oboler's intention to lead the listeners away from seeing the plays as purely fictional. A notable exception comes at the end of the unlikely but possible horrors of "Valse Triste" (December 29, 1942), when Oboler insists:

> Ladies and gentlemen, believe me, the story you just heard was just a story intended purely for amazement and amusement. The young ladies were purely fictional characters and the villain existed only for the brief space of the twenty-nine minutes during which you listened to the play. So stop breathing hard, permit your blood pressure to fall to its normal, healthy rate....

Oboler loves the thrill of the dramatic experience of radio, and for him commercials are a potential bugbear:

> [The] commercials in a drama should be at the opening and at the close; they should never interrupt the play. Always the story must be tied up with the listeners; mere excitement is not enough. The play must run smooth. That is impossible if an announcer interrupts the show and destroys the scenery and illusion built up in the listener's imagination [*New York Times*, July 23, 1939].

Here is an indication of Oboler's ideal structure around this period (all timings are approximate, due partly to possible fluctuation in recording speed):

> ANNOUNCER: 30 seconds
> MIXED SOUND: CHIMING BELL, HOWLING WIND, GONG: 48 seconds
> PLAY SECTION ONE: 7 minutes
> GONG AND BRIEF SILENCE: 10 seconds
> PLAY SECTION TWO: 2 minutes
> GONG AND BRIEF SILENCE: 8 seconds
> PLAY SECTION THREE: 2 minutes, 20 seconds
> GONG AND BRIEF SILENCE: 7 seconds
> PLAY SECTION FOUR: 2 minutes, 27 seconds
> GONG AND BRIEF SILENCE: 11 seconds
> PLAY SECTION FIVE: 3 minutes, 25 seconds
> GONG AND BRIEF SILENCE: 8 seconds
> PLAY SECTION SIX: 2 minutes, 1 second
> GONG AND BRIEF SILENCE: 9 seconds
> PLAY SECTION SEVEN: 6 minutes, 51 seconds
> GONG AND BRIEF SILENCE: 7 seconds
> PLAY SECTION EIGHT: 1 minute, 37 seconds
> GONG AND BRIEF SILENCE: 7 seconds
> ANNOUNCER: 8 seconds
> ["Cat Wife," April 6, 1938]

We can see that the play is broken up into eight unequal sections. However, the interruptions are not for commercial sponsorship or even a return to the narrative frame. Each interruption is, in fact, a dramatic enhancement: the crashing gong ends each section on a dramatic highpoint of horror or suspense and escalates the overall narrative development of the play.

In contrast, the narrative structures of other horror radio programs are far more complex. While some programs clearly break down into blocks for purposes of syndication that permit advertisements at the start, middle and end, others are more intricate.

To give a detailed example, here is the broadcast structure of "The Black Seagull" (*Inner Sanctum Mysteries*, March 7, 1943):

MUSIC ALONE: 9 seconds
ANNOUNCER including details of commercial sponsor with music continuing in background: 6 seconds
MUSIC ALONE: 5 seconds
GOVERNMENT ANNOUNCEMENT encouraging women to join war movement, without music: 56 seconds
MUSIC ALONE: 6 seconds
ANNOUNCER, without music: 3 seconds
THE CREAKING DOOR OPENS: 5 seconds
RAYMOND plus music in background: 45 seconds
MUSIC ALONE: 4 seconds
ANNOUNCER including details of commercial sponsor, without music: 26 seconds
MUSIC ALONE: 10 seconds
RAYMOND with music in background: 48 seconds
PLAY SECTION ONE: 11 minutes, 41 seconds
MUSIC ALONE: 10 seconds
RAYMOND with music in background: 44 seconds
ANNOUNCER including details of commercial sponsor, without music: 57 seconds
MUSIC ALONE: 11 seconds
RAYMOND with music in background: 24 seconds
PLAY SECTION TWO: 8 minutes, 47 seconds
MUSIC ALONE: 12 seconds
RAYMOND with music in background: 48 seconds
ANNOUNCER including details of commercial sponsor, without music: 23 seconds
MUSIC ALONE: 6 seconds
RAYMOND with music in background: 26 seconds
THE CREAKING DOOR CLOSES: 5 seconds
MUSIC ALONE: 10 seconds
ANNOUNCER including station identification, without music: 6 seconds

We can see how complex is the layering of the program's structure. The actual play is a little over 20 minutes in duration, which means that approximately a third of the broadcast is other material, namely commercial and government announcements, and the music with or without the host. Although we can sympathize with Oboler's lament that "Blah ruins the emotional flow" of drama (*New York Times*, July 23, 1939), the multiple layering of this example of *Inner Sanctum Mysteries* can still create an intricate auditory experience. Raymond returns several times with his usual puns and comic morbidity — in contrast to the eerie central story of death and resurrection. Also the music (played on a Hammond organ) threads and weaves through the broadcast, tying up the narrative and establishing the uncanny world of the Inner Sanctum — in contrast to the world of CBS, Carter's Little Liver Pills or government labor drives. By the time Lipton sponsors *Inner Sanctum Mysteries*, things are interwoven even more tightly, with the Host's pun-filled dialogues with "Mary" merging into advertisements rather than demarcating from them:

HOST: ... When they ask you who you were with last night, you can always say, "That was no lady, that was my *knife*."
MARY: Well, I'm glad you could put a new *point* on that old joke, Mr. Host.
HOST: Ho ho, I like to sharpen up an old saw now and then, Mary.
MARY: Well, let me see what I can do along those lines. How about, the best things in life are *tea*.
HOST: Mary ... I'm afraid your enthusiasm for Lipton's has got the best of you.
MARY: Ha ha ha, well maybe you're right, Mr. Host. But it's so easy to be enthusiastic about Lipton's....

["Blood of Cain," January 29, 1946]

As painful as these puns are, it nonetheless demonstrates an effort to intermingle and merge advertisements into the macabre world of the Host, which is bolder than the segregation found in some advertising campaigns.

It is easy to defend *Inner Sanctum Mysteries* in comparison to the situation seen at the end of, and after, the golden age of radio when "blah" really triumphed. Jim Harmon states that, "Radio proudly proclaims that it is making more money than ever ... with up to twenty-five minutes per hour taken up with commercials" (Harmon, 1967, 262); and Vincent Price, in a 1971 radio interview, spoke of his disappointment with modern radio because of the over-commercialization of the form, whereby programs are constantly interrupted by advertisements. For Price, this abandons one of the great potentials of the medium: "radio has a *continuity* that is just marvellous, as a play does, you know: three acts. I miss it very much" (Chuck Shaden interview with Vincent Price, Chicago, 1971).

The use of the host in the structure of narrative framing is just one distinctive feature in a range of narrative techniques and formal strategies used in horror radio. The 30-minute format demands great economy, especially when, as we have seen, the actual play might only amount to 20 minutes of the total broadcast time. The plays employ a variety of strategies in their dramatic structure. The categories of horror plot structures outlined by Noël Carroll in relation to films and fiction (Carroll, 1990) could easily be supported using examples from radio. Horror plays utilize a range of pace and suspense techniques, which means that one play might spend considerable time establishing a location and atmosphere as a setting for horror, while another might open with a violent shock. The issue of intimacy is important for the way we become "involved" with the characters in a play. Unlike the host, the characters are vulnerable inasmuch as we do not know what will happen to them in their short animation within a one-off horror play. Sometimes there is a deliberate manipulation of trust. For example, in "Two Men in a Furnished Room" (*Mystery Playhouse*, September 27, 1946) the narrator and focal character, Red (John Neill), invents a plausible alibi for his roommate Dixon (Sam Wanamaker) after the latter's girlfriend has gone missing. Having made this decision, Red finds himself embroiled in the investigation of a murder. In the final minute of the play, however, it transpires that Red—whom we have listened to, followed, and trusted throughout—is himself the murderer.

Another strategy that exploits the intimacy of radio is the type of play that places us inside the head of a lunatic. There is an exceptional claustrophobia when we listen to the various adaptations of "confessional" masterpieces such as Poe's "The Tell-Tale Heart" or Charlotte Perkins Gilmore's "The Yellow Wallpaper." Similarly "confessional" is the virtuoso performance of William Conrad as the shell-shocked war veteran in "Confession" (*Escape*, December 31, 1947), based on an Algernon Blackwood story, and described by John Dunning as "one of the greatest pure-radio items ever done in any theatre ... [a] creepy sleight-of-hand that keeps a listener guessing until the last line" (Dunning, 1998, 233).

As Martin Shingler and Cindy Wieringa emphasize, "Radio is a medium of mass communication, but presenters and producers learn to deliver to one person, *the listener*" (Shingler and Wieringa, 1998, 145). This observation implies that radio offers an extraordinary intimacy, and the implications of this for horror radio are profound. It was something that was recognized by Orson Welles, who developed what became known as *The Mercury Theater on the Air*'s "story-teller" or "first person singular" technique of radio drama as a response to radio that approached drama in the manner of eavesdropping, a process, in Welles' words, "somewhat akin to overhearing a conversation, let's say, in the next apartment; the listener seems to be entirely out of the picture" (*New York Times*, August 14, 1938). In contrast, Welles describes, in the same article, the ethos of the *Mercury Theater* in the following terms:

> While our aim is to reach many thousands of people, the listeners should be considered as small groups of two or three, and then the idea of intimacy can be best achieved. For intimacy is one of radio's richest possessions.

If the *quality* of intimacy is one of radio's richest possessions, the *potential* of intimacy is never more fully exploited than in horror drama, and it is an aspect of the medium that will be examined further in the next chapter.

Aside from the spoken word, one of the most important languages of radio drama is music. Whether in the form of the crashing gong of *Lights Out* or Bernard Herrmann's brooding orchestral composition for *Suspense*, non-diegetic music has an extremely important place in horror radio. Sometimes it is a signature tune, like the use of Mussorgsky's *Night on Bald Mountain* at the start of *Escape*, or Cesar Franck's melancholic *Symphony in D Minor* for *Quiet, Please*. Albert Buhrmann, the organist on *Quiet, Please*, also makes minimal but extremely effective use of various musical accents and "stings" to provide scenes or lines of dialogue with emphasis or irony. After all, as Robert McLeish says, music in radio drama can "create *overall style, mood,* or *passage of time*" (McLeish, 1988, 206). The eerie, now archaic, moaning of the organs in *The Sealed Book* and *Inner Sanctum Mysteries* undoubtedly capture the style and mood of the respective shows. As Himan Brown explains:

> On *Inner Sanctum* for fourteen years I had a Hammond organ ... but I didn't use it for music—I used it as a sound effect so that the stab was repeated by the Hammond or the gunshot was repeated or the woman's scream suddenly became a musical scream and so on. And the Hammond lent itself to that kind of thing [Bob Morgan interview with Himan Brown, April 9, 1984].

Jim Harmon goes into more detail:

> [Himan] Brown even used music as a sound effect. His organist was warned never to play a recognizable song, or, if he could help it, even an original sound of

> melody. The man at the somber Hammond organ was to play sharp "stings"— a high musical note struck to emphasize an important piece of dialogue. He sounded "doom chords." He played "bridges" between scenes. There were two kinds of bridges: somber marches to disaster, extensions of "doom chords," and staccato frenzies of pell-mell movement, the chase [Harmon, 1967, 75].

This use of music demonstrates horror radio's roots in sensationalistic popular performance. Even more than being akin to the incidental music of cinema, the performance strategy can be traced directly back to the heightened theater of nineteenth-century stage melodrama.

We should not think, however, that the dramatic use of non-diegetic music in radio drama amounts solely to the use of extemporized and clichéd dramatic chords. Raymond William Stedman celebrates *I Love a Mystery*'s use of sound:

> So adept were the makers of this mystery program that they could effect an extreme of terror through a sound that in itself was not frightening. The soft tinkling of a collar bell warned of the approach of the savage wolf Prometheus, who, save for the click of his paws on a bare floor, was totally silent. Gentle organ music, seemingly coming from nowhere, brought to another sequence possibly the most singularly chilling impression in the entire series, for it meant that a crazed murderer was once again announcing a new victim. Anomalous as it may seem, the melody that told of death was the lovely "Cradle Song" of Brahms. Those who remember the sequence know well how effective the juxtaposition of tenderness and horror can be [Stedman, 1971, 178].

The potential of music in radio drama is such that, in an example given by Shingler and Wieringa, music can represent a "storm more effectively than the actual recording of thunder and lightning, conveying the emotional effects that often accompany such an event" (Shingler and Wieringa, 1998, 64). In fact, such technical decisions about whether to use music or sound effects are not always "either-or" propositions: "The Roman" (*The Croupier*, September 21, 1949) is not the only example in which a storm scene is created by using a combination of Rex Koury's organ music *and* storm sound effects.

Because music is an exceptionally useful tool available to radio drama, it is no surprise that there are some interesting examples of the diegetic use of music in horror radio. Lucille Fletcher's "Fugue in C Minor" (*Suspense*, June 1, 1944) is an extraordinary horror play in which Theodore Evans (Vincent Price) is a man who has killed numerous women and buried them in the organ that he has built into the structure of his house. The play is replete with sexual innuendo and symbolism, and possesses an almost absurdist quality. The play has a veritable score, mixing the sound of orchestra, chamber music, piano, cornet, pipe organ, and even the eerie laughter of Evans' two children, Daphne and David. In "Symphony in D Minor" (*Quiet, Please*, September 13, 1948), a blind hypnotist discovers that his wife is having an affair. He hypnotizes her lover into murdering her so that the hypnotist will escape suspicion with a watertight alibi. The plot is, at least for Wyllis Cooper, something of a cliché. However, the play is distinguished by its irony and self-reference. The impulse to kill will be triggered when his wife's lover hears Franck's *Symphony in D Minor*, the theme tune to *Quiet, Please*. The broadcast mixes Albert Buhrmann's keyboard recitation of the tune with an orchestral recording. In a twist ending, just when it looks like the murder has been averted, the lover puts a recording on and kills the hypnotist. This was the 65th *Quiet, Please* broadcast, so the audience was familiar with the framing theme tune; consequently, the use of it as a trigger for murder is an intriguing interpolation whereby the diegetic and non-diegetic is ingeniously mixed.

One of the most important technical resources in radio drama is sound effects. Indeed, for some people it would seem that it is not the script or the acting, but sound effects technology that lies at the very heart of the medium. As Robert L. Mott says, radio sound effects are "the art of painting pictures for the imagination" (Mott, 1993, vii). Peter Lehman and William Luhr state that, "Radio's total reliance upon the world of sound points to an area of potential creativity within the form" (Lehman and Luhr, 2003, 227), and perhaps sound effects technology is the best example of this. Recorded sound effects could even become a creative inspiration: Erik Barnouw reveals that Arch Oboler "loved to sit listening to sound effect records [and] some exploded into scripts" (Barnouw, 1968, 72). Live radio sound effects were a creative technology that evolved through trial, error and experience. Although some techniques could be imported from the stage, many could not. Moreover, some of the techniques that developed may surprise us because of their simplicity, tricks that could nonetheless sound more "real" in broadcast than a recording of the thing itself. After all, things do not always sound like themselves when broadcast on the air, and, by the same token, the unlikeliest of objects could create aural verisimilitude. Examples include beating a hunk of liver on a marble slab to sound like leeches devouring human flesh (Grams, 2002, 27), blowing through a straw into a bowl of water to imitate any boiling liquid — including, for episodes of *Lights Out*, blood (Mott, 1993, 78) and "break[ing] an egg to sound like someone's eye being splashed out" (*Washington Post*, July 27, 1955); while the discovery that chopping a watermelon sounded exactly like a skull being cleaved was, to Arch Oboler, "the ultimate orgasm" (quoted in Maltin, 2000, 89). Whatever the source sound, the human imagination worked to make the sound real. As the *Chicago Tribune* (April 7, 1935) reported with regards to *Lights Out*, it "may only be the head of a cabbage in the studio, but it's red with gore when you hear its dull thud on the floor." In addition, many elaborate pieces of equipment were invented to achieve these specific effects. The sound effects technicians became an indispensable member of the performance ensemble in the days of live radio, some of them acquiring celebrity status. They were performers in their own right, and the best in the field were highly prized and respected by the whole production team. In broadcasts with a studio audience, the sound effects technicians were much-loved and a focus of attention. This creative domain of performance was comparatively young, and its development was followed with interest. Newspapers — including the *New York Times* — devoted articles to revealing the ingeniousness of the sound effects technicians and their astonishing practices. The numerous handbooks and guides devoted to sound effect technology produced in the golden age of radio are a testament to the challenge and importance of the field. In the early days of radio drama, the development of sound effect technology captured the public's imagination:

> Until television arrives the broadcasters must depend upon sound effects to give the dramatic programs "auditory realism." They use numerous novel devices and simple things to convey the radio "scenery" to the listener [*New York Times*, April 19, 1931].

Sound effects, however, were not without their critics, including Orson Welles:

> I believe that they are overdone in most radio plays, having a tendency to clutter up the action. Sound effects which are used to merely paint the scenery should be used intelligently and economically and should have as much value to the play as the spoken word. I don't wish to be misunderstood. Sound effects and music are essential to any air drama; we are using all the equipment that radio offers, but economically and, we hope, intelligently [*New York Times*, August 14, 1938].

In the area of horror radio, sound effects have a pivotal significance. Let us compare two descriptions that celebrate radio actors. The *Chicago Tribune* (March 20, 1935) summed up the fate of one leading actor on *Lights Out*:

> [Sidney Ellstrom has] been put to death in this show more than 100 times. And his endings have all been grisly and gruesome. He's been skinned alive, boiled in oil, devoured by a man-eating jungle plant, strangled by a vampire. He's been drowned, electrocuted, poisoned, buried alive, decapitated and dismembered.

Compare this with Grams' description of the diverse fates of one of the grand dames of *Inner Sanctum Mysteries*:

> [Lesley Woods] was shot, stabbed, drowned a few dozen times, poisoned, strangled and bludgeoned without end. One of her most horrifying and difficult performances involved being clawed to death by a mythical panther. Equally difficult to effect were the screams of a woman burning to death [Grams, 2002, 24].

As colorful as these descriptions are, it is important to consider that although the virtuosity of each actor was important, sound effects were essential and instrumental in the successful creation of the majority of these imaginative deaths.

Lights Out's "most famous sound effect" (Maltin, 2000, 89) has probably become the most famous sound effect in horror radio: the turning inside out of three unfortunate victims in "The Dark" (sometimes said to have been broadcast December 29, 1937, Oboler's personal directing copy is dated "January 19, 1938"). The play develops slowly, with two on-duty medics— Ed and Sam — waiting for their next call. After a careful establishment of their characters and lives, the two men are called to a house: "Somebody hurt out at 433 Pine." Ed and Sam force their way into the house, where they find an insanely cackling woman. On the floor they discover a corpse whose "skin is the inside and the *flesh* is the *outside*!" They see the "dark" creeping up from the floor like "black smoke," and reaching up to the insane woman and turning her inside out. Although the sound effect used has become quite famous, there seems to be some ambiguity as to exactly how the illusion was created. John Dunning sums up the most popular account when he explains that it was "accomplished by soaking a rubber glove in water and stripping it off at the microphone while a berry basket was crushed at the same instant" (Dunning, 1998, 399). Erik Barnouw paints a more elaborate version:

> In one program they had to turn a man inside out. The task was solemnly divided into three components: for *flesh* sounds, a technician put his arm in a length of inner tube, grasped the end firmly, and yanked; for *blood-and-guts* sounds, warm spaghetti was attacked with a bathroom plunger; for *bones crunching*, Lifesavers

were ground between the teeth, very close to the microphone [Barnouw, 1968, 72–73].

Whichever version is correct, it is interesting to read in the original script Oboler's direction and suggestion:

> THE NEXT SOUND IS TO PAINT THE PICTURE OF THE WOMAN BEING INSTANTLY TURNED INSIDE OUT — IT'S A SOUND SOMEWHAT LIKE A RUBBER GLOVE BEING TURNED INSIDE OUT — IT CAN BE ACCOMPANIED BY A HISS.

Perhaps Oboler's suggestion was made more sophisticated by a technician when the play was broadcast. It has to be said that the extract from the play included in the *Arch Oboler's Drop Dead!* (1974) album sounds like it is solely dependent on the manipulation of the wet glove. Such is the folklore of old-time radio.

The dimension of sound on radio encompasses the voice, music and sound effects, but it also encompasses silence. As Andrew Crisell contends, "In various ways ... radio is positively besieged by silence — a silence which portends non-existence, annihilation" (Crisell, 1994, 160). Oboler would concur, telling the *New York Times* (July 23, 1939):

> Often a silence or a pause between words is more important than the spoken word, because the listener, in the mind's eye, during the pause, is contributing to the play. His imagination gets a chance to work; he is experiencing the play more emotionally.

There are many excellent exploitations of silence in horror radio, whether it is the silence of realization before a scream of terror or the silent presence of an abject monstrosity. By the same token, little can sober or focus the mind as effectively as the few seconds of silence between Ernest Chappell's first and second utterance of "Quiet, Please." As Crisell argues, in contrast to film, television or theater, silence on radio "is a quality which is noticed, heard, *listened* to" (Crisell, 1994, 159).

Radio drama is a commanding experience. We take in what we hear and fill in the gaps to create the totality of the dramatic world being broadcast. The languages of sound can encompass the human voice, music and silence, as well as sound effects that can sound more "genuine" than the real things they imitate. Nothing can place you inside the head of a lunatic, a monster or a victim more profoundly than radio. When it comes to terrifying a listener, we are our own worst enemy: by default, nothing is more frightening than the demons within our own minds. As Himan Brown insists:

> The key to radio drama is sound — is imagination — is what you can do by stirring somebody. You can't do that with television. You can show them the pictures and say, "This is what it is." But so what? So you sit there like a dummy and accept the car crashes but you can't add anything to it. *There's nothing bloodier than the blood you see in your imagination.* What are they gonna do? Pour a lot of ketchup on the television screen? It's still bloodier in your own mind [Bob Morgan interviews Himan Brown, April 9, 1984].

No two imaginings will ever be the same: we create the optimum pool of blood as far as our own imagination is concerned. Looked at it in this light, radio drama makes severe demands. You cannot be a "dummy" when it comes to the medium of radio drama. There is an unspoken contract: whatever is "on the air" has to be held "in the air" by the listener's mind. If a listener is unwilling to play the radio drama game and hold the artifice of a play's universe and scenario aloft and alive in the ether, the play will not work and the listener will fall asleep or re-tune their receiver. Martin Grams, Jr., looks at the listeners' letters to *Inner Sanctum Mysteries,* and, on the basis of their meticulous observations and queries, reaches the convincing conclusion that, "Radio audiences apparently did not play bridge, read a book or carry on a conversation while tuned in for a program" (Grams, 2002, 36).

The fact that the audience gave their full attention to the broadcast is part of the serious demands of radio drama, which means that, as Andrew Crisell stresses, we are forced not only "to build the scenery," but to "'construct' the appearance and movements of a character as much as or more than the actor who plays it" (Crisell, 1994, 153). Persistently in horror radio we are the show's premier technician and director, and nothing will enthral or frighten us more than the scenery we construct or the dramatis personae that we assist in creating. As Jim Harmon argues:

> Some of radio's stars were a gigantic, pulsating chicken heart and a battered old squeaking door. It was a world of faceless things and faceless people, but a master showman could bring it to life. The greatest impresario of radio was not Cecil B. DeMille or Orson Welles. The one who really ushered you into the world of strange and commonplace delight that was radio, the guide through the mind's inner rooms, was always yourself [Harmon, 1967, 92].

However, before we render radio drama as a medium entirely dependent upon the process of reception, let us return to aspects of production. Ideally, the listener should not "notice" the framing, music and sound effects in a radio play; these elements should be conduits that imperceptibly facilitate our imagination. What we do notice and consciously "listen to" is the actor. The presence of the actor remains the quintessence of performance on radio as much as it does on stage or screen. Our imagination may orchestrate what we hear into a personal acme of horror, but nothing is more important in this process than the actor. In addition, nothing can compensate for other technical or creative shortcomings better than the actor. The performance of the actor lies at the heart of horror radio's intensity, and it is to the actor that we will now devote our attention.

3

The Cult of the Actor: Acting and Genre in Horror Radio of the Golden Age

Radio drama is a recitative form. The demands—primarily temporal—placed on the participant means that the script must be adhered to rigorously. One would expect that such strictures would threaten to destroy any potential of spontaneity, but, if anything, they enhance it. The ideal radio actor relishes working intimately with a script in a way that permits a profound exploration of role, voice and mood. The fact that the performer cannot deviate from the script makes the process like that of singing from a score: the challenge of the performance is not one of memory but of interpretation (of a, for the most part, fixed text). For the live radio actor, everything depended on the voice and it was a form that could permit a performer to explore everything from a whisper to a scream, along with a whole range of accentuation, pace and intonation. Himan Brown defines the quality of the best of the golden age performers:

> Their voice. What they did with their voice. What they did with the words. You can't write pauses in. You can't say pause, pause, pause. They didn't read—they played. They touched.... They felt.... There was a tremendous relationship in everything. And the skilful actors were absolutely brilliant [Bob Morgan interview with Himan Brown, April 9, 1984].

Voice may have been everything, but the best radio actors had other resources upon which to draw. Waldo Abbot, in a handbook for the radio industry, stresses that the "physical exertion of acting for the radio is just as great as that expended by the stage actor" (Abbot, 1941, 157), while Robert Wise goes so far as to say, "Radio acting demands a higher degree of skill and art than does the legitimate stage" (Wise, 1941, 60). Waldo Abbot urges that the "actor should actually throw himself into the part" (Abbot, 1941, 157). Abbot recalls how actors in a play in which they were pursued by a pack of wolves went through the physical motions of running and the body language of terror, albeit (except for a few moments when an "eight-ball" mobile microphone was used) without ever deviating from the strictly demarcated microphone position, generally "one foot from the mike" (Abbot, 1941, 157). Another radio manual from the same era emphasizes the importance of the "total body":

> Radio acting is not simply "voice acting." Although the listener knows the radio actor only through the voice, the actor uses his whole body in portraying a character, just as does the stage or film actor. Good acting for any medium requires total bodily response, but it is even more important in radio because the voice reflects the muscular and emotional state of the whole body [Kingson and Cowgill, 1950, 3].

Kingson and Cowgill go on to stress that, in contrast to Abbot's example, literal re-enacting is not always desirable or feasible but the tension or relaxation of appropriate muscles is obligatory if a convincing performance is to be achieved: "the radio actor... must learn to act with his whole body, but control overt action to suit the conditions of radio broadcasting" (Kingson and Cowgill, 1950, 3).

Many photographs of performers in action during a performance, including the ones in this book, reveal acting with the total body. The performers demonstrate intensity and dynamism: the actors can be seen with scripts in hand and yet utilizing highly dramatic, even melodramatic, posturing and facial contortion. These physical exertions will not even be seen outside of the studio, but they represent ways of generating a voice for "on the air" horror radio in an attempt to realize all the potential of emotion and intensity offered by the genre. The actors did not have the option to explore a stage or a set: tape marks on the floor would ensure that the actor strictly maintained the correct position from the microphone. All the same, the actors would use their bodies—clutching at their hair seems a recurrent example—or visualize an imaginary world around them. For instance, Agnes Moorehead, in photographs of various performances of "Sorry, Wrong Number" (pages 40 and 42), seems to find differing points of focus: unquestionably aided enormously by having her dialogue memorized (Dunning, 1998, 649), Moorehead variously mimes a telephone, addresses the microphone directly, and targets her focus across the studio before collapsing exhausted.

In a discussion of Miriam Wolfe's acting, Michael Ross (her son) recalls that Wolfe "never really spoke about technique." Nonetheless:

> It was plain to see, though, how easy it was for her to turn any role on and off. She was frequently asked to utter her witch's cackle and it came out quite "naturally," although she would visibly "tense up" her body to produce it.... She was certainly not trying to physically portray a witch in her acting, as radio only required her sounds and she did not have to perform visually. The cramped-up hand is especially noteworthy [Michael Ross, email to Richard J. Hand, July 30, 2004].

Like all the best actors in the intense and terse medium of live radio, Wolfe is able to step in and out of a role with ease. In the last line of the above quotation, Ross refers to the photograph of Wolfe in performance as Old Nancy (page 43). Wolfe can be seen to employ facial contortions: her neck cranes slightly, her brow furrows and her mouth opens uncomfortably in a manner which evidently helps to generate, physically, the

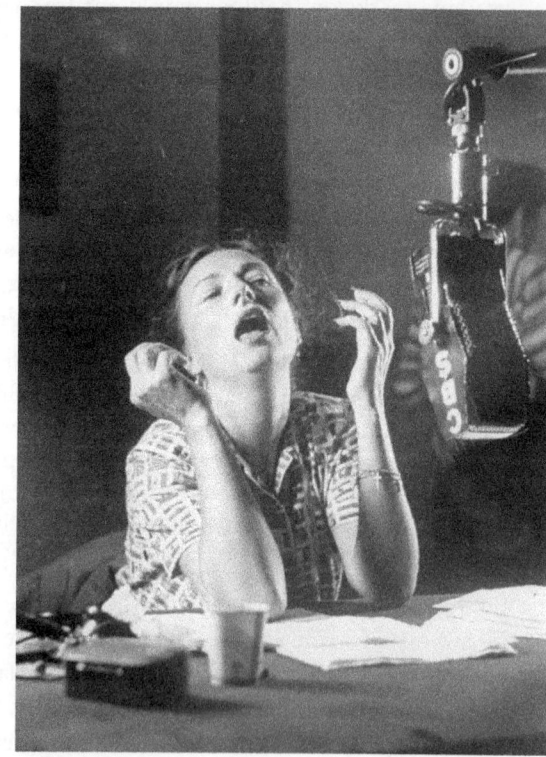

geriatric voice of the old Salem witch. Although voice is everything, it is interesting to observe that Wolfe's right hand is contorted: this gesture may have contributed to the physical creation of Old Nancy's voice, revealing that Wolfe is using muscles beyond the neck, face, mouth and throat; but it is also possible that the "cramped-up hand" is an emblem that facilitates the persona of Old Nancy in terms of characterization. Her left hand holds the script and she stands in the optimum microphone position for a radio actor, but her voice and her right hand are entirely Old Nancy.

The radio studio could vary in size depending on the type of broadcast (most obviously in relation to the size of musical accompaniment, presence of studio audience, etc.), but was often remarkably small. John S. Carlile provides several examples of studios and also explains how the construction and flexibility of each example can facilitate optimum results for the type of program being broadcast (Carlile, 1942, 196–209). Typically, the actors shared the same microphone, and so their area of the studio was characterized by intimacy. Although Frank Sinatra (page 44) may be pictured in almost vulnerable isolation, the proximity of Rita Hayworth and Hans Conried (page 45), and Alan Devitt and Mark Smith (page 46), reflects a familiar performance practice of the studio. Sometimes actors would be in direct physical contact throughout a performance, leaning over one another or pressed against each other, crowding around the microphone. This extraordinary physical intimacy of the studio is another major factor that contributes to the intensity of the performance practice of horror radio.

The dynamics of performance within the studio was not limited to the performers themselves. An extraordinary sign language of directing developed. In the theater, the director is supposed to become a mere spectator by the time of performance, but on live radio the director is needed to orchestrate the performance. Waldo Abbot describes the requirements demanded of a good radio director at every stage of production, and implies that these exceed the demands of visually-based performance media: simultaneously coordinating the actors, music, sound effects and other technical issues, all with one eye strictly on the clock. It seems that the best directors in the era of live radio drama needed to be a type of performer in their own right, inspiring and orchestrating each participant and element of the production. Indeed, "orchestrate" is an apposite word in this regard: in performance, Orson Welles as actor-director of *The Mercury Theater on the Air* resembles a conductor, the focal point of the studio and in a position to coordinate the performances of the actors and the actual orchestral conductor (page 47). Arch Oboler was also aware of his performative dynamic as director, whether leading his actors through rehearsal (page 48) or on the air (page 48).

During the golden age of radio, what could be described as a cult status sometimes developed around horror radio specialists and virtuoso performers, whether it be Sidney Ellstrom (*Lights Out*) or Agnes Moorehead. Cults even developed around fictional constructs. The most celebrated example of this is *The Shadow*. Such was the mystery

Opposite: Agnes Moorehead in various performances of "Sorry, Wrong Number." **Top left:** The image of propriety with focus across the studio (Wisconsin Center for Film and Theater Research, University of Wisconsin–Madison). **Top right:** Miming the telephone (Ralph Crane, Getty Images). **Bottom left:** Rage (Ralph Crane, Getty Images). **Bottom right:** exasperated and exhausted (Ralph Crane, Getty Images).

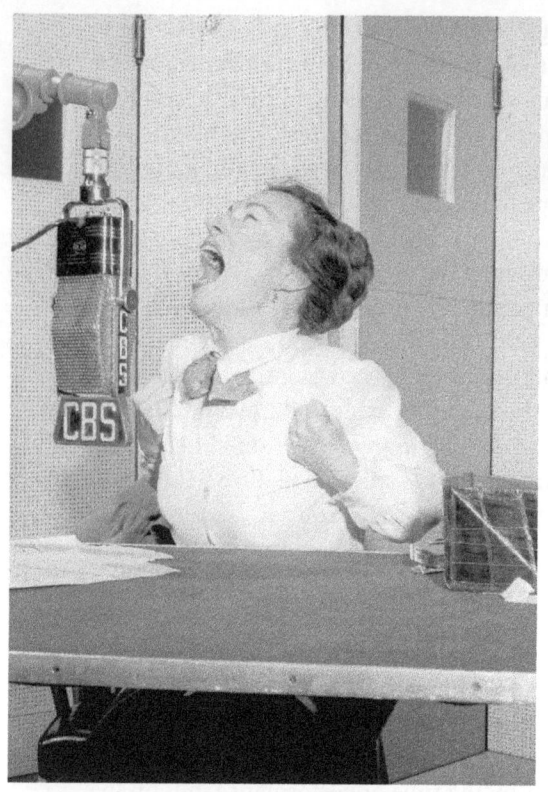

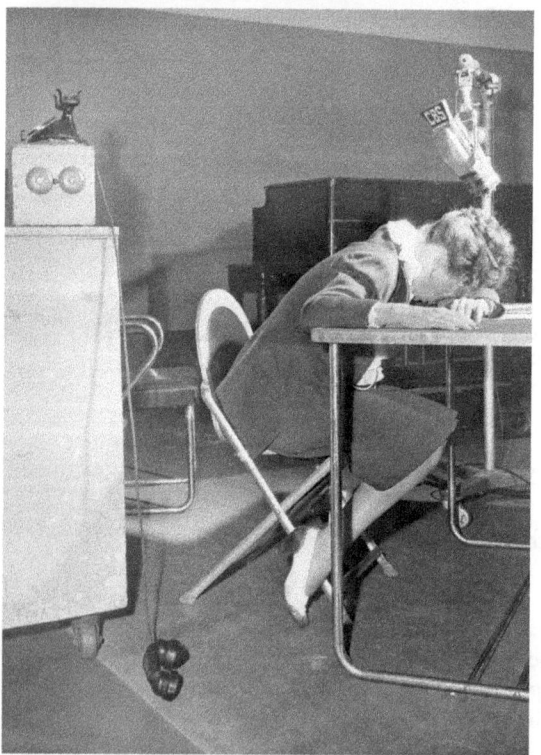
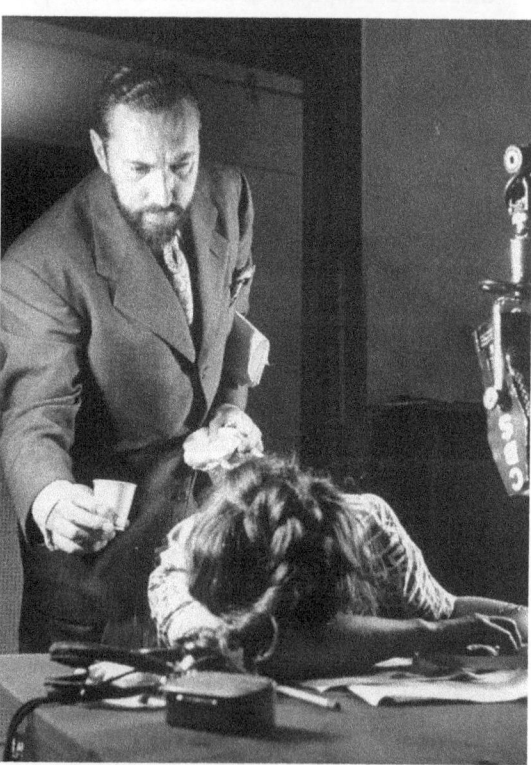

surrounding the superheroic protagonist that *Detective Story Magazine* staged a competition inviting readers to describe what they thought "the Shadow" looked like. Furthermore, on radio the *Detective Story Hour* made the following announcement: "That no man may know his identity, the Shadow will broadcast in a cloak with his face completely masked." Although a small studio audience watched the program's staged performances, the impact of this announcement went much further, inviting the listeners at home to visualize the Shadow completely covered. What is interesting here is that although the announcement acknowledges that the audience is aware that the Shadow is an actor reading from a script, the boundary between fiction and fact is consciously blurred: while the play is either purely fictional or a dramatic reenactment of "true" events, the Shadow himself is always *real*. Of course, this phenomenon is not restricted to radio. It may remind us of the tradition of children sending letters to Santa Claus "care of

Miriam Wolfe as Old Nancy the Salem Witch on *The Witch's Tale* (courtesy of Dunwich Press, publishers of *The Witch's Tale*).

the North Pole," or the phenomenon of Sherlock Holmes fandom whereby people would send letters to 221B Baker Street inviting Mr. Holmes to solve new mysteries. In the case of the Shadow on radio, however, the blurring between fiction and reality is perhaps far more complex. Some broadcasts of *The Shadow* announced that the hero's true identity was even a mystery to the other cast members. This type of publicity spin is rather like that employed by Universal's 1931 *Frankenstein,* which, at the beginning, rather than crediting Boris Karloff as "The Monster," simply includes a question mark. This can be traced back to traditions of early nineteenth-century melodrama, where anonymity was used in order to develop a sense of mystery and horror. This strategy demonstrates that there was a complex interplay between performer, character and audience. It also reflects one of the ways in which a cult could be created around a fictional construct, but also around the actor: at the end of *Frankenstein* Boris Karloff receives his credit.

Opposite: More of Moorehead in "Sorry, Wrong Number." *Top:* two good screams (Photofest). *Bottom left:* Collapse (Wisconsin Center for Film and Theater Research, University of Wisconin–Madison). *Bottom right:* Director William Spier gallantly offers water (Ralph Crane, Getty Images).

Frank Sinatra performing in "To Find Help" on *Suspense*, January 18, 1945 (Gene Lester, Getty Images).

In the golden age, all Hollywood stars made significant appearances on radio. It was partly a contractual obligation and partly an important form of publicity for their work. Probably the most significant example of this is *The Lux Radio Theatre* (1934–55). This long-running drama program presented one-hour versions of Hollywood movies. Sometimes these adaptations would be made a long time after the Hollywood films—for example, Judy Garland recreated her 1939 role of Dorothy in *Lux*'s version of *The Wizard of Oz* on December 25, 1950—but frequently they were contemporaneous with the release of the movie. On these occasions, the *Lux* broadcasts were equivalent to a trailer, or a prose and photo magazine adaptation; but the *Lux* plays were also a precursor to video/DVD release: a slice of Hollywood to be enjoyed in your own home. Although the

Rita Hayworth and Hans Conried performing in "Three Times Murder" on *Suspense*, October 3, 1946 (Gene Lester, Getty Images).

Lux radio adaptations of films were shorter, they usually featured the same actors. Many of the *Lux* dramatizations remain superb examples of adaptation. As "movie tie-ins" their function as publicity vehicle was profound. After all, we are talking about an era when countless more people listened to the radio than went to the movies. Moreover, although the status of Hollywood in the general perception of cultural history remains hegemonic, as the 1950s progressed, Hollywood would become, as John Belton and James Spellerberg make clear, "more like Broadway. Hollywood was less a mass medium and more a specialized form of entertainment" (Belton and Spellerberg, 2002, 242). Arguably, Hollywood developed a special place as a type of entertainment — maybe even an extravagant "live event," like Broadway — and did not, contrary to the general assumption of hindsight, permeate the audiences' lives in the way that radio (and, by now, television) did.

Although radio could simultaneously reach an audience in the multi-millions, its localized effect was a thorough infiltration of domestic lives and environments, and is therefore an intensely *intimate* form. Radio had a colossal role in making actors household names: it made them familiar to their listeners. Also, we should remind ourselves again that the radio during that era was a *live* medium. It was not pre-produced like movies, but reached its audience "live." When a listener tuned in to a broadcast they were in the company of somebody speaking directly to them. The broadcasts may have come from studios in California or New York, but the listeners were in the intimate presence of a performer talking to them: a live voice within the same room. Robert S. Cathcart argues that although Charles Lindbergh's transatlantic flight in 1927 was an event of international triumph publicized through print and even word of mouth:

> It was radio that made the audience members feel they were part of heroic performance. It is this quality of instantaneousness that radio provides that makes people feel that there is very little that separates them from the hero/celebrity [Cathcart, 1994, 44].

Alan Devitt and Mark Smith performing on *The Witch's Tale* (courtesy of Dunwich Press, publishers of *The Witch's Tale*).

Cathcart is talking about true historical events and real people, but the implications of this in relation to radio drama are easy to see: the instantaneousness of radio means that very little separates us from the actor and/or the fictional construct being portrayed.

Radio drama did not merely serve to enhance or consolidate the careers of Hollywood stars, ensuring that they were household names made familiar through the instantaneousness of radio. Many radio dramas were also extremely adventurous. The most sustained example of this probably comes in the form of *Suspense* (1942–62). The vast output of *Suspense* reflects an incredible body of drama (including horror), many paradigmatic in quality. On *Lux*, actors merely had to recreate the same roles in substantially shorter versions. In *Suspense*, however, we are generally looking at broadcasts that are pure one-off radio plays, not adaptations, which presented a freer rein for the actor. *Suspense* offered actors plenty of opportunities to explore the strategies they were good at as performers. But one of the most interesting things in relation to the role of the actor on *Suspense* is the opportunity the program offered supporting actors to take center stage, or leading actors to go against type. As Allison McCracken explains:

> *Suspense* provided opportunities for the Hollywood actors, usually supporting players, in films to take center stage as complex, subjective protagonists in their own twisted narratives [McCracken, 2002, 184].

As examples, McCracken cites Agnes Moorehead, Eve Arden and Joseph Cotten, as well as figures we shall analyze in-depth in due course: Peter Lorre and Vincent Price. In addition to allowing the supporting player to take the lead in intense and often violent drama, *Suspense* also permitted major stars the chance to play against their Hollywood typecast image. Performers such as Lucille Ball (page 49), normally associated with comedy, were able to play victims or femme fatales. In "Dime a Dance" (January 13, 1944), Ball plays Ginger Allen, a "dime a dance" girl, while reports of a serial killer (Hans Conried) circulate. The killer murders redheaded women (the listener is supposed to visualize, as much as hear, Lucille Ball in a fictional role) and then dances with their corpses to the

Orson Welles on *The Mercury Theater on the Air* (Archive Photos, Getty Images).

Left Arch Oboler in rehearsal with Alla Nazimova (John Florea, Getty Images). *Right* Arch Oboler giving the directing symbol "Take it easy," June 26, 1949 (Photofest).

song "Poor Butterfly." The use of a murderer's theme tune — like Peter Lorre's whistling in *M* (Fritz Lang, 1931) — has a fetishistic and uncanny effect which works especially well on radio. Inevitably, Ginger finds herself trapped with the killer, and at the play's climax the killer assaults the woman to the sounds of screams and a violent physical struggle (which the listeners can make as horrible as they fear or wish it to be).

Judy Garland would usually be seen in singing roles or light comedy: in "Drive In" (*Suspense*, November 21, 1946), Judy Garland plays a waitress who hops into the car of a customer. Although the character she portrays simply wants a lift to the bus stop, the audience would have been surprised at the implications of loose morality.

Other examples include Frank Sinatra and Gene Kelly, who both played the same role in a play called "To Find Help" (Sinatra on January 18, 1945; Kelly on January 6, 1949). In this superbly crafted suspense play by Mel Dinelli, Frank Sinatra, although widely recognized now for his versatility, did not play the young "heart throb" crooner that he was known as at the time, but a dangerous psychopath. In this excruciatingly suspenseful play, a young handyman has been employed to help a vulnerable old woman, Mrs. Gillis (Agnes Moorehead in 1945, Ethel Barrymore in 1949), in her home. Once they are alone, he gradually descends into psychosis (and Mrs. Gillis descends into terror), locking all the doors, breaking the telephone and roughly tying up Mrs. Gillis. Although she is finally rescued, the play is a terrifying study of sadistic menace and vulnerability, distinguished by the dialogic power play in which Mrs. Gillis attempts to placate or gain control over her assailant. Both Sinatra and Gene Kelly evidently relished the opportunity to play such an antithetical role, the type of part that Hollywood at the time would not have dared let them play.

As well as allowing actors to go against type and demonstrate their versatility, the implications of *Suspense* are more far-reaching. The dynamics are fascinating when we consider that in radio, the most intimate of all performance media, we are witnessing actors playing the dangerous and the insane. In a review for the *New York Herald Tribune* (November 2, 1948), John Crosby playfully complains that in stark contrast to the misery that the genre usually presents, a recent soap opera presented an episode in which "every blessed soul ... was blissfully happy." He uses this as a springboard to complain about *Suspense*'s "Night Cry" (October 7, 1948):

Lucille Ball performing in "Dime a Dance" on *Suspense*, January 13, 1944 (Gene Lester, Getty Images).

> As if that wasn't enough to shake my faith in the established order of things, there was the case on *Suspense* of Ray Milland playing the part of one of those tough, extraordinarily competent detectives who is tracking down a murderer. He thought he had his man, a very suspicious character, but the guy wouldn't answer questions. In a moment of anger, the cop slugged the murder suspect, who instantly drops dead. The rest of the story was devoted to Milland's efforts to beat a murder rap himself. I can't think what drove the writer of that program to shatter an ancient tradition in such an uncouth manner, to make a cop behave in a way that no cop has ever behaved on the radio. Iconoclasm? Desperation? Or simply the belief that radio hasn't long to live anyway, and we might just as well start breaking up the joint right now?

In playing a "bad guy," Ray Milland was not necessarily going against type, but what is interesting here is Crosby's concern about genre, society and morality. Crosby and millions of listeners heard the good guy metamorphose into the villain in the space of a 30-minute drama. *Suspense* was challenging the traditional order of the genre in which things are governed by a black and white morality, and the law is always good. An article on censorship in *Radio Stars* magazine (September 1940) provides further elucidation:

> Phil Lord, for example, on his various dramatic programs insisted that every cop must be a good cop. No dramatization portraying a dishonest police officer would be countenanced on his *Gang Busters* and other shows.

Despite the fact that this article is written in the past tense, a few years later we find the same Phillips H. Lord stressing his responsibility in an article for *Radio Review* (December 10, 1945):

> In the past 10 years, I have attempted to present cases of hardened adult criminals and to demonstrate to the adults as well as to the novices or potential criminals that crime does not pay. But with the tremendous increase in juvenile crime, I have decided to dramatize more cases of youths in an effort to reach the youth and effectively demonstrate to him that his lawlessness will only lead to prison, at best.... Radio knows that it has this social responsibility—and we, on *Gang Busters*, are continuing to do everything in our power to bring radio's crusade against crime to the public attention.

This demonstrates how issues of genre and narrative were very closely tied to issues of social responsibility. In the light of this, we can add that in the same way that it was a shock to hear a policeman turn into a murderer, it must have been a surprise to hear a well-loved and familiar actor playing the psychopath. In an analysis of radio personalities, Joshua Meyrowitz discusses some of the dynamics of intimacy:

> Radio personalities were close in aural space and often entered people's homes daily, but their "presence" during these visits had no visual dimensions except in the listener's imagination. Media performers who were experienced through the radio were like friends at a pajama party who came after the lights were turned off and left before morning. There was an odd mix of intimacy and distance, of knowledge and mystery [Meyrowitz, 1994, 65].

When an actor was cast against type, issues of intimacy and distance, knowledge and mystery, were further compounded by complications of surprise and suspense, and possibly even betrayal (albeit an immensely enjoyable betrayal that would last up to 30 minutes and would merely confirm the versatility of the performer). Meyrowitz talks about the pajama party with the lights off. This phrase captures the level of intimacy—what Andrew Crisell describes as the "paradox of technology" (Crisell, 1994, 153), whereby the voices of the actors makes them seem closer to us than if we were with them in the literally shared spatial environments of live theater—but Meyrowitz's emphasis on the *darkness* leads us neatly into the area of horror radio. After all, *Lights Out* was the name of one of the most celebrated horror shows. The quintessential horror voices of Hollywood—stars such as Boris Karloff, Peter Lorre and others—invaded the aural space of the golden age listener. However, as we shall see, their performances and presence have their own complicated dynamics.

Horror stars such as Bela Lugosi and Boris Karloff have become synonymous with 1930s horror, primarily because of Universal Pictures. However, despite their association with each other, their fortunes were very different, and the contrast becomes most evident if we look at their careers on radio. Bela Lugosi first appeared on radio giving a speech about the film *Dracula* (KFI, March 27, 1931). His greatest contribution to horror radio was probably as the lead actor on *Mystery House* in 1944. *Mystery House* was a short-lived horror series remarkable for being an overt adaptation of plays from the French Grand-Guignol Theater, a venue and performance tradition with a massive influence on the history of popular horror culture. To date, only one recording from *Mystery House* has come to light. The play "Thirsty Death" is an enjoyable mixture of horror and love, as only a play about adultery and rabies could be. Despite *Mystery House* pointedly declaring that it is adapting plays from the Grand-Guignol in Paris, the program fails to cite the specific plays. One can only assume that "Thirsty Death" is, in fact, an adaptation of the play *Une rage d'amour* (1916) by Alphonse de Beil. Aside from this, Lugosi appeared on *Suspense* in a play called "The Doctor Prescribes Death" (February 2, 1943). He also appeared with Boris Karloff on the *Ozzie and Harriet Show* in the late 1930s, and appeared with Karloff and Peter Lorre on the quiz show *Kay Kyser's Kollege of Musical Knowledge* (September 25, 1940). If in the *Suspense* play Lugosi was used for mysterious and horrific effect, his appearances with Karloff and Lorre were used to much more ironic ends. Other examples of Lugosi's presence as an ironic figure — typical of Lugosi's radio career as a whole — include his appearance in a cameo role on *The Abbott and Costello Show* (May 5, 1948) and as a shopkeeper of ghoulish curios on *Candid Microphone* (ABC, 1947). In both these works Lugosi's performance mode is that of simple self-parody. It is sometimes argued in film history that because Bela Lugosi did not fully master the English language his Hollywood career languished after his Universal heyday. If this is true, the implications for a radio career are immediately obvious. Lugosi's voice may have been distinctive and unmistakable, but he arguably lacked a vocal range, and his status in popular horror culture is greatest as a visible presence, a brilliant visual icon.

In contrast to Bela Lugosi, Boris Karloff's fortunes were very different. Karloff moved into motion pictures having had extensive experience as a classical and melodramatic theater actor, which was probably an excellent grounding for American cinema. By the time Karloff entered radio he was already a Hollywood star. His first appearance was as a guest on *Hollywood on the Air* (January 27, 1934), but within a few years radio became a very important aspect of Karloff's career. As Cynthia Lindsay writes, "In the late '30s, in a spirit of ominous gloom, Boris stomped through a great many varied radio shows" (Lindsay, 1975, 10). Specifically, 1938 was a key year for Boris Karloff's contribution to horror radio. In January 1938, Karloff caused controversy when he read "The Evil Eye" — an adaptation of Edgar Allan Poe's *The Tell-Tale Heart*— on the *Chase and Sanborn Hour*. In the words of S. A. Nollen, the "gruesome nature of the broadcast" (Nollen, 1991, 334) provoked a Senate debate, with at least one senator advocating radio censorship. Although this went no further, the furor surrounding the *The Mercury Theater on the Air*'s "The War of the Worlds" was only a few months away. It is fair to assume that Karloff's "The Evil Eye" was an adaptation (or extract) of the stage play *The Tell-Tale Heart* that Karloff had been touring across the United States during the same year (Underwood, 1972, 134). Among admirers of Boris Karloff as a radio performer we may include Arch Oboler, who, in an article for the *New York Times* (July 23, 1939), states:

> Among the actors Boris Karloff is top-notch. I rate him as the hardest working radio actor with intelligent approach. There is nothing hit and miss about his technique. In broadcasting, voice personality is not enough. Intelligence must be brought into the part, Karloff does just that.

Karloff was also "top-notch" as a radio performer because he used his rich, distinctive voice and his stage experience in the handling of spoken language, characterization and narrative. It is ironic that Karloff came to prominence playing the Monster in *Frankenstein*, a creature who, in the first of the Universal films, could merely growl.

Arch Oboler's celebration of Karloff as a radio performer was based on personal experience. In that key year of 1938, Karloff took what Peter Underwood describes as a deliberate vacation from movies (Underwood, 1972, 134), touring in *The Tell-Tale Heart*, and also joining Arch Oboler to help inaugurate the fourth year of *Lights Out*. According to Paul M. Jensen, the short series of *Lights Out* plays starring Boris Karloff was specially written by Arch Oboler with Boris Karloff in mind (Jensen, 1974, 113). "The Dream" (March 23, 1938) is an example of Oboler's incorporation of modernist technique, with the narrative becoming a stream-of-consciousness within the thoughts of a protagonist as he sits in a courtroom on trial for his life. For Karloff, the play provides the opportunity to deliver an immaculately paced monologue distinguished by a range of emotion from bewilderment to anger to terror. There are also sections of remembered dialogue as well as effective moments of soundscape, such as the sound of his own heartbeat, the voices of the muttering jurors ("Guilty... Guilty...") and the chilling "strange wordless murmur" of the "miserable white faces" that haunt him. Above all, he is haunted by the hallucination of a woman who whispers a mantra of "Kill... kill..." inside his head. "Cat Wife" (April 6, 1938) is, for many people, one of the greatest *Lights Out* plays and an example of horror radio at its best. The performance of Karloff in this play is remarkable for its pace and transmutative shifts: just as the eponymous character undergoes an abject metamorphosis from a woman into a gigantic cat, Karloff presents an impeccably measured performance in which he moves from being a resentful and vindictive husband to a terrified, guilt-ridden weakling. In both these plays, Karloff succeeds in hooking the listener with a descent into narratives of terror, but he does so with an extraordinary quality of empathy.

It was not just on *Lights Out* that Karloff succeeded in this technique. In discussing Karloff's numerous guest appearances on *Inner Sanctum Mysteries* in the 1940s and '50s, Martin Grams, Jr., reveals:

> Almost invariably, he managed to play a villain in such a way that members of the audience felt sorry for him, along with their natural desire to kill him in order to make the community safer [Grams, 2002, 17].

Moreover, it was through this technique that, Grams reveals, some critics "speculate that Karloff altered the whole technique of the horror drama" (Grams, 2002, 17): just one aspect to Karloff's remarkable career with the result that, according to Jonathan Lake Crane, Karloff continues to be "hailed as the interpretive master of horror" (Crane, 1994, 12).

Nearly ten years after his 1938 appearances on *Lights Out*, Karloff returned to *Lights Out* for its 1947 revival. The recording of "Death Robbery" (July 16, 1947) demonstrates that Karloff had lost none of his abilities as a horror radio performer. Once again we find Karloff playing a role that combines qualities of empathy and madness. In this play Karloff is a mad scientist who endeavors to bring his dead wife back to life. He succeeds, but her brain is damaged. As in "Cat Wife," Karloff is married to an abject woman; on this occasion, however, she is not a monstrous feline but a figure who screams with demented laughter and is eventually shot dead by her husband.

In between his two seasons on *Lights Out*, Karloff also played the lead in *Stay Tuned for Terror*, which featured 15-minute radio plays written by Robert Bloch and broadcast in the mid–1940s. And the close of the 1940s brought another horror series, this one called *Starring Boris Karloff*, which broadcast fifteen 30-minute dramas on ABC from September to December 1949. Interestingly, this particular radio program was developed with a television tie-in, so that the same scripts were broadcast on radio on Wednesdays and then performed as television dramas on the following day. *Starring Boris Karloff* was well received, *Newsreel Magazine* declaring in September 1949:

> [With] practically no advance warning, Boris Karloff crept into millions of homes via radio and television [offering audiences] some of the creepiest entertainment yet broadcast and televised [quoted in Nollen, 1991, 138].

It is clear that Karloff managed to sustain a career as a popular horror icon even after the golden age of film in the 1930s ended. Although it could be argued that in Hollywood horror moved away from Transylvanian terrors into Abbott and Costello–style parody or the authentic horrors of film noir, it is interesting that someone like Karloff still managed to sustain a performance career as a horror star, thanks to radio. In an analysis of film stars and issues of genre, Andrew Britton contends that, "stars like Karloff and Lugosi who are enveloped in the ethos of a specific character" (Britton, 1991, 202–3) were unable to cross genres. However, if we look at the work of Karloff on radio we find that the issue is far more complex. Certainly Karloff did manage to sustain a career as a horror star on radio in the 1940s, but on a number of dramatic broadcasts Karloff demonstrates his non-horror virtuosity, including radio adaptations of Eugene O'Neill's *The Emperor Jones* (*Theater Guild on the Air*, November 11, 1945) and H. G. Wells' *The History of Mr. Polly* (*NBC University Theater*, October 17, 1948). Elsewhere Karloff was able to be "himself": on *Boris Karloff's Treasure Chest* in the early 1950s Karloff acted as a disc jockey, playing folk music and other cheery songs for a children's audience, with no suggestion of horror. On other shows he was able to explore his persona as an English actor with great knowledge of his profession. Several appearances on the quiz show *Information Please* provided some fascinating insights into the "real" Boris Karloff. According to Cynthia Lindsay, *Information Please* was "one of the professional activities from which Boris derived the most enjoyment" (Lindsay, 1975, 104).

On *Information Please* (January 24, 1941) we find Karloff answering cryptic questions on Joseph Conrad, as well as demonstrating an impressive knowledge of the history of popular theater and Victorian poetry. Nevertheless, Karloff is still presented as a horror icon: at the time he was playing the psychopathic Jonathan Brewster in Joseph Kesselring's *Arsenic and Old Lace* in the theatre; and they sit him next to Lewis E. Lawes, warden of Sing-Sing and author of *Meet the Murderer!* (1940), a bestselling work of popular criminology. The host makes repeated jokes about Karloff being dangerous and murderous. In a publicity still from the day of the broadcast, we see Karloff demonstrating to Lawes how to use an axe (page 54). In another broadcast on *Information Please* (May 17, 1943), Karloff joins the program via a live link-up from Hollywood, where he decides that rather than interrupt for an answer by using a bell, he will furnish a growl like *Frankenstein*'s creature in the 1931 film. This is a great moment of horror comedy, with the audience laughing every time Karloff growls, and it is portentously ended when host Clifton Fadiman declares it too disturbing.

Karloff's role on *Information Please* was not dissimilar to the kind of role he took in April 1950 when, at the Imperial Theater on Broadway, Karloff played the dual roles

Boris Karloff and Lewis E. Lawes on *Information Please*, January 24, 1941 (Hulton Archive, Getty Images).

of George Darling and Captain Hook in a highly successful production of J. M. Barrie's *Peter Pan*. Karloff's persona is like this in many ways, the father figure and the dreaded villain at one and the same time: a figure that succeeds in being frightening, worthy of respect and strangely comforting — even comic — all at once. In the culture of terror, however, there is always a fine line between comedy and horror. In terms of golden age radio, horror always has an important place outside of the genres that explore it directly. For instance, we might think of Jack Benny's pastiche of *The Whistler* as "The Fiddler" (*The Jack Benny Program*, October 20, 1946), and also the numerous Halloween "specials" that were an important part of the comedy genre. *Spotlight Revue* may have been dominated by the madcap comedy of Spike Jones and the City Slickers, but when Dorothy Shay, "the Park Avenue Hillbilly," sings the deceptively melodious "Mountain Lullaby" (November 21, 1947), we are presented with a satire of hillbilly America — unhygienic, violent and felonious — which concludes with monstrosity and inbreeding: "Close your sleepy eye/That's right, now the other one/That's right, now the *other* one." All these examples feature an aspect of symbiosis, horror draining into comedy, just as comedy will influence horror.

The place of the cameo role is also extremely important in the development of the horror actor on radio. Boris Karloff appeared in cameo roles on numerous horror broadcasts. In the Dorothy Lamour vehicle *Sealtest Variety Hour* "Halloween Special" (October 28, 1948), Karloff steps into and out of character in the conventional variety/comedy formula of sketches and songs. Karloff appeared on the same show the following year, but in a much more adventurous format. In the *Sealtest Variety Hour* episode called "The Stranger Arrives" (June 23, 1949), Karloff plays himself, having toured the same route as a serial killer, announcements about whom frequently interrupt the show. Karloff sustains a menacing persona with the horror-comic ingredients that one expects from horror radio, such as gathering a collection of human heads in the refrigerator. However, one of the radio announcements reveals that the real Boris Karloff is in New York. Hence an announcement broadcast within the radio show reveals that Boris Karloff is not really playing himself but is an impostor. In other words, Boris Karloff is playing someone who is playing Karloff. It is a humorous conceit that is skillfully and enjoyably played and sustained for the entire broadcast. It is rather similar to his role as Jonathan Brewster in the stage production of *Arsenic and Old Lace,* in which Karloff plays a serial killer who at one point explains that he was driven to murder because someone likened him to Boris Karloff. The cameo role often seems to have a simple function, but these moments of oscillation between the authentic and the constructed demonstrate how complex the function of the cameo can be. In terms of reception, the cameo role can only enjoy its full horror-comic potential when playing to an audience that can recognize the dual role of the guest star as character *and* actor. In discussing *Arsenic and Old Lace*, Denis Gifford states that "in harness with Peter Lorre, Karloff found himself sending up the genre he had helped create" (Gifford, 1973, 60); the audiences that watched the play recognized that Karloff and Lorre were playing horror-comic characters but were simultaneously iconic actors of the horror/mystery genre, a receptive process that was repeated by millions of radio listeners.

The casting of Peter Lorre in *Arsenic and Old Lace* was as much of a coup as securing Karloff. In Lorre we have another great horror icon whose function in the play was an exploration of cameo, but who proved integral to the generic subversion of the work. Lorre made his debut on American radio on the *Fleischmann Hour* (May 7, 1936), in which he played the "fiendish" (Youngkin et al., 1982, 48) Doctor Millaire. This shows him being cast in the kind of role that Hollywood would also offer him. In the late 1930s he also appeared on the *Rudy Vallee Show*, but it was not until he moved to Warner Brothers in 1941 that his radio career really bloomed. Youngkin et al. argue that 1942–46 was a prolific period for Lorre on radio, during which he played many "eerie and macabre" (Youngkin et al., 1982, 48) roles. During this period he often appeared on *Suspense*, with 1943 being a particularly prolific year. In 1945 he played the lead in *Suspense*'s play "Nobody Loves Me" (August 30, 1945). Lorre's performance is outstanding: he plays a psychopath who, in an intensely psychological tale, recounts his life of tragedy in which from earliest childhood he was neglected or abused. Lorre manages to bring to the role a genuine pathos.

The zenith for Peter Lorre as a radio actor came with his performances for *Mystery in the Air*. For John Dunning, Lorre's performances will always be "supercharged masterpieces of radio virtuosity" (Dunning, 1998, 477). This short series from July to

Peter Lorre performing on radio, June 11, 1947 (Photofest).

September 1947 was a showcase for Lorre, who delivered performances of extraordinary virtuosity in adaptations of masterpieces of mystery and horror literature. *Mystery in the Air* was a summer replacement for NBC's *The Abbott and Costello Show*, once again bringing to mind the close interplay between horror and comedy, with a horror show temporarily filling the same slot as a comedy show. Peter Lorre, like Bela Lugosi, was another non–Anglo-American who succeeded in creating a distinctive persona. In contrast to Lugosi, however, Lorre's radio career proved far more successful. This probably reflects his strength as a performer. Lorre demonstrated diverse and sophisticated characterization as an actor, succeeding in embracing horror, mystery and comedy. Lorre was able to play comedy as proficiently as suspense or horror; he could play weak men as well as dangerous maniacs. Lorre came with an impressive theatrical pedigree, having been a key actor in the epic productions of Erwin Piscator and Bertolt Brecht in Berlin; and one of his early film roles remains one of the greatest portrayals of a serial killer on screen: *M* (Fritz Lang, 1931). After his self-imposed exile to America with the rise of Nazism, Lorre may always have played the Hollywood "foreigner"; but whether in *Mad Love* (Karl Freund, 1935), the *Mr. Moto* movies (1937–39), *The Maltese Falcon* (John Huston, 1941), *Casablanca* (Michael Curtiz, 1942), *The Beast with Five Fingers* (Robert Florey, 1946) or giving a fine comedy performance in which he simultaneously deconstructs his own persona and the horror genre (in other words, Professor Einstein in the original play and film version of *Arsenic and Old Lace* [Frank Capra, 1944]), Lorre always seems able to place a stamp on his character that is as complex and memorable as his voice. As Steven Youngkin et al. argue:

> He was a natural radio talent. Soft rhythmic whispers, childlike mewling, the frantic inflections of a tortured soul, the ranting and raving of an unhinged mind — all and much more comprised his varied vocal repertoire [Youngkin et al., 1982, 48].

Nothing provides a better example of this natural radio talent than *Mystery in the Air*. As in *M*, Lorre does not simply create the portrayal of a monster, but of a human being with an extremely complicated psychology, finding a complexity of character in his *Mystery in the Air* portrayals. *Mystery in the Air* was one of the few horror radio shows broadcast before a studio audience. Certainly the presence of an audience would not have distracted a seasoned stage actor such as Lorre; on the contrary, it probably inspired him. Harry Morgan describes Lorre's performance on *Mystery in the Air*:

> [Peter Lorre had] terrific intensity ... the things that he went through, contortions of the face and his whole body — everybody remarked on that. And he'd be dripping with sweat after the hour was over because he had not only done a great vocal performance, he'd been through a lot physically [quoted in Youngkin et al., 1982, 48].

In a now legendary anecdote, costar Peggy Webber recalls:

> Lorre threw his script into the air and watched helplessly as the pages fluttered to the stage. Some quick work by the cast and judicious ad-libbing by Lorre got them to the mid-way break, at which point the script was retrieved and put in order [quoted in Dunning, 1998, 477].

The *Mystery in the Air* repertoire included adaptations ranging from Edgar Allan Poe's "The Tell-Tale Heart" and "The Black Cat" to Dostoevsky's *Crime and Punishment* (Lorre had already played Raskalnikov in Josef von Sternberg's 1935 film version of the novel). Although Peter Lorre plays the central role in all of these plays, they are by no means monologues; there was a supporting cast. They are, to a degree, conventional plays of dialogue; yet Lorre has a close relationship with the audience in the studio and at home, and in many of the plays talks directly to us. One of the most successful plays on *Mystery in the Air* was the adaptation of Guy de Maupassant's "The Horla."

Maupassant's short story is one of the quintessential masterpieces of horror fiction, and its appeal for horror radio never diminished. Before the *Mystery in the Air* production, it had been dramatized on *Inner Sanctum Mysteries* (August 1, 1943, starring Arnold Moss) and *Weird Circle* in the 1940s. Maupassant's tale also emerged as an allusion or tangential influence. In *The Hall of Fantasy*'s "Shadow People" (September 21, 1953), for example, the listener is presented with a house in which strange homicidal beings dwell in the darkness. Maupassant's original story is presented to us by a central narrator who recounts the arrival and increasingly threatening presence of an invisible being in his home, and we follow his gradual descent into lunacy, never sure if this is a simple tale of a madman or a genuine record of supernatural phenomena. In "Shadow People," the Maupassant allusion becomes a direct reference at one point in the narrative when we are informed that Maupassant did not know that he was writing about the truth when he wrote "The Horla." Despite all these variations on "The Horla," the most authentic adaptation of Maupassant's horror masterpiece was performed by Peter Lorre in what is one of his most powerful radio performances on *Mystery in the Air* ("The Horla," August 21, 1947). Lorre captures the character of the central narrator with his usual intensity, and we witness his descent into despair and madness. At the end of the broadcast, Lorre expands the horror beyond the narrative frame:

> There is one thing I can do. I ... I can destroy myself ... yes, yes, yes! I must destroy myself! I'm going to destroy, destroy myself! Destroy! Yes! Let me go! Yes! I know I feel alright! I know! I know it's a story! I know it's by De Maupassant!

> Yes! I know it's Thursday night! And we're on the air ... but ... but it's the Horla! Oh, I ... I beg your pardon. I ... I'm sorry I got so excited but I ... I warned you at the beginning, it's a very uncomfortable story.

The above demonstrates Lorre's extraordinary skill at developing an intensity of narrative; the combination of hesitation and repeated words, and the use of faltering ellipsis and exclamatory statements, are compounded by the semantics of the speech in which Lorre, as the central character, is trapped within the role and yet simultaneously reaches out beyond the boundaries of the story. Lorre knows he is on the air, he knows it is Thursday night on NBC. What Lorre captures is almost like an alienation effect in the epic theater mold. At one and the same time Lorre plays a role within the narrative while also drawing attention to the formal conventions of the piece and the medium. There is also a delightfully comic dynamic to the speech.

It is worth commenting on Peter Lorre's performance practice. Like Boris Karloff and the fast emerging Vincent Price, Lorre was capable of doing extraordinary things with the script. We have seen how in the closing speech of "The Horla" Lorre mixes hesitancy and assertion. He is also capable of mixing menace, humor and horror. Sometimes Lorre will deliver a word or a line with a slight nervous laugh. Other times he may utter a line with leering menace. He is capable of speaking with a very gentle voice one minute, and transmuting it into a guttural roar the next. He can speak with irony and sarcasm one moment, and seem deadly earnest the next. Furthermore, his mode of delivery is not necessarily dependent on the sentiment of the speech. As a performer he enjoys establishing a juxtaposition so that the same line delivered differently has an enormous impact on psychology, characterization and the reaction of those around him — including the audience. It is his intelligence as a performer — the kind of intelligence that Oboler praised Karloff for possessing — that makes Lorre such a formidable performer in the intimate world of radio drama.

Like Boris Karloff, Peter Lorre was also a frequent guest on *Inner Sanctum Mysteries*. The show's producer, Himan Brown, recalls:

> You carried the image of Lorre into your imagination when he was playing. I mean, we didn't make him a seven-foot giant, as I might do with Boris Karloff. You fit the character to him, and the sinister, restrained, maniacal, homicidal: the face, the manner of speech. He didn't speak that way normally. That was his living [Grams, 2002, 17].

The *Inner Sanctum* writers played to Lorre's strengths, revealing that in the case of Lorre there was a very close intersection between visual memory and the spoken voice. Lorre's manner of speech and its nuances and rhythms was tied in to the memory of his face and physique. These qualities were exploited, whether Lorre was playing a role within a play, or, for example, acted as host of *Nightmare* (1953–54), or appeared in a comic cameo role.

Peter Lorre made numerous cameo appearances on comedy shows. For example, in stereotypically violent or insane guise, guest-starred on *Amos n' Andy* ("Locked Trunk's Secret," November 5, 1943) and *The Abbott and Costello Show* ("Abbott and Costello Visit a Sanatorium," January 13, 1944). Even when playing "against type" on *Skippy Hollywood Theater* (1941–50), the introduction offers Peter Lorre in self-parodying mode, which the script finds difficult to relinquish:

LES MITCHELL: It's ... it's a great pleasure to welcome our star this week ... Peter, I can't talk with that knife against my throat–
PETER LORRE: Come on, come on, read the introduction the way I told you, will ya?
LES MITCHELL: Yeah, sure, of course. It's a great pleasure to welcome our star this week ... the "young," "handsome," "loveable," "leading man"... Mr. Peter Lorre.
PETER LORRE: Well, thank you.
LES MITCHELL: Will you take the knife away now?
PETER LORRE: Alright. But you do have a nice throat...
LES MITCHELL: Ha ha ha, well I hope our writer's satisfied, Peter, now you can be serious. You see, friends, our writer thought you'd recognize Peter Lorre best in a menacing role. He is not playing a menacing role in this week's play and I'd like to say that it's a great pleasure to be able to present him in a part that shows his ability to play a completely different character than those he usually does but, er, you can leave that knife in your other suit, Peter...
PETER LORRE: Alright, alright, if you insist... ["Mr. God Johnson"].

Another Lorre comic cameo could be heard on *The Dean Martin and Jerry Lewis Show* (August 5, 1949), in which Martin and Lewis visit Peter Lorre at home. Martin and Lewis, within the narrative of the episode, are desperate for sponsorship for their program, and, in an interesting reflection on the success of the horror genre, claim that they need something gruesome to generate sponsorship interest. When they arrive outside Lorre's apartment, Jerry Lewis is typically nervous; eventually Lorre opens the door and says, "Two nice young ones ... come in!" as the audience roars. The episode emphasizes the success of "Mystery and Horror and Suspense," and Martin and Lewis persuade Lorre to join them as a member of the "Sunshine Boys," who will sing songs with a macabre twist. This celebration of the mystery genre proves interesting, considering its reception in the early 1950s, when, for instance, Harriet van Horne in *Theater Arts* (May 1952) bewailed the fact that, "Mystery shows ... continue to be in the same old rut."

In other comedy shows Peter Lorre delights in going into self-parody mode. In the *Duffy's Tavern* episode "Missing Salami Sandwich Case" (October 19, 1943), Lorre provides an excellent, ironic performance. In the episode, Lorre professes the desire to move away from his ghoulish image, and he gives an account of a bedtime story for children he has written, which he claims shows the lighter side of his character. In the story he tells, two children are stuck in a cement mixer, their parents' heads are cut off in a freak windmill accident, and elsewhere their uncle is busy barbecuing their aunt.

Lorre's ability to oscillate between horror and self-parody in comedy repeats a process imitated by (or demanded of) other actors. But it is Lorre's abilities in this field that make him the unique horror actor of his time. It is all the more impressive when one considers his life outside of his persona: he was an opponent of McCarthyism and the Blacklist (even if he was, as Youngkin et al. say, just an "armchair socialist" [Youngkin et al., 1982, 49]). He nevertheless joined the Committee for the First Amendment and read a statement on the 1947 broadcast *Hollywood Fights Back*. Lorre also had other concerns around this time — the *New York Times* (May 22, 1949), for instance, announced his bankruptcy.

One of the most enjoyable examples of the Peter Lorre comedy cameo came in the form of the Spike Jones and his City Slickers' song "My Old Flame." The first half of the song is played straight with what seems to be romantic lyrics, but the second half changes the mood by mutating into a song of horror. Paul Frees imitates Peter Lorre in singing the lyrics in what amounts to a spoof of *Mystery in the Air*. "My Old Flame" transforms from a song of gentle and sentimental nostalgia for an old love into a gruesome tale of dismemberment. The song was so popular it enjoyed several broadcasts on *Spotlight Revue*, but the most interesting broadcast (for our purposes) is the one in which, after Paul Frees has given his impeccable imitation of Lorre, Peter Lorre himself comes on stage and revels in playing the monstrous icon (December 10, 1948). It is interesting to note that the target of the song "My Old Flame," Peter Lorre's persona, is already a self-parodic persona in its own right.

The aforementioned Paul Frees was one of the most exceptionally talented radio performers of the golden age, rivaled only by Hans Conried for sheer versatility. Frees strayed into horror drama not just through the "My Old Flame" parody, but as the lead actor — indeed, the *only* actor — on *The Player* in 1948. These 15-minute examples of "one-man theater" (Dunning, 1998, 548) allowed Frees to display his virtuoso acting and masterful use of dialects and accents in intense, often macabre, plays. The fact that the plays were short did not diminish their attempts at complexity and intertextual sophistication.

Like Frees, Hans Conried was similarly versatile and prolific. As Leonard Maltin writes, Conried "mastered a dazzling range of dialects and tackled both serious and comic parts with enthusiasm" (Maltin, 2000, 115). Conried's ability to play roles of menacing humor is well represented by his appearances in such films as *The Five Thousand Fingers of Dr. T* (Roy Rowland, 1953), and as the voice of Captain Hook in Disney's *Peter Pan* (Wilfred Jackson et al., 1953). But on radio Conried demonstrated a tremendous range. Some of his finest roles were realized on *Suspense*. In "Three Times Murder" (October 3, 1946), Conried plays a district attorney, Elmer Garner, attempting to convict Laura Williams (Rita Hayworth) of killing her husband. The play is predominantly dialogic between the two characters, and creates an impressive oscillation in the listener's empathy. Conried may be part of established authority, but he is as "unscrupulous and objectionable" as the widow describes him. Laura is the focus of the narrative, and thus elicits our empathy — the iconic status of the major Hollywood star Rita Hayworth is integral here — although she proves equally ruthless. Acquitted of murder, Laura — knowing that she cannot be tried for the same crime twice — screams her guilt with vindictive delight. The play follows Laura in her new marriage and her shocking discovery that her brother-in-law is none other than Elmer himself. Elmer resorts to blackmail and becomes the villain of the piece, despite Laura's guilt. Conried and Hayworth work very well together in developing the narrative with sequences of dialogic sparring, power play and moments of malicious antithesis: when Hayworth screams Conried leeringly laughs. Elmer murders his own brother to frame Laura, but she commits suicide and thus sends Elmer to his execution for a double murder. It is a short play which leaves Elmer, Laura and her two husbands dead at the end: three murders and a suicide. The material is perfect for Conried, while for Hayworth it offers another example of the "against-type" opportunity that *Suspense* specialized in. At the end of the broadcast the host interviews Hayworth, who expresses her delight at the role:

RITA HAYWORTH: Excuse me, I'm a little out of breath: I don't usually kill so many people, at least not in one day.
KEN NILES: How does it feel to play a murderer?
RITA HAYWORTH: I love it. I've been looking forward to playing on *Suspense* for a very, very long time...

Actors like Paul Frees and Hans Conried were lynchpins in the era of live radio. The two actors appeared together in a classic episode of *Escape*, "The Most Dangerous Game" (October 1, 1947), a version of Richard Connell's 1924 short story in which a ruthless game hunter on an island chases the ultimate prey: a man. The story was first filmed in 1932, and the scenario became a paradigm of horror. The voices of Conried as the hunter and Frees as the hunted on the *Escape* episode create tremendous atmosphere and pace, making the radio version probably the most successful adaptation of Connell's tale.

Another actor who worked prolifically as a radio performer was William Conrad. The range and resonance of Conrad's voice resulted in him becoming a paid radio performer while still a teenager. In the area of horror and suspense, Conrad acted on *The Hermit's Cave* and *Suspense*, and made a central contribution to *Escape* as both announcer and actor. Of his numerous noteworthy performances, the standout might be his role in "A Study in Wax" (*Escape*, February 1, 1953, and revived on *Suspense* on August 16, 1955). The play, based on an Anthony Ellis short story, is a superb two-hander, perfect for radio, in which two men are confined to a cabin together for the duration of a Northwest Territories winter. The play is a study of claustrophobia and conflict: the habits and personalities of the two men begin to irritate each other, and the play charts their mutual descent into madness. Although the William Conrad character is the narrator and survivor, while his cabin mate becomes murderous and insane, the play is not all black and white: in this study of privation and psychological despair, one character is as dangerous and insane as the other, and the listener knows it.

Another noteworthy Conrad performance came in "Evening Primrose" (*Escape*, November 5, 1947), a genuinely chilling tale based on the short story by John Collier. Conrad plays an arrogant misfit who takes up residence in a department store, sleeping during the day and evading the night watchmen after hours. He discovers that the shop mannequins come to life at night. Conrad's narrative control allows this eerie story to unfurl effectively: the play is a kind of grotesque fairytale, with the mannequins, like the toys in many children's stories, coming to life when no one is looking. However, the play also succeeds as an ironic critique on retail capitalism, grotesquely humanizing the material objects of commerce. The fact that the misanthropic protagonist falls in love with one of the animated dummies also adds an ironic eroticism to the work. The same John Collier story was the source for Rod Serling's *The Twilight Zone* episode "The After Hours" (June 10, 1960), praised by Marc Scott Zicree for its "spooky, unspoken, oppressive quality" (Zicree, 1992, 127). *The Twilight Zone* version adapts the story by abandoning the male protagonist and centering on the female mannequin. As fine and distinctive as the television version is, it does not capture the sheer eeriness that the radio version creates, with its rich atmosphere and evocation of the mannequins coming to life (including the "shadowy matriarch" of the mannequins—a female dummy, "wrinkled and cracked and emaciated"—who crawls down the wall like "an ancient spider.")

William Conrad was a stalwart performer of golden age radio who would become most famous as Matt Dillon on *Gunsmoke* (1952–61). When *Gunsmoke* moved to television, Conrad, to his eternal chagrin, failed the audition, although he would later become a television icon as the detective Frank Cannon in *Cannon* (1971–76). But the work that most fully demonstrates the potency of Conrad's range and ability as a narrator and character actor — and which continues to reward the listener — is his radio work from the late 1940s to the early 1950s, especially in the thrilling or eerie fantasies of *Escape* and *Suspense*.

If William Conrad would be typecast as the voice of Matt Dillon and, on screen, as the corpulent Cannon, another actor who made a major contribution to golden age radio would also become typecast — not as a specific character but as an icon of a genre. Vincent Price, like Karloff, Lugosi and Lorre, is one of the twentieth century's icons of popular horror. Price did not begin his career in horror; as far as many critics — and Price himself (as evidenced by a 1971 radio interview with Chuck Shaden) — were concerned, his first "horror" role came in *House of Wax* (André de Toth, 1953). By this time he was well established as a theater actor and star of dramatic film, having appeared in film noir milestones such as *Laura* (Otto Preminger, 1946) and Gothic romances such as *Dragonwyck* (Joseph L. Mankiewicz, 1946). As for radio, Price's most sustained radio role was as the heroic Simon Templar in *The Saint* from 1947 to 1951. However, Price made a number of significant explorations of the macabre in his radio career that were contemporaneous with, and even prior to, *House of Wax*, which can be seen as shaping his future status as an icon of horror culture.

Vincent Price performing on *The Saint*, July 30, 1950 (Photofest).

Vincent Price first appeared on radio as early as June 18, 1936, on *Standard Brands Radio Hour* with Rudy Vallee in a scene from the play *There's Always Juliet*. In his own words, Price reveals, with typical playfulness:

I started to do radio work in 1936, and for more than twenty years I did a bit of everything at the microphone.... But hardly anyone remembers radio as it was then, so there is no point in going on about what fun it used to be [Price, 1978, 71–72].

This reveals the nostalgia Price would always feel for the medium of radio and the diverse range of roles he created for it. His extraordinary vocal ability was the key to his aptitude for the medium. As Victoria Price explains:

[His] immediately recognizable voice and his aptitude for learning his lines fast made Vincent a natural for radio, where actors were often asked to work with scant rehearsal time, disorganized or unfinished scripts, and cramped conditions. Actors who could master the medium often found they were in high demand [Price, 1999, 111].

If the versatility of Paul Frees and Hans Conried was the key to their prolific radio careers, for Price it was, like Karloff and Lorre, partly a case of exploring a distinctive and memorable voice. If we analyze the horror trio's vocal techniques we make some interesting discoveries: Karloff uses his deep, English theatrical tones and pacing; Lorre employs modulations between the simpering and the menacing, shifting from unhinged but self-effacing laughter into homicidal fury; Price has a delicate voice and invariably lucid enunciation. Price uses these qualities to hold an audience's attention; but they can easily be manipulated to create a sense of menace and psychological complexity. For his own part, Price said that, "I have never played a part in which I was really a monster. My specialty is playing men who have been hurt by life, men who have been betrayed" (Price, 1978, 51) — a statement that reveals that in most of his horror roles he plays men that are driven by passions and desires. James Robert Parish and Steven Whitney observes that Price possesses the "ability to emulate a grand style of macabre vivacity without being foolish" (Parish and Whitney, 1974, 94). Interestingly, Parish and Whitney make this statement specifically regarding Price's performance in *The Fly* (Kurt Neumann, 1958), but it seems a helpful definition in relation to Price's unique contribution to horror as a whole. Price was an actor of irony and humor, and yet he always maintained a gravitas of horror. He never played a role over seriously or pretentiously, but was still able to be convincing *within* the role, drawing an audience into a personal world of obsession, peril or insanity.

Parish and Whitney acknowledge how important radio was as a precursor to Price's horror status when they admit that radio "was painting the way to Vincent's professional future" (Parish and Whitney, 1974, 74):

> Although he continued as Simon Templar in *The Saint* on NBC, he did three CBS radio dramas that were significant: "Bloodbath," "Three Skeleton Keys" [sic], and "Present Tense." All were dramas of the macabre, a form in which Vincent excelled because of the rich deepness of his voice. The subtle menace contained in his full-bodied voice was naturally suited to scaring the wits out of most pliable souls, a fact that moviemakers had not as yet comprehended. Certainly he was playing villains in films, but these parts tended to resemble the Sir Jaspers of Victorian melodrama more than the frightening bogeyman of the macabre [Parish and Whitney, 1974, 74].

"Bloodbath" (*Escape*, June 30, 1950) presents a group of oil prospectors encountering every imaginable peril of the jungle, including vampire bats, piranhas, electric eels and boa constrictors; "Three Skeleton Key" (*Escape*, March 17, 1950) is a paradigmatic lighthouse horror tale; and "Present Tense" (*Escape*, January 31, 1950) is a vivid convict-on-the-run story after the protagonist has survived a gruesome train crash. The plays are all masterpieces of the radio form that utilize Price as both narrator and lead — a storyteller who recounts his story in past or present tense, with substantial sections of dialogue and action revisited as they happened or unfurl in the present. "Three Skeleton Key" is Price's most celebrated contribution to horror radio, and was revived several times on *Suspense* in the 1950s. Interestingly, although it became synonymous with Price as a radio actor, he was not the first to play the main role in "Three Skeleton Key" when it first aired on *Escape* (November 15, 1949). Despite Elliot Reid's memorable performance in the premiere of the play, it is an ideal role for Price. The play, based on George Gustave Toudouze's 1937 short story, is set on a lighthouse in which three keepers become besieged by a legion of rats. It is a play that brilliantly creates a sense of urgency, panic, claustrophobia and increasing madness. The play has a very powerful soundscape, exemplified by the various noises of the lighthouse itself and the chilling cacophony of rats, which was partly created by rubbing wet corks on glass (Maltin, 2000, 108). Price's virtuoso roles on *Escape* and *Suspense* in the 1950s are recognizably precursive to his later horror roles, but we might also consider earlier Price performances, such as his appearance in Lucille Fletcher's "Fugue in C Minor" (*Suspense*, June 1, 1944), a post–Gothic murder play in which Price plays Theodore Evans, a widowed man who has built a massive pipe organ into the structure of his house, and charms Amanda Peabody (Ida Lupino) into marriage. Evans' children are convinced that their mother is alive and trapped inside the walls of the house/organ. It is a play that, like all of Lucille Fletcher's finest radio offerings, utilizes the gifts of the medium to the full, via the sound of the organ, the voice of the "trapped" mother, the miserable children and the dialogic attraction/menace of the lead characters. It is also a work that in its literal implausibility and eroticized irony succeeds as an example of heightened post–Gothic intensity and nightmarish fantasy.

It is Price's performances in works such as "Fugue in C Minor" that had, by late 1947, comedy shows lampooning the actor's typecast image as a killer. On one broadcast of the variety showcase for the armed forces, *Command Performance* (November 30, 1947), Vincent Price co-hosts with Hy Averback:

> HY AVERBACK: ... It seems to me that in every picture you've done lately you go around knifing beautiful women or strangling pretty girls.
> VINCENT PRICE: Oh yes, Hy, and I'm so tired of that. I'd like to forget knifing and stabbing for a while. I'd like to invite girls over for dinner ... and poison the food.

Later in the same broadcast, Price's serious acting credentials are emphasized. In a sketch with comedienne Joan Davis, Price proclaims:

> VINCENT PRICE: Joan, say you'll remain in pictures and I'll teach you the Stanislavsky Method of acting.
> JOAN DAVIS: The whozaswitchy?
> VINCENT PRICE: Stanislavsky! Why, that's where you let the audience know you feel what you see.
> JOAN DAVIS: I feel what I see?
> VINCENT PRICE: Yes.
> JOAN DAVIS: That's not Stanislavsky. That's the Navy method.

This mixture of lurid "villainy" and "serious" acting is recurrent in Price's image, and reiterated in uncanny plays like "The Roman" (*The Croupier*, September 21, 1949), in which Price plays the ghost of a treacherous Roman doomed, "Flying Dutchman" style, to roam the world on a mysterious ship. The role permits Price moments of high drama, as his character somewhat anachronistically (for a Roman soldier) quotes Shakespeare's

Macbeth and thunderously attains redemption. It is this mixture of the uncanny and the classical theater that will characterize Price's role in the film *Theater of Blood* (Douglas Hickox, 1973), where Price, in one of his greatest screen performances, plays a Shakespearean actor who strives to exact retribution on his critics. The delightful melodramatic theatricality that Price employs in this film is familiar from his roles in Roger Corman's Poe films. But Price's voice remains the most powerful element to his acting, and this is amply demonstrated by his voiceover role in Michael Jackson's *Thriller* (1983), and in *The Abominable Dr. Phibes* (Robert Fuest, 1971), where he has no throat and stands a mute figure, with his eerily disembodied voice projected through an electronic device, making this a role that is curiously allusive to Price's triumphant career on radio).

Despite the celebrated performances of Boris Karloff on *Lights Out*, Peter Lorre on *Mystery in the Air* or Vincent Price in "Three Skeleton Key" and other examples of horror radio, the most celebrated "horror" performance in the history of American radio drama is Agnes Moorehead in Lucille Fletcher's "Sorry, Wrong Number." The play was performed on *Suspense* eight times from 1943 to 1960, with Moorehead in the lead role on each occasion. As Allison McCracken writes, the interest and controversy surrounding "Sorry, Wrong Number" represents "the most attention given a single radio broadcast since Welles' 'War of the Worlds'" (McCracken, 2002, 188). "Sorry, Wrong Number" is a phenomenal example of radio writing and remains a paradigm as an example of radio performance and, specifically, of horror acting. In the play, Mrs. Elbert Stevenson, an invalid, attempts to phone her husband, and in a crosswire overhears two hit-men discussing a plan to kill a woman and make it look like a burglary. In the subsequent action Mrs. Stevenson repeatedly contacts the operator, the police, and her husband in an attempt to save the intended victim. Of course, for many listeners it is immediately apparent that Mrs. Stevenson is the intended victim, and that the reason her husband has remained late at the office is to provide himself with the perfect alibi. This plot twist is not designed to surprise the listener, it is designed to build to the point where Mrs. Stevenson realizes that she is the victim. It is a very voyeuristic play (albeit about *listening*), in the sense that just as Mrs. Stevenson accidentally overhears, the listener is the intimate witness to the final half-hour of Mrs. Stevenson's life; we cannot intervene, we can only listen. It is quintessential radio (Anatole Litvak's 1948 film version was obliged to develop and expand the story) which is about listening, claustrophobia and technophobia. The fact that the majority of the play consists of telephone conversations works superbly as radio. Radio, like the telephone, is an electro-mechanical device entirely dependent on sound and voice. The first use of the telephone in horror performance can be traced back to the André de Lorde and Charles Foleÿ Grand-Guignol horror play *Au téléphone* (1902)— a pioneering masterpiece of technophobia (Hand and Wilson, 2002, 156) in which the audience watches the central character as he listens helplessly to his wife and son being murdered at the end of a telephone line. The use of the telephone also emerges in contemporary folklore or "urban legends." In one example, popularly known as "The Babysitter" (Brunvand, 1981, 53–57), the eponymous character receives a number of menacing phone calls before checking on the children upstairs, only to discover them murdered or missing. While "The Babysitter" may differ from "Sorry, Wrong Number" in that the telephone is used as a specific "weapon" rather than a gruesomely ironic crossed line, the urban legend's ingredients of, in Michael Wilson's words, "violence (threatened or actual) and a steady increase in tension" (Wilson, 1997, 223) makes it indisputably akin to the *Suspense* play. Moreover, Dunning reveals that by its fourth broadcast in 1945, "Sorry, Wrong Number" had acquired "the characteristics of an urban legend" (Dunning, 1998, 648). The classic framing of urban legends—the opening gambit that the story is "real" and happened to a "friend of a friend"—ties in with the reception of "Sorry, Wrong Number," which, it seems, may have been regarded by some listeners as a true story or even a recorded event. Certainly, after each broadcast the phone company would be harangued by callers complaining about "the insensitivity of its operators" (Dunning, 1998, 649). Arguably, "Sorry, Wrong Number" is a more intimate and compelling experience for an audience than *Au téléphone* or the recounted narrative of an urban legend, inasmuch as we clearly hear both sides of all the conversations as they happen. This means that we are not simply in the presence of Mrs. Stevenson, we share her ear. The telephone is a not a lifeline but a frustration: the mechanical voices are distant or dehumanized, making Mrs. Stevenson seem increasingly trapped and doomed.

Between them, Fletcher and Moorehead create a masterpiece of characterization: Mrs. Stevenson is not particularly likeable. She is pompous, officious, and egotistical. The fact it takes the character a while to realize that she is the intended victim reflects her self-love which rapidly transforms into paranoia when she finally comprehends that she is the intended target. Fletcher and Moorehead provoke the listeners by making them understand why her husband may despise her so thoroughly. Mrs. Gillis in "To Find Help" is the unequivocal victim on the "good" side of the black and white universe of melodrama. Mrs. Stevenson, in contrast, may be vulnerable, but the unpleasant side to her character makes the play much more gray and modern than the melodramatic unambiguousness of some suspense radio. Although the listener pities her, the dynamic of the character can make the listener feel not only guilt for disliking Mrs. Stevenson, but even complicity in the crime. Mrs. Stevenson's 30-minute journey to her death explores an astonishing range of attitudes and emotions. In each of the live performances of "Sorry, Wrong Number" for *Suspense*, Agnes Moorehead proves herself to be a formidable actor. According to Dunning, Moorehead would rehearse for an intense six hours with director William Spier and sound effects technician Berne Surrey prior to the performance (Dunning, 1998, 649). During the broadcast, her sharp and clear voice shifts convincingly between talking to people on the phone and talking to herself, as the dramatic tension of the play develops and she impeccably integrates the story with the intensity of her performance. Moorehead captures Mrs. Stevenson's self-importance and bullying temperament, and meticulously shifts into other moods, such as condescension, exasperation, self-pity, frustration, despair, terror and, ultimately, the prolonged scream and abrupt, eerie silence of death. Photographic stills demonstrate the physical demands of the role (pages 40 and 42): Moorehead may be sat at a studio table with a script, but she is evidently bringing the world of Mrs. Stevenson to life around her. The attitudes and emotions of Mrs. Stevenson are explicitly animated on Moorehead's face and reflected by her posture, from superciliousness to absolute horror. We also see the physical techniques Moorehead employs in order to create the role, and the psychology and voice for it. The photographs show her variously clenching her teeth and fists, her face in exaggerated confusion as she mimes the phone, and her arms and face drooping as she collapses. In the two images of her screaming we can see how she develops two distinct screams: one achieved by facing forward and clutching her face, the other by raising her head up and back, pushing out her chest and pressing her fists close to the body. Both screaming techniques must have had an intense psychological and physical effect on Moorehead at the climax of the play. One imagines that the second posture allows Moorehead to attain the raw, primal death scream that concludes her role in "Sorry, Wrong Number." Martin Grams, Jr., reveals that at the end of every performance of the play, Moorehead would always be "completely exhausted, lying on the table, worn down emotionally from her work" (Grams, 1997, 22), a fact demonstrated in the studio photographs.

"Sorry, Wrong Number" remains a paradigm of horror radio because it is by turns a humorously ironic and deeply disturbing play. It is also distinguished for the concision and resonance of a script that completely comprehends the medium and its outstanding central performance. It is a play that explores a range of emotions and time constraints — an impressively classical unity of time, place and action — which all contribute to the creation of an intense horror experience and a study of alienation and despair in modern technological society. Agnes Moorehead in "Sorry, Wrong Number" should be regarded as one of the great live performances of the twentieth century. The fact that the play was performed an unprecedented eight times on *Suspense* is a tribute to Moorehead's performance. Following the first performance of May 25, 1943, many repeat listeners would already know the story, but what they listened to was not so much *what* happens to Mrs. Stevenson but *how* Agnes Moorehead enacts the character's grim fate, live and on the air. As such, the reception of "Sorry, Wrong Number" becomes a study of a virtuoso performance. In its own time the play was much discussed and alluded to in other programs. In *Inner Sanctum Mysteries*' revival of "Listener" (July 20, 1952), Agnes Moorehead was in fine self-parodic form: in the opening minutes she plays a vulnerable old woman — Aunt Ellen — talking to the operator in desperation as she hears strange noises in her house. Ironically, it is revealed that Aunt Ellen hides a guilty secret: she has killed her husband and buried his corpse in the house.

Outside of radio, too, "Sorry, Wrong Number" became a point of reference. Nearly a year after her final performance of the play on *Suspense* in February 1960, Agnes Moorehead took the lead in one of the greatest episodes of *The Twilight Zone*, "The Invaders" (January 27, 1961). It is a half-hour thriller in which Moorehead plays an old woman whose house is infiltrated by what appear to be two tiny aliens from outer space. There is only one short speech in the entire play, and this is not uttered by Moorehead. Apparently, when she first read the script Moorehead was perplexed, as she could not find her part; in other words, she could not find any dialogue for her character. However, the director of the episode, Douglas Heyes, was determined to cast Moorehead in the role:

> The reason I suggested [Agnes Moorehead] was that she had done a radio show called "Sorry, Wrong Number," which was a half-hour *tour de force* where she used nothing *but* her voice, and I said, "Here's a half-hour *tour de force* where she doesn't use her voice at all!" [Zicree, 1992, 172].

Even in such an antithetical example of pure television — 30 minutes of virtually soundless visuals — the paradigm of pure radio, "Sorry, Wrong Number," remains the source of inspiration and creative impetus. Generally, however, the influence of "Sorry, Wrong Number" can be detected in the use of the telephone in performance horror. In many horror films the phone lines are cut, or the cellphone cannot receive a signal. Whenever the telephone keeps working—in films as diverse as *Scream* (Wes Craven, 1997), *Phone Booth* (Joel Schumacher, 2002) and *Phone* (Byeong-hi Ahn, 2002)—and leads the doomed listener into the nadir of absolute terror, echoes of the frantic Mrs. Stevenson will always be heard.

4

The Grandmother of Horror Radio: Alonzo Deen Cole and *The Witch's Tale* (1931–1938)

We have already highlighted the major significance of *The Witch's Tale* as the earliest horror program, and have celebrated the show's creation of Old Nancy, the Witch of Salem and grandmother to all horror hosts. Aside from that achievement, some critics have found it easy to dismiss the program. Dunning argues that *The Witch's Tale* repertoire featured plays that were nothing more than "one-dimensional affairs, calculated for a single effect" (Dunning, 1998, 724). Nevertheless, regarded in its context, the one-dimensional stories spun by Old Nancy are an interesting reworking of classic horror formulae contemporaneous with the nascence of Hollywood horror (in the guise of Universal Pictures). Moreover, during its long run the program did attempt to give these horror fables an individual treatment, and many were presented in a style of passionate melodrama. In addition, we must credit Cole for an impressively broad selection of fiction chosen for adaptation, which includes, but is not confined to, the most well-known classics of horror literature.

Alonzo Deen Cole was the genius behind *The Witch's Tale*, and his versatility as writer, producer and principal male actor leads David S. Siegel to liken him to Orson Welles (Siegel, 1998, 3). Cole was born in 1897, and his early interest in theater led him to pursue a modest stage career as an actor before being enlisted as an army medic and serving in France during World War I. After the war, Cole returned to the stage in both theater and vaudeville. Siegel draws special attention to Cole's vaudeville comedy act *The Honeymooners* (1925–26), which Cole performed with Marie O'Flynn, the woman who would become Cole's wife and the female lead on *The Witch's Tale*. When Cole broke into radio, he used *The Honeymooners* as the basis for his first major radio program, *Darling and Dearie* (1931–32), which successfully ran as a weekly 15-minute comedy serial on WOR. Soon afterwards, *The Witch's Tale* premiered with "The Queer House" (May 28, 1931), a 30-minute horror play also on WOR. The program was an immediate success, and remained so despite the mind-boggling number of scheduling changes the show was forced to undergo over its broadcast history (Siegel, 1998, 6–7).

Cole served as the principal writer and producer, while, according to Siegel, the core performance team consisted of Cole and Marie O'Flynn, plus Alan Devitt and Mark Smith, forming an "ensemble that was only occasionally added to" (Siegel, 1998, 4). The other pivotal member of *The Witch's Tale* cast was a female performer who played a number of small parts within the central narrative but specialized in the role that would prove to be an incalculably important invention: Old Nancy the Salem witch, who, with her cat Satan, was the framing narrator for each broadcast. In many ways, the concept of the horror host is the single most important contribution that *The Witch's Tale* made to horror radio, yet I believe that this major innovation should not distract us from subjecting some of Cole's unfairly marginalized plays to serious analysis. But before we look at the plays themselves, we will, appropriately enough, devote some attention to Old Nancy.

The role of Old Nancy was dominated by two actors during *The Witch's Tale*'s seven-year run. The performer from 1931 until her death in 1935 was Adelaide Fitz-Allen, a veteran stage actress who may not have been as ancient as the woman she portrayed but was nonetheless a respectable 75 when she took on the role. The story of Adelaide Fitz-Allen's replacement has entered old-time radio folklore. After a number of "'try out' Nancys" (Siegel, 1998, 5), Nila Mack, the producer-director of the long-running CBS children's drama series *Let's Pretend*, brought one of the program's young performers to Cole's attention: Miriam Wolfe. Her performance in the audition so impressed Cole that he gave her the role, which she played until *The Witch's Tale* came to an end in 1938. The remarkable thing about Wolfe was that she was only 13 when she auditioned, a fact that is undetectable when listening to her cackle and croak her way through a script. Another favorite anecdote associated with *The Witch's Tale* is the fact that Satan, Nancy's familiar black cat, who provided a meowing and caterwauling accompaniment, was played by Alonzo Deen Cole himself.

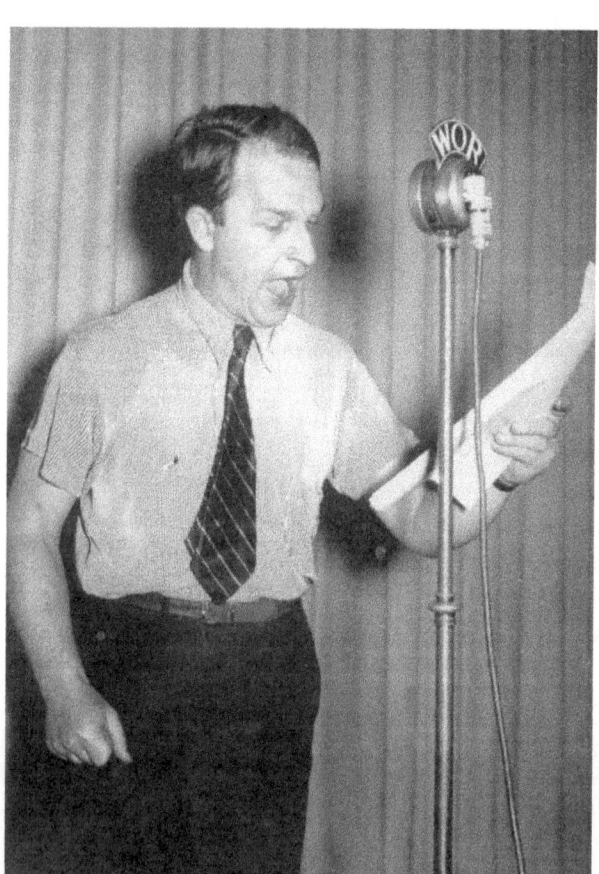

Alonzo Deen Cole performing on **The Witch's Tale** (courtesy of Dunwich Press, publishers of **The Witch's Tale**).

Old Nancy was the framing narrator for each broadcast. Her cackle and the meowing of her feline familiar Satan would open every episode. She would begin with ironic self-reference, announcing that it was her birthday (although her age would vary each week — and sometimes vary within a single broadcast — she was always at least "one hun'ned year old"), and then make a topical joke about anything from chocolate to radio advertising. After this preamble, Old Nancy would invite us to "douse out them lights" so that she could get down to business. After setting the scene and giving the listener the title of the story, Old Nancy would fade and the dramatization would begin. Midway through a play, Old Nancy might share a few words with the listener, recapping and emphasizing the plot before the concluding half of the play. At the end of the episode, Old Nancy would return and close the broadcast, very swiftly, in her inimitable manner. Sometimes her closing speech would include some brief comment about the tale we have heard, but the prime function of her last words was simply closure. Old Nancy's epilogue to "Mrs. Hawker's Will" (June 20, 1935) is a typical example:

> NANCY: He he he... (CAT) Weel, that's th' end o' that un, Satan! Yew folks come see me nex' Wensday on m' buthday, an' me an' Satan'll have anuther cheerful yarn t' spin ye! Dunt fergit — nex' Wensday night at Noo York time ov ha'f pas' ten o'clock! He he he he he he... (CAT) [Siegel, 1998, 179].

As well as demonstrating the function of *The Witch's Tale*'s epilogue for the purposes of closure, this case includes a reiteration of the program's day and timeslot. This example, like all of the scripts included in Siegel's anthology, also demonstrates the importance of dialect in *The Witch's Tale*. The notation provides a fascinating clue as to vocal performance, and although most of the dialogue in the central stories are in standard English, Cole often marked the need for emphasized accent for characters, whether French — "dee vase ees yours" (Siegel, 1998, 80) — or Texan — "Ye know we made up our minds t' insist on sump'n else b'sides jest carved woodwork an' fancy staircases" (Siegel, 1998, 64). As Siegel writes on the issue of dialect:

> [Without] the visual stimulation of television, radio, particularly radio drama that was being broadcast in the 1930s, depended to a large extent on the broad dialect that was viewed as typical of the various ethnic groups who were being portrayed [Siegel, 1998, 10].

The accents may often sound like stereotypes, but they served the important and necessary function of *differentiation* within the plays, which were performed by a relatively small ensemble of *The Witch's Tale*, often demanding that the actors "double" and play more than one role. Moreover, at a time when it seemed that spoken language within performance steadily shifted towards the homogeneous, the variety and texture of the accents on *The Witch's Tale* and some other examples of old-time radio drama proved fascinating and rewarding. The voice of Old Nancy herself is no exception. A first listening to the few extant broadcasts of *The Witch's Tale* can be a surprise, as Old Nancy's voice is not like the other witches of the 1930s, being neither the rich aristocratic tones of the evil Queen (Lucille La Verne) in *Snow White and the Seven Dwarfs* (Walt Disney, 1937), nor the malicious screech of the Wicked Witch of the West (Margaret Hamilton) in *The Wizard of Oz* (Victor Fleming, 1939). Perhaps this should come as no surprise after all: Old

Nancy may be one of the greatest 1930s witches in American performance media, but she is not a melodramatic villain. Old Nancy is unquestionably the listener's friend, albeit a rather eccentric one.

Regardless of her voice, the invention of Old Nancy was a major and indelible innovation, and all subsequent horror radio hosts can be traced back to this particular witch of Salem. As we have seen, the host is one of the trademarks of golden age horror radio as a whole: the role fulfils the function of "hooking" the listener, but also adds an original and individual stamp on what are frequently formulaic stories. Siegel provides an apposite summary of *The Witch's Tale* repertoire:

> Mad scientists, haunted houses, ghosts seeking revenge, ancient curses, creatures out of control (insects, tigers, wolves, snakes, etc.), witches, magicians, vampires, were-wolves, the Reign of Terror, tales of African or Latin American jungles, the Wild West, statues coming to life and simply bloody murder were the stuff that made *The Witch's Tale* plots flow [Siegel, 1998, 8].

This is a fascinating summary, as we can immediately see that *The Witch's Tale* produced plays that use the same themes that reoccur throughout not just horror radio but the history of popular horror culture. Certainly Cole's plays include generic tales of vampirism, lycanthropy and the occult, adhering to a formulaic approach. Nevertheless, in his approach to a generic choice of story, Cole often makes a concerted effort to grace his work with an original take on the theme, and add effective surface detail and color, not least through the aforementioned use of dialect. Moreover, it was not simply a matter of *approach*: Siegel's list also demonstrates that Cole produced plays that strayed away from the formulaic and the clichéd. At least, we could argue that "Latin America" might leap out as a more unusual setting, as would the specific historical setting of post–Revolutionary France and "the Reign of Terror." Cole set stories in these atypical geographical and historical locations, while his plays of "statues coming to life" reflects Cole's wide-ranging research and reading as a source for adaptation, an important component in *The Witch's Tale* repertoire. We will look at *The Witch's Tale* and adaptation in due course, but first of all we will look at Cole's treatment of an archetypal horror formula by comparing two scripts about lycanthropy included in Siegel's anthology.

"The Lord of the Jungle" (November 16, 1937) is a conventional horror tale of archaeological/anthropological exploration. Such tales are often set in Egypt, but in this instance we witness explorers from the United States searching for relics of Mayan civilization in the jungles of Central America. They discover an ancient pyramid graced with the statue of a jaguar, the "Lord of the Jungle" of the title. The suspense builds, with a menacing jaguar heard in the jungle and seen at a distance. Ironically, the lycanthrope turns out to be Archie, one of the scientists in the group, who is dismissed as being as weak as a "rabbit" (Siegel, 1998, 218) by his adulterous wife Janis, who, in ironic contrast, is described by the stage directions as being *"feline, savagely passionate"* (Siegel, 1998, 217). In the final scene of the play we witness Archie's transformation when he argues with Britt, the man who has been having an affair with Janis:

> ARCHIE: We're in the jungle ... where there's only jungle law — that law says that two males cannot share a mate between them and, of those who try it, one must die! One of us is going to die tonight.

BRITT: You little fool, I can break you in two!
ARCHIE: (*Madly*) hah ha — suppose we see! Suppose we — (*His voice changes to the snarl of a jaguar.*)
JANIS: (*Screams in horror.*)
BRITT: (*Terrified*) Good God!
(*Two heavy bodies meet, as though a jaguar had sprung upon a man, snarling and tearing.*)
JANIS: He snarled like a jaguar!
BRITT (*Cries in agony.*) He's clawing my eyes — his teeth are at my throat!! (*He struggles then is still.*) [Siegel, 1998, 234].

Britt is killed, and Archie, having relished the "sweet" blood of his victim, runs off to join his kindred jaguars, explaining to the treacherous Janis that "my breed of cats and yours are different" (Siegel, 1998, 235). In the end, the real monster is an entirely human one: the adulterous Janis is robbed of her lover and loses her husband, yet there is a degree of nobility in Archie's departure into the wilderness, where this betrayed man will be protected by "the Lord of the Jungle" in the company of his fellow beasts. Janis, the spiteful cat, is left irredeemably alone: her actions drove her husband to murder and metamorphosis, but through this her husband finds salvation and communion. It is easy to see the play as a celebration of a masculine impulse which can turn an emasculated "rabbit" into a potent jaguar, but can only do so through tasting blood and liberating the self from female control.

"The Lord of the Jungle" is perhaps the polar opposite of one of the most acclaimed examples of lycanthropy in horror radio, "The House in Cypress Canyon" (*Suspense*, December 5, 1946). We will look at this latter play in more detail in the chapter on *The Mysterious Traveler*, but it is worth mentioning that in this play it is the woman in the marital relationship who is a lycanthrope, and her transformative and disruptive power lends the play, as Allison McCracken argues, a remarkably radical socio-sexual resonance (McCracken, 2002, 201). "The Lord of the Jungle" is reactionary in comparison, as it presents women — in the form of Janis — as destructive, and celebrates a romanticized vision of the quintessentially masculine myths of "law of the jungle" and, to an extent, the "noble savage." Nonetheless, these same features make the play an interesting example of the lycanthrope scenario: not only does the play prefer to present an unusual "were-jaguar" — a few years before *Cat People* (Jacques Tourneur, 1942) — in preference to the favorite werewolf, but it also decides to end the story not with silver bullets or exorcism but eternal freedom for Archie. Technically, the episode is an interesting example of horror radio: Archie's rapid, mid-speech metamorphosis and the bloody murder of Britt is an excellent example of horror radio technique for both its dramatic impact and its ability to exploit the listener's imagination.

An example of a lycanthropy play in *The Witch's Tale* repertoire that displays a similarly effective transformation scene but opts for the more conventional werewolf is "The Image" (February 8, 1932). In this play, the lycanthropic transformation is governed by the use of "a girdle of human hide" (Siegel, 1998, 28), a magic belt that can mutate the wearer into a werewolf. This plot element is unfamiliar to those whose experience of lycanthropic folklore is restricted to cinema. Cole, however, draws on various traditional werewolf legends that cite the wearing of "a girdle made of wolf's skin" (O'Donnell, 1912,

57) as a key component in the process of transmutation. In the final scene of "The Image," the innocent Claire mistakenly picks up the human skin girdle:

> TERRY: Claire—don't touch that girdle!
> CLAIRE: Why—I can't let go!
> TERRY: Don't touch it with your other hand, too—it completes the circuit! For God's sake—Claire!!
> CLAIRE: (*A growl.*)
> OFFICER: Jees! She's changing!
> TERRY: Keep away from her—she'd kill you now! I'll try to hold her from behind! I've got her!
> CLAIRE: (*Screams and growls like a beast.*)
> TERRY: Get that belt! Not with your hands—use those fire tongs! Quick! She's trying to get at my throat! She'll kill me! Claire!!
> OFFICER: I got it—struck it from her hands!
> TERRY: Thank God! Claire! Claire!!
> CLAIRE: (*Sobbing*) Oh Terry—Terry—I knew what I was doing—and couldn't help myself! [Siegel, 1998, 29].

The male lycanthrope in "The Lord of the Jungle" commits an "honorable" murder in killing his love rival, and succeeds in taking the moral high ground when he condemns his "catty" wife and nobly joins his feline soul mates. In contrast, Claire in "The Image" would kill the Officer—an emblem of authority—and then lunges at the throat of her husband. The men are only saved by Terry's swift (we might even contend, sexually resonant) grabbing hold of the bestial Claire "from behind." She is sandwiched between a police officer and her husband: representatives of the conventional forces of patriarchal society in relation to a woman. The most profound aspect to the episode is that *she knew what she was doing*. Claire's mental identity and awareness was not lost (as it so often is in werewolf tales), but she *wanted* to kill the policeman and wanted to tear her husband's throat out with her bare teeth. In that moment she is a disruptive woman, a danger to society (specifically male, given the gender of her adversaries) and forerunner to the deadly female lycanthrope in "The House on Cypress Canyon." The Officer's action with the "fire tongs" saves the men and retransforms Claire into a "*sobbing*" woman, not the menacing beast who endangers both those present and the overarching masculine order. The mental image the listener momentarily creates of the policeman lunging at the entrapped Claire with fire tongs even suggests an element of torture (and witches). The play ends with the girdle of skin (rather than Claire) consigned to the flames, and equilibrium (both matrimonial and social) is restored—a stark contrast to the desolate conclusion of "The House on Cypress Canyon."

We can see that Cole's approach to formulaic horror is varied, and offers interesting levels of meaning and complex ramifications when subjected to close analysis. The plays also include exciting moments of performance virtuosity in their rapid and ferocious transformation scenes.

The templates of horror are never far away, even when *The Witch's Tale* broadcasts quasi–science fiction in the form of a "mad scientist" play. "The Entomologist" (January 7, 1935), for example, is a tale set in tropical Africa in which a mad scientist conducts experiments with spiders. The heroes discover and kill the creature responsible for a mysterious murder: a giant spider "two foot long," a thing so horrific the witnesses say they would prefer to believe in the local superstition of vampires. In other words, we are presented with "real" science that has consequences more terrifying than the concept of vampires, yet belong in the same narrative territory. The sentiment also succeeds in grounding the play in the horror drama genre by having characters within the play signposting the vampiric, hence Gothic, aspect of the work.

As well as utilizing the core formula of horror themes and narratives for his plays, Cole also turned to legends as a source, such as "The Flying Dutchman" (February 1, 1932; revived April 26, 1934) and "The Golem" (in both single [September 24, 1936] and two-part [September 25 and October 9, 1933] formats). *The Witch's Tale* also makes significant use of literary adaptation, with notable dramatizations of the greatest horror classics: *Frankenstein* (broadcast three times: August 3, 1931; March 7, 1932; and July 17, 1935); *Dr. Jekyll and Mr. Hyde* (in both a one-part [November 23, 1931] and two-part [August 19, and 26, 1937] version); and a free adaptation of Ambrose Bierce's "An Occurrence at Owl Creek Bridge" as "The Deserter" (January 23, 1933; revived May 30, 1935). It may come as a surprise that the program also produced adaptations of less well-known literature of the supernatural, such as a two-part version of the first vampire novel in English, John William Polidori's *The Vampyre* (June 5–12, 1933); a three-part adaptation of Edward Bulwer-Lytton's 1842 novel *Zanoni* (July 10, 17, and 24, 1933); and a number of adaptations of Théophile Gautier's fiction, such as the 1836 ghost story "Clarimonde" (August 16, 1932; revived November 26, 1935), and the Italian-set "evil eye" novel *Jettature* (1857) as "The Evil Eye" (August 27, 1931) and revived as "The Jettatore" (July 3, 1933, and July 6, 1936).

Cole also adapted the greatest "statue coming to life" horror story, Prosper Mérimée's "The Venus of Ille," as "The Bronze Venus" (July 2, 1931; revived July 18, 1932, and August 22, 1935). In Mérimée's tale, a young man called Alphonse is betrothed to a beautiful young woman but is somewhat reluctant in his affections. Cole's version keeps the French setting but renames the Alphonse character as Henri. Henri is not so much reluctant as he is increasingly fascinated by the antique bronze statue of Venus he and his future father-in-law have unearthed. Georgette, the bride-to-be, is jealous of the attention her fiancé devotes to the statue, and in a central scene Henri passionately describes the statue as "So beautiful ... So beautiful ... *So beautiful*...." In both versions, the bridegroom makes the mistake of placing the ring on the finger of the bronze statue after looking for a place to put it, and the statue seems to bend its finger to hold onto the wedding ring. In the radio version, the beguiling power of the statue reaches a climax at the wedding scene, with Henri hesitating through his vows because of the recurrent metallic chime of the bronze Venus. Unable to finish his wedding vows, Henri expresses his adoration: "Venus, I am yours forever!" He runs to the statue, which starts to move as though alive and crushes Henri to death in front of the aghast congregation. In Mérimée's original, Alphonse dies, crushed to death in his wedding bed, and with his wife gone insane, but the actual cause is not spelled out to the reader.

Michael Dirda sees "The Venus of Ille" as a sophisticated tale and an "oblique commentary on love" (Dirda, 1986, 289), to which we might add that it is a masterpiece of the grotesquely erotic. Although *The Witch's Tale* adaptation does not fully capture the sensual and sexual horror of Mérimée's original, it is still present in latent form. If the sexual resonance is more subtle, the dramatic treatment is more blatant in *The Witch's Tale*: we have no cause to doubt the animation of the bronze figure, as it occurs in front of a congregation of witnesses rather than behind the locked door of the not-altogether-happy newlyweds' bedchamber. The 30-minute horror play of *The Witch's Tale* is no place for inference and suggestion, so Cole's decision for a scene of explicit horror in the finale is a logical one. The clumping sound of what could be the animated statue is heard at a distance in the original story, while in Cole's version the dull, metallic chime of the bronze Venus as it moves is an intermittent and haunting sound effect.

If the works of Prosper Mérimée are somewhat neglected, especially in dramatization, the same cannot be said of Mary Shelley's *Frankenstein*. As a final example of literary adaptation on *The Witch's Tale*, we will turn our attention to the 1935 broadcast of "Frankenstein." This production is the revival of a 1931 broadcast contemporaneous with Universal's hugely successful *Frankenstein* (James Whale, 1931); despite this, it succeeds in adhering to Mary Shelley's novel to a surprising degree. The play works on the kernel of the story, beginning with Frankenstein having created his monster, the scientist's regret and the Creature's subsequent rampage. The Creature is given the sophisticated characterization that Mary Shelley allotted the original fictional character. Although the Creature speaks with a snarling voice, he is nonetheless as articulate as the creature in the original novel (and in the many melodramatic versions on the Victorian stage), but poles apart from the inarticulate Boris Karloff incarnation and the subsequent popular cliché. As an example, when Frankenstein is lured into the wilderness by the Creature, he asks where he has been brought. The Creature responds that this is all that he can call "home":

> This barren cave upon the mountainside exposed to the wind and the howling beasts. Here I, the monster you created, live whilst you reside in comfort. I want to show you my solitude whilst you are planning marriage!

The eloquence of the monster allows for moments of melodramatic characterization, with the voices of Dr. Frankenstein and his creation in constant juxtaposition, defining the dramatic structure and impetus of the play. The performance style at certain moments is not far from Victorian melodramatic practice. When, for example, Frankenstein shudders on beholding the monster, the Creature responds with the words: "Even you cannot bear to look at my repulsive being! Even you, my maker! You, my God!" The speech is delivered with heightened emotion, a trembling, ponderous voice on the brink of desperate melancholy.

Having described Frankenstein as "God," the Creature likens himself to "Adam" and thus commands Frankenstein to make him an "Eve." After the scientist refuses, the Creature pledges to destroy Frankenstein's bride. Once this tragedy occurs, Frankenstein spends decades pursuing the Creature across the world before locating him in the icy wilderness. While in the novel the Creature brings Frankenstein to his death and the monster survives, the play provides a sentimental and melodramatic finale in which the Creature begs for forgiveness, and both "creator and created" let themselves sink together into watery oblivion. In her closing narrative, Old Nancy describes what the listener has heard as "the true facts" behind the *Frankenstein* story; as playful a statement as this is, it is accurate inasmuch as, despite some major differences and inevitable omissions, *The Witch's Tale*'s "Frankenstein" remains one of the most loyal dramatizations of Mary Shelley's masterpiece.

Cole's use of adaptation for a significant portion of *The Witch's Tale* reflects a trend that will be repeated in many other programs in the horror radio genre, and will be of central concern in *The Mercury Theater on the Air* repertoire, where Orson Welles and John Houseman will specialize in the adaptation of "Literature." However, while the *Mercury Theater* may have produced classics of literary horror like *Dracula* and *War of the Worlds*, this was not the dominant part of its repertoire. *The Witch's Tale*, on the other hand, was unabashedly a specialized *genre* show, and its overt penchant for *literary* adaptation will find its best equivalent in the following decade with *The Weird Circle* (1943–47), a series that will focus entirely on literary adaptation, with a bias towards horror and grotesque mystery.

In addition to its plays of formulaic horror and literary adaptation, *The Witch's Tale* also explored specific historical settings as a forum for the weird and horrific. "The Physician to the Dead" (November 8, 1934) uses the Reign of Terror after the French Revolution as an historical backdrop, offering a mixture of scientific themes ("citizen doctors" experimenting on the corpses of guillotine victims) and romance of the "Scarlet Pimpernel" ilk (with the hero, a doctor called Rene, saving a beautiful woman, Solange, from execution). In a superbly grotesque denouement, Rene, having left Solange alone for an evening to conduct an experiment to see if consciousness survives after decapitation, receives a sack full of some of the 93 heads removed that day. Rene is unnerved by the sack, deciding that he should return to Solange. His assistant urges him to regain his composure: "Science should come before everything, Rene." With mounting horror, Rene lifts the severed heads out of the sack while endeavoring, with difficulty, to consider them merely as "specimens": "Here was an old woman ... Here was a child..." Suddenly Rene recoils when something warm moves inside the sack, touching him on his hand with something that felt "almost like a kiss." His assistant is thrilled that this may be the proof of consciousness they have hoped to discover. At this moment they are interrupted by the eerie voice of Solange, who, Rene decides, "must be outside." Of course, she is not just inside the laboratory, she is inside the sack. Rene "must see" and opens it up, shrieking in terror as Solange's head utters, "Even in death ... I love you..." and the play ends. Solange's decapitated head is eerie in concept and in voice, and is one of the ultimate examples of the disembodied female voice. The horror of the situation is enforced by Solange's awareness of what has happened to her — the fact that she is dead — and renders the romantic notion of the enduring power of love after death into something deeply disturbing: in the world of horror, perhaps a bitter or vengeful victim might be easier to contemplate than a human head that kisses your hand and tells you it loves you. Either way, Cole creates a powerful and surprising conclusion to a play that has explored romance, political intrigue and scientific speculation in a comparatively detailed historical setting. The spiritual home to the guillotine in horror culture is to be found in the (unsurprisingly) Paris-based Théâtre du Grand-Guignol, a stage that had featured many guillotine plays in its repertoire, and, in 1928, just a few years before "The Physician to the Dead," had produced René Berton's *L'Homme qui a tué la mort*, in which a scientist manages to revive to consciousness the severed head of a guillotine victim (Hand and Wilson, 2002, 122–23).

The French setting and use of the guillotine in "The Physician to the Dead" had already been explored in "The Altar" (November 8, 1933), and *The Witch's Tale* would revisit these motifs with the revival of the same play as "The Altar of Hate" (January 13, 1938). "The Altar of Hate" is a tale of retribution in which the son of a condemned aristocratic family, the des Lauriennes, is told his life will be spared by the dreaded "Butcher Carrier" if he will execute his own parents on the guillotine. He is unwilling, but does so to obey their final command to save his life, denouncing his tormentors with the vow to reap his revenge "a hundredfold!" A generation later, France is in more stable times, and we find that the unwilling executioner the Count des Lauriennes has grown old but has never forgotten his vow of revenge. He dies, revealing to his son Henri a grotesque emblem of his pledge: in his lifetime the Count had gradually constructed an altar made out of dozens of skulls of the people who willingly participated in the Terror and their descendants, with spaces remaining for two final heads that Henri must fill. Like "The Physician to the Dead," the play moves in a romantic direction, with Henri falling in love with the niece of Carrier, who has been captured by Guinard, the late count's servant. Guinard intends to make Henri complete his father's altar of hate. Early on in their whirlwind romance Henri and his love decide to marry, viewing their ironic family backgrounds as a demonstration of the triumph of love. In the closing scene of the play, Henri carries his bride over the threshold, but before they have reached their wedding bed we hear their piercing screams and the servants rush in to see two "freshly severed heads" completing the altar of a hundred skulls.

"The Altar of Hate" exists as a recording; and we are fortunate that Siegel includes the script of "The Altar" in his anthology, which allows us to compare the earlier incarnation of the play to the extant 1938 broadcast. The Old Nancy framing narrative is entirely different, which makes it clear that in revivals of early plays Cole nonetheless wrote completely new speeches for the second Nancy, Miriam Wolfe. Both plays share the same story and characters, and adhere to the same structure and number of scenes. There are, however, a great number of slight alterations to the dialogue. Some changes give greater emphasis to character: Butcher Carrier is a melodramatically villainous character in both versions, but only in the 1938 broadcast does he insist on calling the Countess des Lauriennes "she-dog," thus giving more emphasis to his despicable character. Some changes have a rhetorical effect: des Lauriennes' oath to "punish and avenge a hundredfold" in 1933 becomes "avenge a hundredfold! *Avenge a hundredfold*!" in 1938. The repetition of this snappier phrase allows the performer greater dramatic emphasis, and is well-suited to the end of the scene, emphasizing the theme that will dominate the remainder of the play. Similarly, we can compare the two versions of young des Lauriennes as he looks at the painting of his father:

> The — the eyes do look at me as though — (*Slight hysteria.*) But that's just imagination! It's only a painted figure standing in that frame! You have hounded me so much my mind is being weakened by your ghoulish chatter! Leave me alone, I shall keep my promise — but I must have more time!! (Siegel, 1998, 107)
>
> They — they do look ... alive. But that's imagination! My mind is becoming weakened by your ghoulish chatter! Oh, leave me alone, I must have more time! [1938 broadcast].

We can see in the latter version that Cole employs greater economy of expression, which does not alter the meaning but does make the speech more direct, thus making the action of the play faster-moving. In another description of the painting, Cole finds a more appropriate word: in 1933 the eyes of des Lauriennes "gleam" (Siegel, 1998, 110) while in 1938 this becomes a more menacing "glare."

The most profound difference comes at the end of the play when the severed heads of des Lauriennes and his wife are discovered. In both versions, with only the slightest adjustment, Guinard shouts triumphantly:

> Now the altar is complete! Not even the grave could keep my master from fulfilment of his vow! He has avenged an hundredfold! And hate has triumphed!

In the 1938 broadcast these are the final words of the play, and we are back with cackling Old Nancy. In the earlier script version, Cole lets Monsieur le Curé have the last line:

> No—for love lives on and hate, as ever, has defeated its own ends. Your master's hate was born that a name might not perish; with hate fulfilled that name is ended on the earth [Siegel, 1998, 112].

This speech displays a conciliatory and romantic ethos inasmuch as, despite what has happened, it celebrates the triumph of love. The trajectory and finale of the plot in both versions of the play may be no surprise, but the story is nonetheless startling in the gruesome dispatch of the innocent young newlyweds and the vindictive servant's celebration of his final, damning words: "hate has triumphed!" The fact that in 1938 there is no romantic celebration of the redeeming strength of eternal love merely strengthens the horror and impact of the finale.

The last play we will analyze in this case study of *The Witch's Tale* is "Hangman's Roost" (July 4, 1932). In this play, two wealthy Texans, Walter and Ella Reynolds, have bought an old mansion in England. The play begins as a satire of the American *nouveau riche* in the world of old Europe. As Walter explains, "Mrs. Reynolds an' me lived in tents, shacks, an' cheap lodgin' houses for a good many years 'till I brought in them oil wells"; now they plan to have "mansions in Noo Yawk, San Antone, an' over here in England," and "commute between" (Siegel, 1998, 64). Ella explains that she wants a property in England because her grandmother was English, but they are not merely generations but worlds apart. The enthusiasm of Ella and the slow drawl of her husband contrast with the "*Stiff and precise*" (Siegel, 1998, 64) voice of the English real estate salesman. Having established the situation as one of comic satire, Cole promptly begins leading the play towards horror. The best victims in a ghost story are skeptics: in the classic ghost story formula (the short stories of M. R. James, for example) the victims begin the narrative confident in their rational worldview, and the story charts their encounter with suggestions of the supernatural and culminates in irrefutable proof. "Hangman's Roost" begins with a similar structure. The Reynolds do not believe in the supernatural, but insist that part of buying into traditional English country life means that they want nothing other than "a real, certified haunted house with a genuine, eighteen karat ghost" (Siegel, 1998, 64). The "Hangman's Roost" of the title is a house formerly owned by the notorious judge Merrick, who had a passion for sending the guilty to the gallows. Merrick hanged himself in the house in 1792, and after that time there were a further ten suicides before the house was vacated and left unoccupied for 50 years. The story does not discourage Walter and Ella; in fact, it precipitates the signing of the check—for them it is a "romantic hist'ry" (Siegel, 1998, 66) rather than an ominous one. But the supernatural aspects commence immediately: the Reynolds have already seen a man they presume is the caretaker walking around upstairs with his head lolling on one shoulder. Cole wastes no time in exacerbating the horror: as soon as the second scene, the Reynolds' servant is found hanged, and their skepticism is gradually worn away. The couple are pestered by a rat as "big as a kitten" (Siegel, 1998, 72), which seems to have the same eyes as the portrait of Merrick. Eventually, in yet another horror radio transformation scene so beloved by *The Witch's Tale*, the rat metamorphoses into the fully formed figure of the diabolical judge. It is interesting that Cole decides to make the malevolent rat the size of a kitten and resists some implausible description of it as being big as a cat or dog. This allows for a more startling effect in the metamorphosis scene: the listener imagines the creature transforming from the natural into the supernatural, the real into the unreal.

Perhaps the most impressive achievement of "Hangman's Roost" is the final section of the play. Walter and Ella survive their encounter with Merrick, and in the following scene an English doctor explains the authenticity of the supernatural phenomenon to the now much humbler and no longer skeptical Texans. It could almost be the end of the play, but Cole realizes that a dramatic denouement is necessary. In the eerie final scene, Walter and Ella discover that they have been inexorably drawn back, inexplicably finding that, "we have come back here" (Siegel, 1998, 75), despite their desperate determination to keep away. Their return allows for a final reanimation of Merrick, but this time the doctor is present and kills the spirit with the obligatory silver bullets, providing us with a happy ending.

In an editor's note to "Hangman's Roost," Siegel comments:

> Horror writers draw their ideas from many different sources. If this story reminds the reader of Bram Stoker's "The Judge's House" (though it has different elements), the reader may also be reminded that Stoker "borrowed" the idea for "Dracula" from earlier sources [Siegel, 1998, 76].

Siegel's comment about the use of diverse sources is an astute one, and it is clear that Cole read widely in his research process, but would then reshape and even reinvent the chosen story within the 30-minute horror drama format. We could also suggest that as much as direct sources are important, horror is a genre that has underlying structures, motifs and formulae that are limited in number but are shared and exploited by a potentially limitless number of examples. Stoker's short story is clearly the source for Cole's play, but it is very much a free adaptation. The student Malcolmson in "The Judge's House" is pestered by an enormous rat with the eyes of the judge in the painting, and when the spectral judge and his host of rats appear at the end of the story, Malcolmson is executed. "Hangman's Roost," of course, has a happy ending, but it also has major themes of satire and its own specific structure of suspense. Moreover, the play—broadcast on Independence Day no less—is an effective use of horror to investigate American anxieties. The play explores the fears surrounding the concept of modern Americans in old, benighted Europe, and does so with an effective mixture of a fast-moving, atmospheric horror plot and satire. Certainly Cole seems to have decided that if he is going to lead two American victims into hell and back, they should be brash Texan multimillionaires. This decision allows a comic treatment of material wealth clashing with the spirit world: the Reynolds' attempt to buy into tradition with ostentatious affluence and complete skepticism is inevitably punished. The theme of Americans abroad in a dangerous Europe is a pertinent one in a world that was witnessing the rise of tumultuous political times in Europe. The paranoia of the world "over there"—a Europhobia—is clearly being exploited alongside the fundamental horror themes of the real and the supernatural, alienation and *Todesangst*. A hybridization of the same settings and themes was taken to a new level of sophistication in *Lights Out*, the subject of our next case study.

The final broadcast of *The Witch's Tale* came on June 13, 1938, with the concluding part of "The House of the Gargoyles." After *The Witch's Tale* ended, Cole wrote scripts for a number of shows, including *Gang Busters* and *The Shadow*. His greatest success after *The Witch's Tale*, however, was as principal writer on *Casey, Crime Photographer* (1943–55). The series was based on the fictional character created by George Harmon Coxe, and is described by John Dunning as "a B-grade radio detective show" (Dunning, 1998, 140), citing the music as the most prominent feature to the show. Whatever the merits of it as crime drama, some episodes of *Casey, Crime Photographer* allowed Cole to stray back towards horror. In "The Gentle Strangler" (April 24, 1947), for example, we witness a serial killer driven by vengeance who claims that he lives nowhere because he is "dead" and strangles his victims to death with his "awfully strong" hands. The two lurid strangulations we witness, and Casey's ferocious struggle with the killer, contain all the violence, and fulfil the same structuring function, that one would expect in horror.

With the demise of radio's golden age, Cole attempted to break into the television industry, with little success (not least due to failing health). A television pilot for *The Witch's Tale* was made but never sold. Siegel reveals that Cole himself admitted that the pilot had been "done so cheaply it lacked quality" (Siegel, 1998, 9). Around the time of his move from New York to California, Cole destroyed all his personal copies of *The Witch's Tale* recordings, believing "they had lost any further commercial value" (Siegel, 1998, 9).

The Witch's Tale is the first of its kind, and although it may have been superseded, it has never been forgotten. During the great era of American horror comics in the early 1950s, before their annihilation by the censorship of the Comics Code Authority, there was a horror comic entitled *Witches Tales*, a title which would reappear as the slightly modified *Witches' Tales* during the more enlightened 1970s. The most synonymous horror comics of the 1950s—the EC titles—featured three hosts in their horror titles: the Crypt Keeper, the Vault Keeper and the Old Witch. The latter is clearly an homage to Old Nancy, although Stephen Sennitt likens the first Old Witch narrator, "tittering away to herself insanely" (Sennitt, 1999, 55), to the host of the "Tales of Terror" comic script featured in early 1946 examples of *Yellowjacket*. Of course, the witch had been a familiar icon of supernatural and horror culture long before the invention of radio, even in a "host" role. Indeed, we could even consider the Three Witches in Shakespeare's *Macbeth* (1606) as precursors. Although Shakespeare's "weird sisters" are an important part of the action and plot, they function as an equivalent to the familiar "Prologue" character of the Renaissance stage or framing narrator, appearing as they do in the first scene of the play and at other pivotal moments of exposition in the plot. They are able to "comment" on the progress of Macbeth's fate, as well as influence it, but they are also characterized with the same type of macabre humor and eccentricity that will distinguish their descendant Old Nancy, centuries later. Old Nancy's humor is a key feature and stands in contrast to the foreboding presence of *Suspense*'s "Man in Black" or Arch Oboler when in *Lights Out* mode. Certainly Old Nancy sets a precedent for Raymond on *Inner Sanctum Mysteries* and other subsequent humorous hosts, whether in pre–Code horror comics; television horror hosts (such as Vampira and Ghoulardi) in the 1950s and beyond; or the skeletal, wise-cracking host on the television version of *Tales from the Crypt* from 1989 onwards. As Siegel comments, "It would be a mistake to take Nancy too seriously" (Siegel, 1998, 5), a statement which is apt for many other horror hosts who take similar delight in luring us into and out of their lurid tales, with no shortage of laughter in the process.

In his anthologized selection of *The Witch's Tale* scripts, Siegel insists, "Readers must be prepared to suspend their belief in the rational and embrace old fashioned 'melodrama' at both its best and its worst" (Siegel, 1998, 10). These are apt and wise words for anyone approaching not just *The Witch's Tale* but golden age horror radio as a whole. It is a form that can be driven by melodramatic conventions in both its worldview and performance style. *The Witch's Tale* is the "worst" example —for reasons that make it, ironically, the "best": it is the original horror show. The plots and acting are often heavy-handed and slovenly predictable, while others are obfuscated. Occasionally, some of the broadcasts feel weighed down by their extended use of the program's musical theme (Leginski's "Orgie and the Spirits"), which, when it seems to have reached its crescendo, starts again. However, Cole was clearly concerned with keeping the repertoire fresh, and he draws on a wide range of sources in the process of constructing his plays. He was also adept at exploring and using — indeed, pioneering — the potential of "horror radio." Consequently, there is a "spark" to these works that often include a remarkable and surprising exploration of dialect, and, at their best, are impassioned and frenetic journeys into heightened realms of horror. *The Witch's Tale* would remain a central influence on all that followed on horror radio, as well as an indirect influence on other aspects of popular horror culture in the twentieth century and beyond.

5

The Ultimate in Horror: *Lights Out* (1934–1947), Arch Oboler and Horror

Lights Out premiered on WENR in Chicago on January 1, 1934, and broadcast 15-minute plays on a weekly basis until April 1934, when the plays were extended to what is the quintessential horror radio format: the 30-minute drama. The program went national in April 1935 when it was broadcast by NBC, billed as "the ultimate in horror" (quoted in Dunning, 1998, 399). The *Syracuse Herald* (April 12, 1935) took matters further, declaring that the program "achieves the ultimate in horror, not only in radio, but in any form of dramatic representation." The program had been nurtured to this privileged position by Wyllis Cooper, who, after a year of producing *Lights Out* on NBC, used the success of the program as his ticket to Hollywood. His successor, Arch Oboler, felt that Cooper left *Lights Out* for other reasons: "He wore out quickly because you have to be slightly insane to write the kind of plays that Bill Cooper felt was good radio" (quoted in Maltin, 2000, 48). Whether worn out or insane, Cooper would not return to horror radio until *Quiet, Please* at the end of the next decade. Arch Oboler was 26 when he took over *Lights Out* in May 1936, and, far from diminishing, *Lights Out* enjoyed an increasing popularity that would soon make it synonymous with the name of Arch Oboler. Nevertheless, Cooper's founding influence on *Lights Out* would always remain; as Erik Barnouw states, it was Wyllis Cooper alone who "taught Arch Oboler how to write *Lights Out*" (Barnouw, 1968, 163) and "made him aware of undreamed facets of the medium" (Barnouw, 1968, 72). Cooper would be an influence whose tutorage would always be openly acknowledged by Oboler. In August 1939, however, NBC discontinued the program, and *Lights Out* remained off the air until Ironized Yeast sponsored the return of the program for a year-long run on CBS in 1942–43, some episodes of which were revived and re-produced by Oboler for syndicated broadcast as *The Devil and Mr. O* in the early 1970s. *Lights Out* returned to NBC for short summer runs in 1945 (*Fantasies from Lights Out*) and 1946, both of which mainly featured new productions of Cooper's 1930s scripts;

and ABC broadcast a final, very short run of the program from July to August 1947. *Lights Out* made a successful shift to television (NBC, 1949–52), but, as John Dunning states, "the legend of *Lights Out* is firmly rooted in the radio days" (Dunning, 1998, 400). In this chapter we will look at the *Lights Out* repertoire, but by devoting central attention to Arch Oboler we will also consider some examples from *Arch Oboler's Plays* (1939–40, 1945) and his postwar career.

Wyllis Cooper may have been the genius behind *Lights Out*, but Arch Oboler managed to sustain and consolidate the program's status, turning himself into a cult figure in the process. Oboler knew that Cooper was a tough act to follow, especially as Oboler regarded Cooper as more than just an extremely gifted writer, producer and director. In 1951, Oboler wrote an article in *Theater Arts* (July 1951) entitled "'Windy Kilocycles': Arch Oboler's Analysis of Radio Drama in Chicago," which opens thus:

> Radio drama (as distinguished from theater plays boiled down to kilocycle size) began at midnight, in the middle thirties, on one of the upper floors of Chicago's Merchandise Mart. The pappy was a rotund writer by the name of Wyllis Cooper…

Forget the BBC's output in the early 1920s, and forget *The Witch's Tale*; Oboler regards Wyllis Cooper as the founder of radio drama as a whole. The midnight broadcast Oboler refers to is, of course, *Lights Out*, which implies that "pure" radio drama begins with horror. This is a fascinating contention; as it places horror not as a generic subspecies of radio drama but at the heart of its creation and innovation. Wyllis Cooper may not be as celebrated a radio creator as Orson Welles or Norman Corwin, but most radio historians would acknowledge that he is a genius of the form. We will look at Wyllis Cooper in a later chapter while appraising his *Quiet, Please* program, perhaps the greatest aesthetic achievement in the horror radio of the golden age.

Wyllis Cooper was not an ostentatious man, and yet he knew how to play the showman. The *Chicago Tribune* (February 9, 1935) recounts an anecdote whereby a group of 50 *Lights Out* fans were permitted to attend a broadcast at NBC. Cooper ensured the studio lights were "doused during the broadcast, only two narrow lights playing on the actors themselves." This, combined with the efforts of the sound effects team, ensured that the guests had, according to the report, "a nice case of the jitters." In comparison, however, Arch Oboler turned showmanship into a form of art: he carefully constructed a distinctly unorthodox image (especially for the time period), always wearing "a sloppy T-shirt, unpressed pants, a sportcoat, and a porkpie hat" (Dunning, 1998, 39), and carrying with him a pet toad which he nourished with worms. A contemporary account of Oboler by Fred R. Sammis in *Radio and Television Mirror* (December 1940) reveals the complicated reception of him:

> He is too short, he has too little hair, too large a head, wears too thick glasses and talks too distractedly. His one really good point at parties … is his wife, who looks to be a child bride until you talk to her and discover a mature woman. Arch Oboler and neckties were born enemies, just as Arch and sweatshirts are boon companions. Partly because he likes to shock people and partly, I suspect, to make people know he is different, he wears hideous clothes, whether he's in dignified Radio City or studiedly careless Hollywood. But Arch fits that meaning of the

word genius I found, for no one I know has a greater capacity for imaginative creation.

Sammis' description is essentially a "gossip" account that is rather unkind about Oboler's physique, the way he talks, dress sense and even, fleetingly, morality (when Oboler's wife is said to look like a child). But all the same, Oboler is acknowledged as a "genius." In his own time Oboler was often damned by some for being less a genius than a self-serving publicist, but with the benefit of hindsight it is hard to condemn a man who knew how to play the publicity game in the burgeoning period of the modern mass media. Although Oboler succeeded in making a radio star of himself as writer, producer and director, and did so with no shortage of ego — to some of his contemporaries he was nothing short of "objectionable" (quoted in Dunning, 1998, 38) — he was generous when it came to his "rivals." We have seen the generous acclaim he awards Wyllis Cooper, and, although often compared in his time with the great radio dramatist Norman Corwin, Oboler made it clear that he regarded Corwin as the only "fine writer" in the history of radio, conceding, "I was a melodramatist, he was a poet" (quoted in Maltin, 2000, 47).

Oboler became not just successful but famous, and his name is inextricably linked with the radio drama of the golden age. But this status was not achieved without hard work, and his radio career is characterized by a prolific output. In fact, so prolific was Oboler that it is hard to be specific about how many plays he did write: Barnouw attributes "sixty scripts" on *Lights Out* as being by Oboler; Dunning claims that Oboler wrote and directed over 100 plays between May 1936 and July 1938 (Dunning, 1998, 399); while the *New York Times* (July 23, 1939) announces that Oboler has "written 275 broadcast plays." It would seem that in the subsequent ten years his output increased even further; according to Nachman, between 1938 and 1948 Oboler produced nearly 800 radio plays (Nachman, 1998, 312), although it is worth stressing that this figure would have included the numerous repeat broadcasts and the significant revisions and adaptations of his own work. Before Oboler had any success as a radio writer, rumor has it that he wrote some 50 radio scripts before one of them — *Futuristics*, a speculative drama set in 2001 — was produced by NBC in November 1933 to mark the opening of their New York City headquarters. The broadcast may have indisputably marked Oboler's arrival, but the experience was tinged with disillusionment for the 23-year-old aspiring writer. Oboler was paid $50 for *Futuristics*, and explains: "it had taken me weeks to write the play, and I had been trying to sell the thing for many more weeks, and the division of all these days into fifty dollars came to a very small sum" (Oboler, 1945, 19). Indeed, when he realized that actors get paid too, he managed to talk his way into a role in the play to boost his salary. The baptism of fire surrounding *Futuristics* did not stop here, however. Oboler, as performer, delivered one line in such a way that it seemed to satirize a slogan coined by one of NBC's commercial sponsors. Oboler likened the reprimand he received to "immediate disembowelment" with a "short knife" (Oboler, 1945, 20). He added that he managed to extricate himself from a situation that might have prematurely curtailed his career on the grounds of "extreme youth and extreme ignorance" (Oboler, 1945, 20).

Oboler may have extricated himself from danger on this occasion, but his prolific work as a writer and producer did not exclude him from other controversy. We have already seen that Oboler's first play for *Lights Out*—"Burial Services" (June 10, 1936)—

and the many noticeable letters of complaint it received seemed to indicate another controversy, but it was a controversy that signified a healthy audience and guaranteed the program's longevity. The following year Oboler was in danger of being embroiled in the scandal that enveloped Mae West over her performance in the "Adam and Eve" sketch Oboler had written for the *The Edgar Bergen and Charlie McCarthy Show* (December 12, 1937). The sketch is classic Mae West innuendo, with the snake getting stuck in the fence around the tree of forbidden fruit: "Oh, shake your hips! Yeah, you're doing all right. Get me a big one, I feel like doing a big apple" (a line greeted with spontaneous applause from the studio audience). NBC received a thousand letters of complaint, but the case soon became a furor when it was taken up by the newspapers, politicians and, most critically, the sponsors (Standard Brands). The result: Mae West was unofficially banned from radio for well over a decade. In contrast, Oboler, the author of the sketch (but, luckily for him, not the author of Mae West's style), received no punishment or reprimand. Indeed, periodicals such as *The Evangelist* (December 17, 1937), which vehemently denounced the sketch, did not even mention that there was a writer equally responsible for it; the only sinner was that "lascivious West woman" contaminating the homes of America with the "animalistic lure of lewdness."

Returning to Oboler, even when established as one of radio's most well-known figures, he was still able to cause upset. R. LeRoy Bannerman informs us that during World War Two, "Oboler created a mild controversy by his advocacy of anger and hatred as pragmatic attitudes for radio and people at war" (Bannerman, 1986, 99).

To return to the rise of Oboler in the early– to mid–1930s, the young writer was determined to build on the success and prestige of the *Futuristics* broadcast. Erik Barnouw describes Oboler's activities after *Futuristics*:

> Oboler then wrote a number of short, startling sketches for *Vallee Varieties*. On the basis of their success he tried to persuade NBC in Chicago to let him start a "maturely experimental" series on the lines of CBS's *Columbia Workshop*.
> Instead, NBC put him to work on *Lights Out*, a late-night horror series [Barnouw, 1945, 386].

Let us now look in detail at the *Lights Out* that Cooper had created. Although most recordings of the early Wyllis Cooper *Lights Out* broadcasts no longer exist, the mid–1940s revivals of his scripts give a taste of his work, as do the two extant scripts we shall analyze. Neither manuscript bears a title, although one has a series number and both include dates of broadcast. For the sake of the following analyses I will refer to the numbered script as *Lights Out* "#90" (October 23, 1935), and give the other play the plausible working title of "Amoeba" (December 4, 1935). *Lights Out* "#90" explores a "writer's block" scenario in which a writer called Sam Chase sits at his typewriter struggling to complete the crime novel he is working on. He bounces ideas off his friends Stewart and Taylor, but to no avail. Chase insists that his fictional victim needs to die in a sealed room with no weapon, and yet blood stains need to be present. Stewart and Taylor eventually go to mix cocktails in an adjoining room, leaving Chase to finish writing. The play cuts back and forth between the two rooms. After a few moments of typing alone, the door opens mysteriously and Chase is joined by a stranger called Harvey Kerrigan. Chase is only momentarily perplexed by the fact that the stranger shares exactly the same name as his fictional killer. The visitor proves extremely helpful to Chase, who is blissfully unaware of the obvious fact that the stranger does not merely share the name but is the imaginary villain come to life. The play is humorous, with Chase missing the innuendo and threats of Kerrigan but celebrating his creative inspiration: when Kerrigan utters, "I'm going to torture you as I was tortured..." Chase replies, "Hey, wait a minute till I write that down ... that's swell..." Chase remains innocent right up until the end, thoroughly enjoying the collaborative writing and throwing himself into the moments of role play with gusto. Finally, Kerrigan looms towards Chase, ominously repeating, "I'm not forgetting the blood," for which Cooper includes the direction that the actor playing Kerrigan should come closer and closer to the microphone before Chase screams. After the subsequent gong, Stewart and Taylor return to Chase's study with drinks and are amazed to see the neatly-typed manuscript of the novel finished in the mere "three or four minutes" they were out of the room. Taylor reads out the end of the novel: "He tried to scream again, but it was too late. Great fangs met in his throat, and the bright blood..." The fate of Chase's fictional victim is clear. At this moment, Stewart notices the corpse of Chase behind a chair, with "his throat ... all torn out."

The playfulness of this script bears all the hallmarks of Cooper's later work: it is a drama that plays an ingenious time game, a piece of writing about writing, and a satire on the difficulties of being a writer (especially a horror writer who tries to create effective generic stories and summons up vampires in the process). Indeed, Chase consistently tries to find a rational explanation for the murder scene he has invented, but ultimately the conclusion can be nothing other than supernatural—at least in the 30-minute format. It is perhaps a paradigm for the horror writer that the most unsettling and vivid conundrum is explained away by the use of the supernatural—it may be irrational but it unquestionably provides closure. It is a subject that Cooper will enjoy returning to in the *Lights Out* play "The Coffin in Studio B" (which was revived on July 13, 1946), an ironic satire of the process of radio production, focusing as it does on a lackluster dress rehearsal which drives all involved to despair. As well as satirizing the personalities of radio actors and production staff, the play includes humorous lines, with the director cursing the sound effects assistant in charge of the *Lights Out* trademark: "Oh, pay attention, dummy, will you hit that gong!" Cooper does not spare his own principal vocation either: "That's the trouble with writers—no imagination." Cooper will also experiment with the theme of metadrama in *Quiet, Please* with the play "Where Do You Get Your Ideas" (February 20, 1949); but, significantly, it is also a subject adopted and explored by Oboler in his own *Lights Out* work.

In Oboler's "Murder in the Script Department" (May 11, 1943), two secretaries lament having to type up the manuscript of "one of those *Lights Out* plays: blood, and people dying, and murderers and worms..." and speculating what a "screwball" Oboler is, if not a genuine "werewolf." The secretaries become trapped in their office and endure a night of horror they assume to have been precipitated by their typing of the weird works of Oboler. The play ends with a news bulletin announcing that there was an earth tremor and power cut during the night, and two women, trapped in a building, were "frightened to death." Oboler develops the self-referential still further with "The Author and the Thing" (September 28, 1943), a sophisticated exploration of a similar theme, with Oboler playing himself struggling to write his latest *Lights Out* script. In the process,

Oboler thinks of a monster for seven days and seven nights, an inadvertent ritual that summons it to life, after which Oboler believes that he sees the monster devour his brother. During the episode Oboler himself describes the play (in his narrative frame) as "one of those crazy stories inside of a story." The question of structure and identity is particularly complex in this play, as we have a writer called Arch Oboler taking a dramatic role (hence becoming an actor called Arch Oboler) by playing a writer called Arch Oboler. In the script within the script, Oboler ends up confined to a lunatic asylum for life, while in the narrative frame the play concludes with Oboler killed by the summoned monster. "The Author and the Thing" affords a playful degree of self-mockery on the part of Oboler, who clearly enjoys playing writer and performer, host and lead, lunatic and murder victim within the same play. Like *Lights Out* "#90," "The Author and the Thing" is a comedy horror play about writer's block and the perils of creativity, and the expediency of horror. Both plays are also interesting studies of the revenge of the fictional construct, with writers suffering the fate normally reserved for mad scientists and necromancers when their personal creations cause their own annihilation: a portrait of the artist as Dr. Frankenstein, as it were.

Wyllis Cooper's "Amoeba" is a very different, yet equally paradigmatic, piece. The play features the experiments of Dr. Baumeister and his faint-hearted assistant Laferski, who create a giant amoeba-like life form with a voracious appetite and propensity to grow and grow. The amoeba begins to demonstrate intelligence, slurping when its mad scientist inventor (who explicitly likens himself to "Frankenstein") calls it "Amoeba." Laferski's pleas that they destroy it go unheeded, and in the second half of the play the amoeba reveals that it has telepathic skills and is able to change its shape and imitate whomever its subject is thinking of. The amoeba imitates Baumeister when his wife Esther visits the laboratory, and devours her, described by Cooper with this delightful directing note:

> SHE SCREAMS AND OLD AMOEBA GOES SLURP SLURP SLURP. HER SCREAMS ARE MUFFLED AND FINALLY DIES DOWN BEHIND THE SLURPING SOUNDS INTO GONG.

Baumeister is killed in turn when the amoeba imitates Esther. With Laferski the only person left, the play ends with him using an oxyacetylene torch and the sound of "melting protoplasm." The similarity between "Amoeba" and Oboler's now-legendary "Chicken Heart" (March 10, 1937), as well as the nearly-as-celebrated "Revolt of the Worms" (October 13, 1942), is unmistakable. "Chicken Heart" enjoys its status as one of the most famous horror radio plays, thanks in great part to Bill Cosby, who, as Martin Grams, Jr., writes, "immortalized" (Grams, 2000, 288) the episode in a comedy routine about his childhood. In addition, "Chicken Heart" was done no disservice when Stephen King discussed it in his *Danse Macabre*. Both "Chicken Heart" and "Revolt of the Worms" succeed as horror radio because they establish a nightmarish scenario that is all the more effective for the use of sound effects and dialogue, and for being unseen. In fact, the horror of the stories would be diminished through vision. We might consider the protoplasm in *The Blob* (Irvin S. Yeaworth, Jr., 1958) and the worms in *Tremors* (Ron Underwood, 1989): their *Lights Out* precursors are all the more powerful and alienating because of the exploitation of the listeners' imagination, forcing us to envision massive flesh smothering the world or gigantic worms hideously wriggling from the ground. The origin of these scenarios can be traced back to H. G. Wells' *The Food of the Gods* (1904), if not back to the ancient myth of Pandora's Box. But in terms of radio, Wyllis Cooper's "Amoeba" represents one of the original explorations of this theme, predated only by the giant insects in "The Entomologist" (*The Witch's Tale*, January 7, 1935).

The colossal expansion of slurping amoebas, pounding chicken meat and cacophonous garden worms are all absurd stories, but the theme was not always treated in such an unsubtly gargantuan way on *Lights Out*. In Oboler's "Spider" (May 18, 1943), two men discover and attempt to capture a "natural" monster, a spider the size of a dog. The play establishes a highly effective atmosphere in the evocation of the jungle and the psychology of the two hunters. Moreover, the silence of the arachnid itself is an absence that proves extremely eerie. In radio drama the presence of something can be evoked through sound effects and dialogical description, yet, ironically, it can remain as an equally terrifying presence even in absence.

Long after Cooper had departed, some of his scripts were revived for the later seasons of *Lights Out*, several of which survive as recordings, such as "Death Robbery" (July 16, 1947) and "The Coffin in Studio B" (July 13, 1946). "Man in the Middle" (revived August 25, 1945) is a play that demonstrates yet another side to Cooper's versatility, and is also another of his paradigmatic radio plays. The play makes brilliant use of both the spoken voice and interior voice of the central character, Johnny. This device allows for repetition and, most dramatically, hypocrisy. Johnny's affections are split between two women, his wife Lucille and his secretary Patricia. Despite their torrid affair, Johnny's affection for Patricia has waned and, while he continues to flatter and kiss her, his internal voice expresses his disgust. It is Johnny's weakness that allows his marriage to break up and himself to die. However, at the end of the play it transpires that this scenario was merely a daydream, and Johnny redeems himself — and his marriage — by speaking his mind and firing Patricia. It is a play in the suspense/thriller genre with all the ingredients needed for a film noiresque tale of adultery and violence. The virtuosity of Cooper's script means that an ironic juxtaposition between "real" action and interior monologue is created. This is a technique we might associate closely with the modernist fiction of James Joyce and Virginia Woolf, but Cooper was one of the first to demonstrate how effective it could be for radio drama when he makes the language of interiority interweave with spoken utterance.

On the strength of these scripts it is immediately apparent that Oboler owes a considerable debt to Cooper. Some of Oboler's most famous horror works appear to be reworkings of a Cooper paradigm. In the case of Cooper's "Man in the Middle" it is a question of style. Although John Dunning argues that Oboler utilized a stream of consciousness technique on *Lights Out* "two years before [Norman] Corwin came on the scene" (Dunning, 1998, 38), we could justifiably contend that Cooper came first of all. Oboler uses what could be described as a modernist stream of consciousness in a number of *Lights Out* broadcasts. The play "It Happened" (analyzed later in this chapter) uses the technique to build an intensity of horror. Another play, "State Executioner" (March 17, 1937; revived August 17, 1943) concerns Samuel Jones, state executioner at the time of King George III. The story may be straightforward, but its methodology creates a compelling narrative, not least by using its modernist technique to handle a historical subject. Jones awaits the mob that threatens to lynch him, and the play incorporates flashbacks as he recalls 20 years as the official hangman, but the narrative thread is dominated by the stream of consciousness style. The preamble to this "psychological drama" explains that it is a play in which "the principal part is taken not by the character himself but by his thoughts." The episode opens with the interior monologue of the state executioner as he sits "alone in a dismal room":

> I want to be dead, dead, dead. Do you feel anything when you're dead? Are you hungry, are you cold, are you tired when you're dead? No? When I'm dead I'll have peace, peace. I've got to have peace — kill myself. Yes. Bullet in my heart. The pain — I don't like pain, but it can't hurt. They say it doesn't hurt. Only hanging hurts. I know it does. I've seen their faces when they cut them down. Purple, black. I've seen their faces when the masks came off and there's pain in them, pain that twists their faces, grinds their teeth, and gives them living hell until at last they die.

On paper, this section of speech may seem melodramatic. But in the 1943 broadcast the monologue is delivered in a mere 30 seconds, and a similar speed of delivery is sustained for the interior monologue episodes through much of the broadcast. Rather than lending the production a melodramatic feel, the rapidity of the delivery gives the play a quality of breathless and intimate desperation.

Oboler employs a similar stylistic technique for the narrative of "Happy Ending" (June 23, 1937). It is a remarkable play, not simply in terms of form but also in its theme. The play presents the interior monologue of Peggy, a woman who has just discovered that she is pregnant. The story follows her journey home from the doctor as she prepares to tell her husband the news. She explores every repercussion of being pregnant during the Depression. With a soundscape that includes the busy sounds of the street, Peggy's footsteps and sentimental music, we hear Peggy's memories and reflections, creating a panoramic vision of 1930s America. We hear FDR's presidential inauguration juxtaposed with a shoeshine desperate for work; we hear the finale of a grand opera juxtaposed with a woman fighting with her husband ("You think I'm afraid of ya? Go on then — hit me! Hit me!"). We hear the voice of Peggy's husband Bill as she imagines how he will react to the news of the pregnancy. He speaks either in a mantra of domestic worries ("rent, gas, dentist, light...") or in anxiety of the state of a world where war is brewing. The voice of Bill questions the wisdom of having children: why "raise 'em up to blow 'em up"? In its use of flashbacks in its exploration of domestic and global anxieties, "Happy Ending" is reminiscent of Clifford Odets' *Waiting for Lefty* (1935). However, far from ending with a cry of agitation, the final scene of "Happy Ending" presents Bill having received a pay raise and wanting to start a family. If Odets questions the American Dream, Oboler asserts his belief in it. "Happy Ending" becomes, ultimately, a melodrama. Nevertheless, the journey to this point is a thought-provoking and remarkable one. At the conclusion of "Happy Ending" it is clear that, unlike *The Witch's Tale*'s "The Happy Ending" (September 28, 1934), the title is not ironic, although one imagines that an audience familiar with the shocks and twists of *Lights Out* would be wary of the title until the play is over.

We will now look specifically at Oboler's horror drama in *Lights Out*. In the large body of work that is *Lights Out*, the plays encompass a broad range of themes and types of horror. The *Lights Out* repertoire includes plays that range from conventional tales of horror to science-gone-wrong scenarios. For example, "The Thirteenth Corpse" (June 15, 1938), "Bon Voyage" (June 22, 1938; revived November 10, 1942) and "Scoop" (December 8, 1942) are formulaic tales of vengeance from beyond the grave; while "Chicken Heart" (March 10, 1937) and "Revolt of the Worms" (October 13, 1942) are classic science fiction fodder about scientific experiments gone awry — although "science fiction" was a term that Oboler always hated simply because, to quote him, "the day after tomorrow it always becomes reality" (Oboler, 1967, 14). The world is yet to be consumed by a giant chicken heart, so it is safe to say that these examples are fantastical. In contrast, some of Oboler's finest horror plays are couched in a recognizable reality: horror tales of the possible that play on the listener's paranoia.

Oboler claims that if he had to put a crest on his notepaper, it would be "a dinosaur rampant on a field of spiral nebulae" (Oboler, 1945, 1), as this would encapsulate his fascination with both past and future. This twin fascination is certainly evident in Oboler's world of horror, many examples of which function through the impact of temporal juxtaposition. For instance, "Subbasement" (August 24, 1943) — revived as "Going Down" in *The Devil and Mr. O* — is set in the vast transportation tunnels (for many listeners a futuristic concept) beneath a city's department stores, which prove to contain a living dinosaur. In "Neanderthal" (November 3, 1942), a group of explorers stumble across a caveman. These stories are blatant instances of what could be described as horrific anachronism, but it is a dynamic that works in other examples. "Gevangenpoort," "It Happened" and "The Ball" are all plays that feature Americans in Europe in the tradition of *The Witch's Tale*'s "Hangman's Roost" (July 4, 1932): the new world visits the old world and experiences the depths of horror.

In "Gevangenpoort" (July 6, 1938), we are presented with Marion and Jim Elson, two American tourists enjoying a vacation in Holland. Their guidebook has led them to visit the Gevangenpoort in the Hague, "Holland's famous and infamous prison." It seems to be closed but they manage to gain entry, let in by a strange curator who then locks them into a pitch dark, echoing room. They move from fear to amusement, believing it to be a sensational set-up and part of the tourist package. The joke soon wears thin when they are dragged out by men dressed like members of the Spanish Inquisition who treat them as spies — they regard Jim as an "Englis'man" — and subject Marion to a very audible torture with thumbscrews. Jim is ultimately condemned to be hanged, after which Jim and Marion are back in the lightless room where they started. They assume it was all a dream and stumble out into the city's busy streets, at which point Marion screams in horror when she sees Jim's neck bearing the rope burn of the noose. "Gevangenpoort" is a successful horror play because of the concision of its scenario, the shock of its climax, and the depth of its characterization. On this latter point, the rather edgy but realistic relationship of Marion and Jim works both as a portrayal of a married couple and as a portrayal of rather jaded tourists, and stands in stark contrast to the stereotypical portrayal of the menacing and heavily accented Spanish Inquisition.

"It Happened" (May 11, 1938) is a play that utilizes, to an extent, Oboler's stream of consciousness technique, but it also borders on the territory of melodrama, even if, as we shall see, the female protagonist refuses to play the simpering victim. In an attempt to prevent the audience from perceiving that the play is straying into one of the stylistic perils of melodrama (namely, the aside), the opening preamble takes pains to emphasize that we will hear "the voice in her throat as she speaks, but also the voice in her mind as she thinks." The story opens with a group of American schoolgirls on vacation in Paris, including one Jean Taylor (Mercedes McCambridge), an overconfident teenager who, in her determination to have "fun, fun, fun," rejects the Louvre and heads off alone, much to the American tour guide's horror. Within minutes she meets an American abroad who claims to know her father. The jovial Mr. Edwards offers to show Jean the "real" Paris, the "living, lusty Paris" that everyone reads about but tourists never see. He promises to give her a Paris "pure and adulterated … ha, ha, and not so pure," to which Jean, lacking a sense of irony (just like so many victims in the horror genre), declares, "Mister, you're the answer to a maiden's prayer!" Trusting him to be a family friend, she is led to a quiet back street and into a dark and sparse apartment, where Mr. Edwards locks the door: "I'm an opportunist," he explains to her. Jean does not play the melodramatic maiden tied to the railroad track: she is assertive, sarcastically commenting "show me the etchings" before explaining she is no "kid" and he will not get away with anything. Mr. Edwards, despite the signposting and development of the narrative, is not planning a sexual assault, and says to Jean with scorn: "You little sap, you don't think I'm interested in you!" In fact, Mr. Edwards is a kidnapper and has carefully planned this abduction to extort a fortune out of Jean's father.

The listeners find themselves a quarter of the way through the play, during which they have been taken through a narrative that sounds like it will be a disturbing tale of the rape of a teenage girl, only (in some ways thankfully) to become a story of kidnap and extortion. But there are more twists in this labyrinthine tale. Jean, once again in a refreshingly different approach to the dramatic stereotype of a very young woman, assesses that she should be able to overpower her abductor. She grabs a candlestick and kills Edwards with a blow to his skull. After this, Jean begins to panic—"My head—I'm all mixed up!" she utters as she fumbles with the keys to escape the gruesome scene. In pitch darkness, Jean runs down a flight of stairs into the basement, where she finds herself wading in water. We are now in one of the great horror locales of Paris: the sewers so beloved by the "Phantom of the Opera" in Gaston Leroux's novel (1911). Now, halfway through the play, we are no longer in crime drama but seem to be in the Gothic territory of classic horror. This is even more the case as Jean meets a mysterious stranger in the sewers, the first Frenchman in the play, talking in a deep, heavy accent. Once again, the listeners are presented with the close interplay of horror and the erotic. Jean is, for the second time, rescued by an older man, one who this time helps her out of the water and promises to lead her safely out of the sewers. However, a subtle ambiguity remains as to whether the Frenchman is a romantic savior or yet another peril. This uncertainty dissipates as soon as the stranger says, "Here we are," when they have arrived at an underground chamber as dark as Mr. Edwards' apartment, and which Louis calls "my workroom." Unfortunately, this time her abductor has no interest in money, despite Jean—the rich American tourist abroad—making impassioned promises of more money than he could earn in a whole year.

We would seem to be approaching the heart of horror, the lair, as it were, of the Minotaur or Medusa. The Frenchman shows Jean what he does in his workshop: he makes "exquisite" jewellery from the bones of corpses. He has no interest in killing Jean but in keeping her as his companion. He enslaves her as his assistant, and in a virtuoso moment of soundscape we hear Jean sobbing as she saws through human bones under the supervision of the jovial Louis. When a half-drowned man washes past, Jean manages to escape while Louis violently finishes the man off. The coda to the play presents two Frenchmen looking at the polluted Seine and seeing a body washed up. They say it is the corpse of an "old woman" who looks like she was an American. To their horror they realize she is alive, and the prematurely aged Jean croaks, "Would you like a beautiful necklace? A beautiful necklace ... Out of bones ... Real human bones."

"It Happened" is a fast-moving play that manages to stray in and out of a variety of styles. It is, to a certain degree, melodramatic in plot but modernist in technique. It is in places a crime thriller (an attempted kidnapping and an actual murder), and in others Gothic horror (Louis is a Parisian sewer dweller like the more famous Phantom). Over all, the play is a fascinating exploration of the American abroad.

Other examples of this sub-genre include Henry James' *Daisy Miller* (1879), a work that may be poles apart from Oboler's horror play but, curiously enough, also ends in tragedy. Indeed, it also possesses a moral framework, if not a similar degree of paranoia: Daisy Miller dies from a mosquito bite, having audaciously visited the Coliseum late at night without a chaperone but with an Italian admirer. In "It Happened" we see another young American who cannot resist the allure and romance of old Europe, and her reckless decision also seals her doom. In both works, the American heroine is resourceful, confident and inquisitive, but both are ultimately punished for being so. Europe, and especially Paris (but James' Rome is as good), has a romantic connotation, and Oboler's play is a nightmarish subversion of the "American in Paris" type of fantasy wherein innocence meets experience across continents and love blossoms. There is a significant sexual subtext to this American fantasy of Paris. When Oboler produced this play in the late 1930s, Paris was still seen as a playground for adults, legendary not only for its clubs and bars but its *maisons de tolérance* (legalized brothels). Obviously Jean is not interested in a brothel, but she is nonetheless lured away by Mr. Edwards' promises of experiencing the Paris that is "lusty" and "not so pure." There is a sexual tension throughout "It Happened," whether in Jean's desire for "fun" (she sees herself as a child no more), the dialogue with Edwards, or Louis' expressed desire to keep Jean as his partner for many years. The fact that Oboler sets out to exploit the fears of his American listeners—especially teenagers *and* their parents—is given particular emphasis in the title, which seems to be the answer to the question, "What's the worst thing that could happen?"

One aspect of "It Happened" is ludicrous—the idea of a sewer-dwelling lunatic who makes necklaces from bones—but apart from that, the play dwells in the region of the unlikely but possible horror. Jean Taylor experiences every tourist's worst nightmare. In this respect, the play follows the Grand-Guignol tradition (appropriate for a play set in Paris). Indeed, the "possible" and distinctly sexualized horrors of "It Happened" would belong very comfortably in the Grand-Guignol repertoire, although Oboler's play is exemplary horror radio in its use of evocative location and Jean's tragic descent. A Grand-Guignol adaptation would have to be set entirely in a well-lit version of Mr. Edwards' apartment or Louis' workroom.

There is a convincing stage equivalent to "It Happened," albeit post–golden age and post–Grand-Guignol, in the form of Jean-Claude van Itallie's *I'm Really Here* (1964), in which all–American gal Doris, another Daisy Miller on vacation in Europe, is shown the sights of Paris by a romantic Frenchman, only to be stabbed to death by him when she takes a chance and lets him into her hotel room. Van Itallie's play may be horrific, but it is nonetheless a humorous and complex satire. Although "It Happened" may not be as absurdly comical as van Itallie's heroine explaining her citizenship to a serial killer after he has stabbed her ("I am pert. I am pretty. I am an American. I don't know anything about this." [van Itallie, 1968, 44]), one suspects that both writers shared a similar delight in playing with the paranoia of their audience in refusing to let the "cavalry" come to the rescue of their precocious protagonists.

While "It Happened" may be a play set ostensibly in the "real" world, Oboler's other great Paris play, "The Ball" (March 9, 1943) — revived as "Paris Macabre" on *The Devil and Mr. O* — is an example of supernatural horror. The play centers on two young American men, Jerry and Paul, on vacation in France, looking, like their doomed compatriot Jean Taylor, for a good time in "gay Paree." The college boys have acquired tickets off some "bozo" for a costume ball which, although the students may not initially detect it, seems more like something out of Poe's "Masque of the Red Death" than the "wild party" they are expecting. One of the masked figures urges Jerry and Paul to leave while they still can, but once the clock strikes midnight it is "too late." Of course, Paul and Jerry have stumbled upon a dance of the dead. There are no heads behind the masks: the revellers are ghosts of guillotine victims. "The Ball" also provides a fine example of the *Lights Out* unhappy ending, the play concluding with the decapitation of both American tourists: Paul is lynched by the headless ghosts and put in the guillotine; Jerry manages to escape into the Paris streets where an automobile knocks him over and cleaves off his head. "The Ball" is a heightened tale of the macabre, but there is an effective texture to the play that makes it engaging and memorable. Jerry and Paul are well-constructed characters, and the play presents the clash of the new world with the old in a humorous way. Jerry, for instance, dances with a masked young woman and, exasperated at her silence, declares, "Oh come on now, beautiful, haven't you read that book on how to win and influence friends? You've gotta give, ha, you know, conversationally, ha ha." It is highly unlikely that a headless victim of the guillotine would have read Dale Carnegie's *How to Win Friends and Influence People* (1937), but there is also delicious irony in Jerry playing the sexually predatory American male attempting to seduce a ghost.

Oboler did not always send his unfortunate American victims across the Atlantic to secure their demise; sometimes it is enough for Oboler to send his protagonists into an alienating American wilderness, like James Dickey would many years later in *Deliverance* (1970). "Poltergeist" (October 20, 1942) — *The Devil and Mr. O*'s "Gravestone" — opens with a group of three young women on vacation travelling across a snowy landscape singing "Jingle Bells." A number of Oboler's plays open with characters singing familiar or popular songs, a classic Oboler technique to lure the listener into a tale of terror; the use of a popular song hooks the listeners' attention and also mischievously disarms and even comforts them prior to a terrifying descent into horror. Martin Grams, Jr., contends that Oboler's use of music is less a formal strategy than a deliberate intertextual reference to the diverse compositions that had motivated or inspired him:

> Oboler was a music lover and required "white noise" in order to write his scripts. As a result, he grew a large collection of classic music on records and often incorporated the music into his scripts: more out of inspiration than intent of empha-

sizing and affecting the audience [Martin Grams, Jr., letter to Richard J. Hand, December 3, 2004].

Returning to "Poltergeist," the singing student and her two roommates are travelling on a cart, but the snow is so deep they are obliged to walk. The three female characters are drawn so as to create an interesting dramatic interplay. Kay is flamboyant, and after the Christmas carol sings the blues, much to the disapproval of the rather pious Edna. Kay replies, "Well, what's wrong with a hot song to keep us warm? If you think 'The St Louis Blues' is gonna dirty up the snow you oughta hear 'Frankie and Johnny' the way I sing it!" The third character, Florence, is the peacemaker with a calming influence over her friends. For a listener of our own time, the idea of three young friends not entirely at ease in a wilderness brings to mind *The Blair Witch Project* (Daniel Myrick and Eduardo Sanchez, 1999). Inadvertently, Kay the extrovert dances on a grave in a cemetery obscured by the drifting snow. The superstitious Edna is horrified and reprimands Kay, who replies, "You superstitious little fool, if you don't stop talking that way I'm gonna slap ya face!" Edna becomes hysterical and anticipates the arrival of a poltergeist. At this moment, a rock strikes Edna on the head and she is knocked unconscious.

In safety, Edna is put into bed, and the three women are forced to cancel their journey home. Kay and Florence are now terrified that dancing on the tomb has awoken a vengeful spirit. They hear Edna scream from the bedroom, and both collapse when they behold what we are only told about in the next scene: Edna lies in bed with her "head crushed flat" by a tombstone. Kay and Florence go through swings of guilt, attempts at prayer and a desire to flee. Waking up alone, Florence realizes that Kay has gone out into the snow, and she follows. In one of the finest examples of the disembodied voice in horror radio, Florence hears the voices of Kay and Edna on the wind of the blizzard as they chant an eerie mantra: "Here we are Florence ... This way Florence ..." Florence follows, and the scene culminates in her scream as she "discovers" her friends. If the first 20 minutes of the play is like a forerunner to *The Blair Witch Project*, the final section of the play commences like a version of *Picnic at Hanging Rock* (Peter Weir, 1975), with two men heading out into the wilderness to find the missing women. They find a shoe and some footprints that lead them to the graveyard. "Glory be! They're alive!" cries one of the men as they see the women "dancing on the graves" in the distance. The intermittent moonlight throws the men into sporadic darkness. As the clouds drift by again, the men find the corpses of Florence and Kay, frozen stiff, with their heads crushed flat under tombstones. With this *Blair Witch Project*–style ending, wherein none of the three friends survive, Oboler produces an uncompromising shock. The listener expects at least one of the disparate women to survive, possibly rescued by the two men at the end of the play in a melodramatic denouement. But this genre of horror is not like the Hollywood movies of the same period. *Lights Out* plays such as "Poltergeist" are like short ghost stories (such as in the Gothic "Shilling Shocker" tradition) or urban legends where happy endings are not guaranteed. In the concluding narrative frame, Oboler attempts to resist the possible interpretation of the story as belonging to a traditional legacy of fiction when he argues that there have been recorded cases of poltergeists (in London in April 1872)—which is rather like the authenticating proviso given to urban legends with the phrase "this happened to a friend of a friend."

Perhaps one of the finest works in the *Lights Out* repertoire is "Valse Triste" (March 30, 1938; revived December 29, 1942), a play that investigates the same themes and fears of other *Lights Out* horror stories but does so in a method and style that is particularly compelling and well constructed. It is even more of a precursor to *Deliverance* in that it terrifies the listener with a tale of *possible* horror: there is nothing supernatural in this play, simply the unpredictability and danger of existence. In the opening narrative frame of the 1942 broadcast, Oboler describes "Valse Triste" as being about "chance," and this concept—that everything is chance and nothing is planned—is investigated throughout the play. It is probably a deep-seated fear for some listeners, as it denies the possibility of preordination and implies that existence is merely a game of chance. Once again we are presented with young people on vacation. Dotty and Laura are two New Yorkers on a canoe on a "healthy" camping holiday in a remote area they chose through a process of "eeny-meeny-miny-mo." The play displays the clash of urban and rural values: Dotty talks about the canoe as if it were a car, is terrified at the possibility of "Indians," and comes from a world governed by "keep off the grass" signs. Dotty and Laura attempt to pick some beautiful posies they see on the riverbank and lose their canoe in the process. Completely lost, they toss a coin to decide which direction to travel. Hearing a violin playing, the women are lured to a remote house to find sanctuary. John Boyd (played by Boris Karloff in the 1938 performance) welcomes the women into his house, and the play develops with an increasing Gothic quality.

The house is dark (Boyd is blind), the sun sets rapidly and a chilly breeze announces an impending storm. Dotty and Laura attempt to leave but are violently prevented by Boyd, who, they suddenly perceive, is hideously disfigured. He explains the deal to them: he will marry one and kill the other, a decision to be determined by the flip of a coin. "Chance must choose my bride ... and the bride of death," he intones. In this single phrase, Oboler captures what are arguably some of the most central components to horror: the frightening and fascinating taboos of sex and death, and chance, the uncertainty of existence. In excruciating humiliation, Dotty and Laura beg to be "married" before Boyd flips the coin. Laura passes out, and Boyd waits for her to wake up before announcing the result. In a grotesquely erotic scene, Boyd withholds the outcome, revelling in teasing the women before he announces the result. Meanwhile, two men from the camp attempt to find the missing women. When they near Boyd's house they flip a coin to decide where to go, but continue searching downstream rather than visit "old man Boyd." Cutting back to Boyd's house, we hear the result of the coin flip. Laura has her throat cut, and Boyd plays his violin to his bride. In a final twist of irony, we hear one of the two men searching for the women confess that he lied about the result of the coin flip, and the play ends with them heading back—as the coin dictated they should have—to see Mr. Boyd.

The play certainly possesses a melodramatic and Gothic quality, with its two maidens trapped in the desolate house of a sinister, disfigured man. Moreover, the play experiments with a notion of sexual horror we might associate with these heightened forms, and with the quasi-melodramatic thrills of the Grand-Guignol. "Valse Triste" shares some similarities with Maurice Level's Grand-Guignol play *Baiser dans la nuit* (1912), in which Henri, a victim of a vitriol attack and therefore as disfigured as Boyd, lurks in a darkened room and, like Oboler's villain, ensnares (spider-and-fly style) a beautiful victim.

But as much as "Valse Triste" belongs to a nineteenth-century and early twentieth-century tradition, it is a forerunner to what has become a standard theme in American horror, a motif repeated in later generations of films such as *Psycho* (Alfred Hitchcock, 1960) and *The Texas Chainsaw Massacre* (Tobe Hooper, 1974), as well as numerous other horror movies in which young, usually attractive and urbane people are lost in remote patches of America and find themselves where no one wants to be — in the lair of the American psycho. Like "Valse Triste," these are works of "real" and possible horrors that often exploit contemporary sexual anxieties. *Psycho* and *The Texas Chainsaw Massacre* may have been loosely based on the true story of the 1950s serial killer Ed Gein, but the narrative structure, characterization, and plot twists and surprises, the treatment of violence, and the pervading bleakness owe a debt, directly or indirectly, to "Valse Triste." Examined in this light we can see that "Valse Triste" is an anti-melodramatic work in that there is no happy resolution — the would-be heroes will arrive too late; and Oboler constructs the image of a universe governed by rules of chance completely indifferent to human aspiration or well-being, rather than a divine and moral universe of black and white certainties where good will always triumph over evil.

The sexual anxieties in Oboler's "It Happened" and "Valse Triste" are to be found elsewhere in the *Lights Out* repertoire, and are sometimes given a less "real" treatment. "Cat Wife" (April 6, 1938) — "Alley Cat" on *The Devil and Mr. O* — charts a woman's metamorphosis into a "human-sized cat" (Dunning, 1998, 400), to the horror of her increasingly simpering and guilt-wracked husband. The scenario, including the giant cat's deliberately human meowing (no need for an Alonzo Deen Cole–style feline verisimilitude in this play), makes the play a grotesque but humorous satire of gender relationships and dysfunctional matrimony. "Little Old Lady" (November 17, 1937; revived May 25, 1943) is another feline lycanthropic horror. In this play two university students, Alice and Lona, visit the latter's Aunt Harriet at her remote cottage. Once inside the old lady's house they think they see a mysterious cat lurking in the shadows, a cat the size of a tiger. Up in the bedroom the women hear scratching on the door, and upon opening it one of them is attacked by the monstrous feline and killed. The other escapes and is intercepted by the local police, who take her back to Aunt Harriet's house. The police only find Aunt Harriet knitting in her rocking chair. The old lady denies knowing the young women, and the police, in the role of archetypal rural cops, physically restrain Alice and begin to forcibly remove her from the building. However, at that moment Aunt Harriet begins to chuckle, and in an eerie transformation scene, her laughter becomes yowling, her lips draw back to reveal cat's fangs, and her fingers are seen to be talons. She claws the eyes of one of the policemen and is shot dead. It turns out that Aunt Harriet died three years before, and in a ludicrous but nonetheless disturbing precursor to Norman Bates, the cat has continued to live as its owner (or "mother"), rapidly fashioning itself into a little old lady. In the closing narrative frame of the 1943 production, Oboler endeavors to make us believe in the plausibility of this absurd tale, rationalizing the story in terms of an interpretation of lycanthropy: "Even we who are, ha, 'normal,' haven't we met women who are catty, men who are brave as lions and others who made you wonder whether they were men or mice?"

Oboler was not the only writer on *Lights Out* in the late 1930s. "The Hounds of Weir" (July 20, 1938) is an interesting example of an Oboler-era *Lights Out* script still in existence that was not written by Oboler. The scriptwriter is Geoff Whalen, and the play is an example of lurid melodrama that is perhaps both more lurid and more melodramatic than anything penned by the self-proclaimed melodramatist himself, Oboler. The play opens with a District Attorney called Meyster stopping at a gas station and asking directions to "Meath's Place." The gas station attendant warns Meyster against his strange destination and its packs of wolfhounds and Great Danes (which we hear baying in the distance). Meyster is also informed that the place is owned by a Dr. Meath, "a peculiar feller [sic] ... a doctor or surgeon," who has retired there. Before Meyster arrives, we are taken into the house itself, where we meet the clearly insane Meath and his equally mad sidekick Graves. Meyster arrives to see his ailing wife, demanding to know who ordered her removal from a sanatorium to "this terrible spot!" It comes as no surprise to the listener when it is revealed that it has all been an elaborate ruse to lure Meyster into a madman's retribution; Meyster's line of work as a District Attorney has already signaled him out as a prime victim for a revenge melodrama (anticipating *Cape Fear* [J. Lee-Thompson, 1961]), just as Meath's former profession contains all the promise of a gruesome revenge. To Meyster's horror he realizes that Dr. Meath is in fact the unsubtly named "David Eath" who he unjustly sent to prison some years before. "D. Eath," indeed gets his revenge, giving Meyster a potion that paralyzes his body and causes his tongue to swell enormously. However, Eath tells Meyster, "I will not let it choke you ... no ... no ... before that happens I will cut it out of your mouth and feed it to one of my dogs." As well as having captured Meyster, Eath and Graves have also abducted Mrs. Meyster, whom they have subjected to sadistic torment. Although we have no recording of the play, the script's directions suggest that a performance would be uncomfortable listening for many because of its sadomasochistic suggestiveness and, quite possibly, titillation. This becomes clear if we look at the trajectory of the sounds Whelan demands of the female performer (the character is never named, beyond being "Meyster's wife"):

SCREAM OF WOMAN WAY BACK AND COMING IN AND FADING INTO MOANS LOW AND AGONIZING CHANGING IN CLOSE TO THREE DEEP INTAKES OF BREATH FOLLOWED BY PRONOUNCED DEEP BREATHING

The woman's agony is superseded by a sexually ambiguous "deep breathing." While Mrs. Meyster's torment has a sadomasochistic connotation, Meyster's torment is one of humiliation, as he begs, while his swelling tongue permits, to be spared or put out of his misery.

Whelan uses Eath's background as a surgeon to develop a theme of mad science, as well as callous revenge and humiliation. With suitably gory sound effects, Eath transplants the heart of one of his howling dogs into the chest of Meyster's wife. Soon after this, Meyster begins to choke on his bloated tongue, so, with the "SOUND OF KNIFE PENETRATING FLESH AND BLOOD OOZING," we are invited to picture its amputation. By this point, the listeners can visualize buckets of blood. The increasing frenzy of the hounds driven as insane as Eath and Graves by the sight, smell and, above all, *sound* of dripping blood (water released by an eyedropper onto paper, Whelan's directions suggest) leads to the dogs breaking loose and killing all four people, Eath dying triumphantly with the words "WE ALL PERISH!" followed by the ultimate cliché that horror has appropriated from the Bible (Romans 12:19): "VENGEANCE IS MINE!" "The Hounds of Weir" is a lurid and misogynistic work that for many people is probably gratuitous in its cruelty, not least as the torture of Meyster takes up the entire second half of the play. Technically, the plot exposition is predictable, and the dialogue is imbued with cliché:

> MEYSTER: Are you a madman?
> GRAVES: The world considers all geniuses madmen.

Although it is a distinct possibility that Whelan intended "The Hounds of Weir" as a tongue-in-cheek horror comedy, it is perhaps too crass for an easy defence. Certainly it lacks not just the complex dramatic and comic irony of Oboler's works, but the careful creation of atmosphere and ingenuity in narrative and characterization that Oboler brought to his horror melodramas, which meant that he could succeed in tempering the excesses of his grotesquery, gore or absurdity with stylistic and technical finesse.

So far we have seen how Oboler (and a less distinguished imitator such as Geoff Whelan) used a range of archetypal situations and strategies to create for the listener a thrilling experience — the adrenaline rush of an aural rollercoaster — to make *Lights Out* "the ultimate in horror." Part of this process involved tapping into the listener's paranoia and anxieties. But we should not think that *Lights Out* was entirely sensationalistic. Oboler can be considered a consciously "political" writer. Erik Barnouw makes the following observation regarding Oboler's *Lights Out*:

> Oboler managed to devote a percentage of these plays to themes of current significance. This suggests the pattern of much of Oboler's career. While capitalizing on his skill in melodrama, he has fought for the privilege of expressing himself, through plays, on world problems [Barnouw, 1945, 386].

While the Second World War raged in Europe, Arch Oboler produced one of his most celebrated plays, "Johnny Got His Gun" (*Arch Oboler's Plays*, March 9, 1940). The play, an adaptation of Dalton Trumbo's anti-war novel *Johnny Got His Gun* (1939), is a masterpiece of stream-of-consciousness technique, and provided a virtuoso role for James Cagney, who was much-lauded for the passion and intensity he brought to the role. The play is essentially a return to the territory of "Burial Services," but is a polemical rather than Poe-like story: the play is the internal monologue not of a paralyzed girl, but of a horrifically wounded soldier as he lies in a hospital bed. Trumbo's original novel is a minor masterpiece in its own right, but in Oboler's 30-minute dramatization we are launched into a narrative that is as terse and compelling as it is technically and stylistically accomplished.

"Johnny Got His Gun," which remains a powerful anti-war play, was broadcast on the ostensibly "serious" drama show of *Arch Oboler's Plays*, but the war was no less significant in the horror dramas of *Lights Out*. Prior to Pearl Harbor, Oboler may have been a pacifist, but he was always unambiguously opposed to fascism and totalitarianism.

One example of an anti-fascist play broadcast on *Lights Out* is "Nobody Died" (December 9, 1936; revived December 16, 1939). The story is set in an unspecified nation in continental Europe, in which Dr. Miller, a female doctor researching cancer, discovers a treatment that has a rejuvenating effect on her patients. The theme of reversing the ageing process is a classic science fiction premise, given memorable treatment in the film

Cocoon (Ron Howard, 1985), but it is also recurrent across genres and traceable back to the myth of the elixir of life in traditional alchemy. Oboler himself returns to an inverted treatment of the same theme in "Speed" (*Lights Out*, January 5, 1943), in which a scientist creates a drug which makes him and another user move at 20 times normal speed, and allowing them to embark on a crime spree. Although the first scene in which the doctor speaks in a hurried gobbledygook may be rather comical, the finale, in which we hear both villains age a year every second, is not: it is excellent radio as the drama comes from the versatility and pace of the actors' voices. Their clothes have fallen away, and they sit naked as their flesh wrinkles and their voices become frail and aged before they die. "Speed" may be the inverse of "Nobody Died," but the chief difference is that the latter play becomes a work that attacks fascism. The first half of "Nobody Died" lies in the territory of the overreaching scientist, as Dr. Miller dares, after extensive vivisection on mice, to experiment on a human subject. The patient is on the brink of death and pleading for life. Miller yields to temptation and injects her with a serum that, within minutes, not only saves the old woman, but makes her younger. As we approach the second half of the play, we see Oboler's political concerns. Hearing of the "miracle," his "Excellency" Joseph Brown, member of the Department of Propaganda, arrives in Dr. Miller's laboratory. At this moment it becomes clear that Oboler is alluding to Nazi Germany.

Brown is a caricature of the Nazi propaganda minister Joseph Goebbels, and the character claims it was "my brains, my catchwords, my slogans" that made them look upon their Leader (a thinly veiled Hitler) as "Invincible." But using Miller's discovery, Brown intends to usurp the Leader. Brown obtains Miller's formula and scientific notes—"a gift to the State from Heaven"—and has her summarily executed. Brown intends to use the formula to create a vast army of eternally young soldiers. In the play's denouement, we hear Brown amassing his army and injecting himself with the elixir. Brown belongs to the tradition of the science fiction megalomaniac, as in H. G. Wells' *The Invisible Man* (1897), in which scientific discovery is exploited for evil. There is, of course, a catch. It becomes clear that the brains of those who have used the elixir continue to grow ever more youthful. In an extraordinary three-minute monologue we hear Brown denying that the injection will have a detrimental effect: "I'm alright, I must be alright!" he insists. Almost imperceptibly, we hear his voice becoming younger and younger, and his words retarding into a child-like singsong. In the last seconds of the play, his mind degenerates into the pre-language phase and we hear him sobbing with the voice of a baby. It is a simple science fiction parable about the dangers of science that attempts to alter the natural scheme of things, but it is also a political parable about fascism's abuse of science for imperialistic and militaristic ends, concluding with the implied moral that the greed and aspiration of fascism will lead it to its own annihilation.

"Nobody Died" is an excellent example of Oboler's prewar anti-fascist stance, and is the type of play the criticism of which must have infuriated Oboler: at the beginning of *Oboler Omnibus* he takes pains to highlight the accusation that he was "prematurely anti-fascist" (Oboler, 1945, 1). By the time the United States went to war, Oboler's anti-fascism became legitimate and ubiquitous, but his earlier anti-war stance did not. Still, Oboler was unhesitating in his enthusiasm to take a patriotic and militaristic stance, in direct contrast to the anti-war ethos of "Johnny Got His Gun." Indeed, Howard Blue describes "Johnny Got His Gun" as "the last anti-war radio drama of the era" (Blue, 2002, 182), and sums up Oboler's pro-war ethos by calculating that during the war Oboler produced more than 70 "Beat the Axis" plays (Blue, 2002, 26). Some of Oboler's plays during the war are allegorical tales about the universal evils of dictatorship, while others have a much more specific focus. "Surrender" (June 3, 1944)—written for his short series of plays *Four for the Fifth* broadcast during the month of D-Day—portrays a GI's encounter with an Axis prisoner-of-war, becoming a dissection of "the terrible warping of the German military mind and the dangers of conditional surrender" (Oboler, 1945, 246). In addition to his wartime writing, the revivals of Oboler's classic prewar *Lights Out* horror plays for the 1942–43 season were placed into a context appropriate for a nation at war. For instance, in advertising the following week's revival of "Valse Triste," Oboler describes it as "a story of chance, that unpredictable chance that makes one man a saint and the next man a Hitler" ("Meteor Man," December 22, 1942), although the play in question (December 29, 1942) could not be further away from the issues of global politics.

We have seen that Oboler's scripts are wide-ranging in theme and purpose. We should not forget that in Oboler we are looking at another wunderkind in the era of Orson Welles. Oboler's writing had the flare and style that led some critics to label him as "radio's top literary genius" (Dunning, 1998, 38). But he was not just a writer; the position he created for himself and the cult that surrounded him was dependent on his skills as a director and producer as much as writer. *Arch Oboler's Plays* may have been the first radio program to include the name of its writer in the title—a reflection of the belief at the time that, as Erik Barnouw puts it, "the growth of the medium would depend, in the long run, on writers" (Barnouw, 1968, 73)—but it reflected just as much his status as director-producer. Barnouw writes:

> Oboler's scripts are always actable, and give the player something to bite his teeth into. Oboler is also an extremely precise and effective director. Under his direction every performer knows exactly what is expected of him; the orchestra leader knows at just what syllable the music must start or stop [Barnouw, 1945, 386].

Over 20 years later, Barnouw still recalled how Oboler's "virtuosity as a radio technician aroused intense interest. His direction was precise. The start or finish of a musical theme or sound effect was always pinpointed to the syllable," even if, with the benefit of hindsight, his "determination to make it yield contemporary meaning had only intermittent success" (Barnouw, 1968, 73). In other words, in Oboler's greatest work we are looking at a master of performance practice and technique rather than meaning: he was not Norman Corwin or Archibald MacLeish, but, as we saw earlier, Oboler never denied that he was first and foremost a melodramatist whereby style triumphs over content. The extant recordings of Oboler's plays confirm the accomplishment of his technical skills. His *Lights Out* scripts afforded his performers the chance to squabble or kill each other, to scream piercingly or put a victim to death with unsettling eroticism. The intensity of performance, the immaculate timing, the orchestration of the gong, sound effects or human voice were all controlled by Oboler's meticulous directing. His performance practice as director was particularly vivacious and theatrical, as evident in the photograph of him executing the "take it easy" gesture in director's sign language (page 48). Dunning describes his typical approach:

> [Oboler's] direction was not done from a glassed-in booth: he got right down on the soundstage with his performers. Sometimes he would stand on a table, com-

pensating for his short stature. In one contemporary photograph, Oboler is halfway up a large stepladder, looming over the cast [Dunning, 1998, 39]. [Author's note: a copy of the photograph is included in Barnouw, 1968, facing 90.]

Oboler also took pains to establish an appropriate atmosphere that would facilitate the horror of *Lights Out*. In fact, he made a deliberately theatrical *mise-en-scene* of the radio studio. The actor Macdonald Carey described Oboler's arrangement of the studio for a recording of *Lights Out*:

> The stage was the biggest stage at NBC. The director would put the microphone in the center of the floor and there'd be a floor lamp there and a light by the piano. Here's this big, big studio and this open little floor lamp with actors huddled around it in the dark reading their lines. There was real feeling of mystery about the whole thing. The sound man was in this umbrella of light way off in the corner. They were very, very spooky shows [quoted in Nachman, 1998, 313–14].

But Oboler's constructed mood of eeriness did not work for everyone. Mary Jane Croft recalls *Lights Out* as her only unhappy experience in radio drama:

> I didn't enjoy working for Arch Oboler. It was never a happy atmosphere. He was not fun to be around, but then the shows he did were also dark and gloomy [quoted in Nachman, 1998, 474–75].

Even if it was not a pleasant experience for Croft, her acknowledgement that the repertoire was "dark and gloomy" demonstrates that Oboler was successful in creating an authenticity of atmosphere for his tales of horror. Whether or not his show was "fun" to be involved in, it certainly made an impact on the public and the profession. As Dunning says, "Hollywood stars listened, and some made the trip to Chicago" (Dunning, 1998, 400) — most famously, the already iconic horror star Boris Karloff for his classic broadcasts with *Lights Out* in the spring of 1938. This would continue into the following decade when, according to Oboler, movie stars would be desperate for the prestige of appearing on *Arch Oboler's Plays,* and would do so for the minimum $21 fee (Oboler, 1967, 10), including the legendary star of early cinema, Alla Nazimova (page 48).

In his radio heyday, Oboler was, in his own words, "NBC's fair-headed boy. You know — I could do anything I wanted on the air" (Oboler, 1967, 10). It was a different story after the war, and even more so during the gradual attrition of radio. Maybe Oboler's status diminished because his propaganda plays during the war effort made him look like past history in a new epoch characterized by peace, prosperity and the rise of television. Furthermore, the political climate of the late 1940s and early 1950s was not a comfortable time to have been perceived as being "prematurely anti-fascist" earlier in one's career. Oboler regarded Wyllis Cooper as being "worn out" when he replaced him on *Lights Out*, but it would seem he himself suffered a similar fate, bewailing that, "radio, for the dramatist, is a huge, insatiable sausage grinder into which he feeds his creative life to be converted into neatly packaged detergents" (quoted in Sterling and Keith, 2003, 1044).

But in the case of Oboler, cultural and technological determinism is of primary significance. Oboler foresaw only too clearly that television would usurp radio. To deny that it would, he wrote in 1945, was "to whistle in the dark of wish-thinking" (Oboler,

1945, 308). In view of this, it is no surprise that Oboler himself made a contribution to television, working for instance, as a producer on the four-episode trial run of *Lights Out* for television in the summer of 1946, and as writer of *The Oboler Comedy Theater* (1949). Ironically, Oboler played no part in the full (and popular) television run of *Lights Out* (1949–52) beyond, for example, selling the rights to adapt his "And Adam Begot" radio script for television. In 1945, Oboler heralded the rise of television, declaring that it would bring "a new opportunity to say the things which must be said until all live in common decency—in simple justice" (Oboler, 1945, 309). His actual experience of the medium left him less than sanguine: "If TV could make money out of the rape of their grandmother, they'd show it" (quoted in Nachman, 1998, 314).

Oboler also turned to the movie industry, where, like his *Lights Out* predecessor Wyllis Cooper, he enjoyed an adequate but decidedly low-key career in contrast to his legendary standing in radio—although Oboler would claim to have made an innovative contribution to cinema. As early as the mid–1940s, the Metro film company invited Oboler to make an experimental film, "a dirty word in those days" (quoted in Oboler, 1967, 10). The result was *Bewitched* (1945), which Oboler did not want released, as he felt, "it was a radio story, not a movie" (Oboler, 1967, 10), not least because it was based on the play known as "Alter Ego" on the *Texaco Star Theater* and "The Voice Within Me" when broadcast as part of *Arch Oboler's Plays*. Metro released the film anyway, and it enjoyed great success and good returns, very little of which Oboler saw. He also made *The Arnelo Affair* (1946) for the same company.

The experiences of the Hollywood studio machine were, over all, rather disheartening, and Oboler decided to become an independent filmmaker. It was in this independent status that Oboler made another experimental film, *Five* (1951). Made by a mere five people, "including crew and everything" (Oboler, 1967, 15), *Five* was filmed in Oboler's own home. Praised by Stephen King as "one of the first films to deal with the survival of mankind after World War III" (King, 147), it remains a classic of the post-apocalyptic genre. Moreover, Oboler even claims that while American critics dismissed *Five* as "a low-budget, low-production, low-key sort of thing" that "they didn't quite understand" (Oboler, 1967, 10), it had an indelible impact on the history of

Arch Oboler in rehearsal on the set of the movie *The Arnelo Affair* (1946) (Photofest).

world cinema: *Five* was not merely the chief influence on French New Wave cinema, but, Oboler asserts, "the start" of it (Oboler, 1967, 10). Less controversial as Oboler's greatest claim to fame as far as cinema is concerned is his key role in the creation of three-dimensional movies: Oboler was the writer and director of the 3-D features *Bwana Devil* (1952) and *The Bubble* (1966). As an example of a science fiction movie, *The Bubble* owes a surprising debt to the world of radio drama. The film is a vision of dystopia, with people living in a type of zombie-like trance, trapped inside an invisible force. As Oboler says:

> ...[Y]ou never see the monster in *The Bubble*. And what a monster I could have built out in Hollywood! You know, a huge scaly hand coming down. But the minute I'd have done that you'd have stopped believing [Oboler, 1967, 14].

The Bubble relies on some action sequences to achieve its impact but chiefly it depends on the performances of its cast, as in the *Lights Out* days. With *The Bubble*, Oboler resists the creation of a focal image of horror. Ironically, in *Lights Out* Oboler could create a focal image of horror without the listener seeing anything at all. The onus is on the imagination of the listener, and Oboler always understood this.

There is no question that Oboler is "one of the great auteurs in radio history" (Sterling and Keith, 2003, 1033). His heyday as a highly successful radio writer-producer-director makes him an icon of the golden age and also, although his star may have faded, a cult figure in the history of popular horror culture. A genuine curiosity in the field of popular horror is *Arch Oboler's Drop Dead!* (1974), a long-playing record release described as "An Exercise in Horror." The album is a highly enjoyable exploration of the potential of aural horror in a time after the golden age is over, and Oboler is addressing an audience whose experiences of horror are shaped by cinema, television, and reality: "In a horrific time, in a horrible world, I have been asked to try and horrify you." The recording allows Oboler, as narrator, to present succinct versions of some of his *Lights Out* masterpieces. It also attempts to demonstrate the experiential nature of the genre whereby the listener's imagination is exploited.

Oboler did not just write and produce horror plays; indeed, the fact that "horror as a genre always left him cold" (Dunning, 1998, 400) is an ironic twist of *Lights Out* magnitude. However, in his horror plays, Oboler is a very fine melodramatist. After all, horror radio was the melodrama of the mass media, and Oboler's best horror plays are masterpieces of the genre in terms of writing and production. Despite Oboler's diverse and occasionally wild scenarios, there is a surprising minimalism at play in *Lights Out*. There may be piercing screams in "Poltergeist," but at those moments we do not know what the victim is beholding; likewise, "Chicken Heart" relies primarily on a simple throbbing heartbeat in a tale of the end of the world. Oboler's dialogue is generally honed and yet succeeds in creating convincing characterization and atmosphere with great economy. Stephen King praises Oboler for rarely overdoing "the dialogue-as-description device" (King, 1982, 150), unlike the writers of *The Shadow* or *Inner Sanctum Mysteries*. For King, Oboler will always be the greatest figure in horror radio:

> Arch Oboler ... utilized two of radio's greatest strengths: the first is the mind's innate obedience, its willingness to try to see whatever someone suggests it to see,

no matter how absurd; the second is the fact that fear and horror are blinding emotions that knock our adult pins from beneath us and leave us groping in the dark like children who cannot find the light switch. Radio is, of course, the "blind" medium, and only Oboler used it so well or so completely [King, 1982, 147–48].

6

Exploring Horror Form and Genre: *The Hermit's Cave* (1935–1944)

The Hermit's Cave was produced by WJR in Detroit from 1935 to the mid–1940s. From 1940 to 1944 a separate version of the show was also broadcast by KMPC in Los Angeles, inaugurated by G. A. Richards (the owner of WJR). After New York's *The Witch's Tale* and Chicago's *Lights Out*, Detroit's *The Hermit's Cave* was one of the earliest horror radio shows. In its opening year, *The Hermit's Cave* followed the early *Lights Out* model of 15-minute broadcasts before moving on to the 30-minute format. Olga Coal sponsored *The Hermit's Cave* from 1937, and the show came to enjoy wide syndication. The Detroit show was produced by Eric Howlett and Geraldine Elliott (a rare example of a female producer in this male-dominated profession), and featured an acting ensemble called "the Mummers," which included actors such as Paul Hughes, Ted Johnstone, Rollon Parker and Bill Saunders, all of whom would have been familiar to an audience that listened to *The Lone Ranger*, "the pinnacle of juvenile western thriller dramas" (Dunning, 1998, 404), which commenced its phenomenally successful history as a program on Detroit's WXYZ in 1931. Aside from the core ensemble, *The Hermit's Cave* boasts one of the most memorable horror radio hosts.

The Hermit was played by a number of actors over the show's broadcast history, commencing with John Kent and including Charles Penman, Toby Grimmer and Klock Ryder. In the West Coast version on KMPC, the Hermit was played by Mel Johnson until 1943, when the role was taken by John Dehner (who, in the late 1950s, would enjoy popularity playing the lead role of Paladin in the radio version of *Have Gun, Will Travel*). The KMPC version of *The Hermit's Cave* was produced by Bill Forman and William Conrad (in actor-producer mode). Both would later rise to greater fame, with Forman becoming a well-known announcer and the lead on *The Whistler*, while Conrad would prove to be one of the most talented and popular radio performers of his generation as Matt Dillon on *Gunsmoke* and in many other broadcasts (indeed, at his peak, according to Thomas A. DeLong, Conrad was "averaging 10 to 15 shows a week" [DeLong, 1996, 60]). As John Dunning states, the West Coast version of *The Hermit's Cave* proved to be "a training ground of sorts for young actors with network aspirations" (Dunning, 1998, 319). Certainly *The Hermit's Cave* offered a great opportunity for a generation of young performers: William Conrad was only 22 when he started acting-producing on *The Hermit's Cave*, having started paid work on commercials on KMPC at the age of 17. Similarly, as Dunning informs us, Mel Johnson was "only 24 years old" (Dunning, 1998, 319) when he played "the ancient Hermit," following in the tradition of the teenage Miriam Wolfe playing Old Nancy on *The Witch's Tale*.

Although it was a long-running show, peaking in popularity in 1942, only a few broadcasts of *The Hermit's Cave* have so far come to light. The extant recordings would seem to be from the Mel Johnson era. But what strikes the listener is how theatrical these pieces are. The writers, Lou Huston (who later wrote *Space Patrol*) and Herbert R. Connor, strive for an original take on classic horror tales and formulae, but so much comes down to the performance practice of its ambitious young actors evidently learning the ropes of their craft and exploring the potential of radio drama. The music on *The Hermit's Cave* recordings is played by Rex Koury and consists of creepy organ tones, serving the usual structural function of interludes and bridges between scenes, but also as a particularly eerie background to unnerving or dramatic scenes. Albert Buhrmann in *Quiet, Please* would later use the organ in a similar style.

For some critics, however, the success of *The Hermit's Cave* had less to do with the central ensemble or the music than with the Hermit himself. Isidore Hiablum goes so far as to assert that *The Hermit's Cave* introduction "was often better than the stories themselves" (Hiablum, 1986, 348). This is a rather harsh criticism. I would prefer to argue that even if the stories were often predictable, despite all the best efforts of Huston and Connor, the delivery was consummate in pace and packaging. Also, to return to Hiablum, we could see her comment as evidence that the introduction was a masterpiece of its kind. Each broadcast opens with the Hermit and his pack of howling wolves deep in an obscure wilderness: we hear the baying wolves, which becomes juxtaposed with the sound of the cackling laughter of our geriatric host, his laugh rising up through the icy breeze. The Hermit narrator and his wolves were blatantly modeled on Old Nancy and her cat from *The Witch's Tale*, but it is a consistently superlative horror frame. After this dramatic establishment, the Hermit speaks:

> Ghost stories ... Weird stories ... and murders too ... He, he, he, he, he, he ... the Hermit knows of them all ... Turn out your lights ... *Turn them out...*

After this trademark introduction, the Hermit introduces the tale. Later in the broadcast (approximately midway or sometimes nearer the end), the Hermit and the wolves return to provide a précis and set the scene for the denouement. The end of each broadcast was signaled by the Hermit ordering us to turn on our lights again.

We will now offer a close analysis of some of the Hermit's stories, which, as his trademark opening narrative makes clear, happily step from the domains of crime to the realms of the supernatural, and in so doing launches into an exploration of horror form and genre.

The opening of "Notebook on Murder" immediately throws the listener into an experience of suspense and horror: after an eerie organ introduction we hear a defenseless woman, Cora Armour, gasping and sobbing hysterically, her panic increasing as her door creaks open. "Who ... Who is it? Who's in my room? Someone's in my room!" It is an effective establishment of atmosphere designed to hook the listeners and compel them to listen on. Cora's supercilious husband comes to her assistance and calls the police when it becomes clear that a "burglar" had broken into the house. It is revealed that Cora is recuperating, having returned from a hospital where she was treated for a nervous breakdown. A police officer, clearly concerned for the vulnerable Cora, befriends her and persuades her to keep a diary, but to hide it from her husband by keeping it under her mattress.

The play is a hybrid of Patrick Hamilton's *Gaslight* (1938) and Charlotte Perkins Gilman's *The Yellow Wallpaper* (1899): the first half of the play is built around Cora's diary account of weird events in her home and her descent into madness. To place explicit emphasis on the fact that it is a diary, the production includes the sound of Cora's nib scratching the paper as she frantically writes. This emphasis on written narrative within the performance narrative raises issues of framing and distanciation (especially in a tale of madness), yet, inversely, it also places the listener in intimate proximity to Cora: we are close enough to hear the nib on paper. Along with the fervid entries in the notebook that establish Cora's deteriorating state of mind, other effective sequences create a sense of claustrophobic atmosphere and soundscape, including the use and description of footsteps. For example, Cora recounts:

> There would be one step ... then a long pause ... and then another ... for a minute I was so scared I couldn't even breathe.... Somehow I just seemed to know that whoever was coming down the hall was coming to my room and to me.

If the first half of the play is dominated by Cora's diary—the "Notebook" of the title—the second half concentrates on the "Murder" portion of the moniker. Cora is killed by a mysterious gunman in the dark. In a long scene that establishes the size and layout of the house, Hubert returns home and, to his horror, finds his wife dead. Despite his feigned surprise, it probably comes as no surprise to the listener that Hubert is, in fact, the killer, as surmised by the police officer and the clues provided by Cora's diary. After a brief interrogation by the police, Hubert incriminates himself when he corrects the police version that Cora screamed:

> She didn't scream, she just called out, "Don't, please!" I admit it, I killed her. She was a stone around my neck, nagging, never well, I hated her! I wanted freedom!

"Notebook on Murder" is one of many radio suspense plays that have turned to the *Gaslight* scenario in which a husband attempts to drive his wife to madness and destruction. If not a clear precursor, the British stage melodrama *Gaslight* was at least contemporaneous with the rise of similar strategies and exposition in suspense radio narrative. The play enjoyed great success on the American as well as British stage, and was a profitable source for two screen adaptations in 1940 and 1944, as well as numerous other indirect imitations for the screen. The play is also known as *Angel Street* and, under this title, enjoyed a vivid radio dramatization on *Theater of Romance* (October 9, 1945), starring Vincent Price, Anne Baxter and Cedric Hardwicke. "Notebook on Murder" may be lacking in originality as a melodrama of psychopathic husbands and neurotic wives, but it is nonetheless consummately paced and delivered. Like many of *The Hermit's Cave* plays, the work takes on an eerie and almost dreamlike quality in the program's 1940s heyday, thanks to Rex Koury's organ music, which is used both as a dramatic structuring device between scenes and as a background consolidation of the atmosphere and mood of the Hermit's tales of terror.

"The Mystery of the Thing" is another play that locates horror in the matrimonial context. The story opens with a series of news reports that announce the disappearance of Dawn Forestier, wife of a celebrated doctor. One report states that her clothes and "underclothes" (radio could include items that Hollywood of the same time may have been reluctant to show) have been found in a cemetery. Keen followers of the news story inform us that Mrs. Forestier herself was the subject of an earlier case: she had arrived in town an amnesiac dressed in an "old-fashioned gown torn all to tatters." Doctor Forestier failed in his attempt to unlock her identity but fell in love with her and made her his wife. So far the play offers a balance between the strange and the suspicious, and we are not sure if this is going to be one of the Hermit's "weird" stories or one of his "murder" stories. The missing woman seems to possess an uncanny quality, with her unaccountable past and strange disappearance, but, in *Gaslight* mode, we find ourselves wary of the doctor before we even meet him. In due course we meet Doctor John Forestier, and at a press conference he reads out a letter that he discovered left to him by his wife, although he states that he will omit the more "personal" passages. This allows for a narrative shift into Dawn's letter and her retrospective account in what will prove to be a tale of the uncanny.

Dawn's narrative is accompanied by the sound effect of howling wind—the "music of the wind," in her words—which emphasizes the eerie and dreamlike. The language used is so highly melodramatic it would not have been out of place on the Victorian stage:

> We met in the dawn, my darling, but I must creep away from you in the darkness of the night. Oh, but John, how I've loved you!

Dawn recounts how she has been visited by an eerie apparition that was at first as invisible as "the Horla," but each night has taken on more form, eventually materializing as an obscure but discernibly human figure in her room. Each night the apparition, with startling intimacy, presses itself against the struggling Dawn and sucks the breath out of her, growing in strength while Dawn weakens. Eventually, Dawn states that she realizes what the "thing" is, a moment which is used as a cliff-hanger. The Hermit returns to provide a summary of the play so far, but refuses to share with us Dawn's revelation. When we are back with Dawn we hear a deep, rasping voice uttering, "Come with me ... Come with me..."

The next cliff-hanger is created by the doctor, who breaks off reading the letter and says he will only complete the final pages after they have visited the cemetery. The dramatic climax to the play comes with the exhumation of a coffin and the forcing open of its screeching hinges: inside the coffin is a "decayed skeleton" wearing Dawn's wedding ring. If we had not already guessed it, Dawn was really dead, and the thing that stalked and eventually "dissolved" her into itself was her true form reclaiming her and returning her to the grave. It turns out that, decades before, Dawn was betrothed to one of Forestier's ancestors but died before her wedding day. It is a melodramatic play of spectral Gothicism, with a heightened language the romanticism of which is enforced by the fact that Dawn's farewell letter was tucked into the couple's beloved copy of Elizabeth Barrett Browning's *Sonnets from the Portuguese* (1850), the lyrical quintessence of Victorian romance. The play may feel clichéd, but it flows with a dreamlike languor, and a few key moments in the play — the apparition's voice, the rusty hinges of the coffin, and the realization that Forestier has been married either to a ghost or to a corpse — have a spine tingling effect.

The romantic horror of "The Mystery of the Thing" is taken to a more sophisticated level in "The Story Without End." This play is a strong piece with a great resonance in the context of war. As we shall see, "The Story Without End" is also a curious precursor to *Quiet, Please*, not just in its style but in its construction of what we could describe as beautiful horror, where love intersects with the uncanny. The lead character is a young soldier called David whose opening speech to the listener captures the melancholic quality that will dominate the mood of the whole play:

> This is a story of love that has no end. Of the deep, dark shadows of sorrow. Of dreams that span the bridge of time. It's my story and ... Lorai's.

After this prologue, we find ourselves in a foxhole at the battlefront, with David and Jim caught under fire, their "bodies targets for death." Jim marvels at David's survival mechanism: the strength of his love for Lorai, his childhood sweetheart. David believes that it is the love of his girlfriend Lorai that has kept him alive and safe. He feels that she is always with him: their love amounts to a personal "faith" and a "shield and protector." We hear Jim wavering in panic, and eventually he screams as he is caught in the shrapnel of a bomb and dies. We flash back into David's idyllic childhood on the farm and his romantic encounters with the ideal Lorai at "their old trysting place" in the woods. The war delays their plans for marriage, and, after their farewell, David walks away from Lorai and refuses to make an Orphean error in turning back to see her. After the end of the war, David makes the long journey home, hides from the public and makes his way immediately to see Lorai in their trysting place. Lorai is waiting for him, "more beautiful than ever," and they reassert their love. Lorai is reluctant to be taken home, and they play hide and seek before Lorai hides permanently. When David speaks to his aunt and uncle, it is revealed that Lorai is dead. This probably comes as no surprise to the listener but, significantly, this is not the climax of the play, but the point when the Hermit can interrupt the tale.

In the speech that opens the second half of the play, David says to us:

> You ask what happens to my life now. You think that I believe that death has separated Lorai and me. Never. As we reckon time on this earth, my Lorai was asleep in death at the time she appeared to me on the battlefield. She was not of this world when I returned home...

David now tends the farm by himself. But he does not do this alone: Lorai is still with him, linked with "a bond between Lorai and me that is stronger than life, deeper than earth and beyond all time and reckoning." At night David hears the door swing open and feels Lorai's presence, and hears her voice explaining that he will not see her again until he dies. David declares to us that whether we believe that his "mind is addled by the horrors of war" or not, his love is real and goes beyond the power of death. The title of "The Story Without End" conveys this romantic idea of the power of love, a statement of faith that, like Dante's *Paradise*, sees love at the heart of the universe. But the title is also structurally significant: the play is an extremely simple exploration of an idea and mood. It is highly lyrical, languid in pace, almost a radio drama equivalent to a tone poem. It is an intriguing celebration of love in the context of an America at war, and is also interesting because rather than seek David's recovery or secure external proof (such as having his aunt and uncle see evidence of Lorai's existence), the story is content to let David remain in what is either shell-shocked fantasy or an enviable condition of true love.

"The Story Without End" remains a startling precursor to some of the more lyrical and languorous narratives of *Quiet, Please* at the end of the 1940s, such as "In the House Where I Was Born" (May 24, 1948), a similarly poetic account of a soldier's return home (but this time it is the soldier who is dead). The romantic idealism of "The Story Without End" is also reminiscent of the haunting love story about two people separated by the worlds of consciousness and dreams in "And Jeannie Dreams of Me" (October 17, 1948), and the troubled life and desperate love of the soldier in "In Memory of Bernadine" (November 24, 1947). In these and several other examples, *Quiet, Please* takes the form of beautiful horror to new heights of pathos, psychological depth and lyricism. Nevertheless, "The Story Without End" stands as a forerunner to *Quiet, Please* that demonstrates the poetical and dramatic potential of the subgenre of "beautiful horror."

Not all of *The Hermit's Cave* plays are examples of beautiful horror. John Dunning reveals that *The Hermit's Cave* was celebrated for the "grisly sound effects" (Dunning, 1998, 319) provided by Sidney Brechner and John Foster in the program's Detroit days, and Dwight Hauser on KMPC. A fine example of a more "grisly" play from the repertoire is "The Search for Life," a gruesome tale of mad scientists, and a startling contrast to the plays we have looked at so far. Hale Browson is a scientist with a *Frankenstein*-style ambition of bringing the dead back to life. His assistant is the forthright Court, who reveals to the woman he loves, Nada, that he intends to change the course of Browson's research, although Nada is worried that this implies that Court will have to commit an even worse transgression and "work *against* creation." To this he replies:

> Hale Browson gave his discovery to the world thinking its greatness might overshadow any evil it might give rise to. Instead, its evils have overshadowed its greatness. And it's gone beyond control.

In the same scene, we seem to be moving towards romance when Court proposes to Nada. This would be in keeping with the moral high ground taken by Court, establishing him as the upstanding hero of the piece. However, this potential shift is subverted when Nada refuses, declaring that she is putting her career first. Her decision propels the play towards a startling twist in the subsequent scene, when Court informs Browson that he intends to kill Nada so that the two men may reanimate her with a reconstructed, "improved" brain. Browson leads us into his laboratory and does not voice any objection to Court's plan beyond saying that the results of the process are not guaranteed. Browson's secret laboratory is a place of horror: the cold science of Browson and Court is divorced from morality or humanity. In a cage we hear the guttural snarls of one of their previous experiments, a heart attack victim who they resurrected with the trademark "reconstructed" brain. The warped scientists dispassionately comment that the specimen was not "insane" before, and observe that the man is like a prehistoric being with superhuman strength: his electrified cage would "kill an ordinary man. It only stuns him." After this key establishment we are back to ironic romance with Court and Nada's farewell scene, during which Court unemotionally murders her with poison, urging her to "Remember only the past" so that her dead brain may "hold" the memories and idealism of young love.

After the Hermit's midpoint narrative we hear the rhythmic gurgling of laboratory equipment. This signals that we are in the experiment scene, mandatory in any drama of mad science. We hear the two scientists painstakingly operating on Nada's exposed brain. The snarls of the demented man in the cage distract them, and, in a line that builds up and signposts the violence of the scene, Court screams, "I'll take the shotgun and blow your head off!" When Browson has finished the procedure he directs Court in a speech that is an excellent example of horror radio (Court's succinct and distant replies have been omitted):

> Hurry! Hand me that piece of her skull that we cut away.... Ah, you bored all the holes in it?... So that we can fasten it in place?... Now help me again. We must replace it exactly as it was cut away.... Now, turn it just slightly. (CLUNK) There. Hold it in place while I fasten it.

What Browson says in the above dialogue would be obvious to another brain surgeon. But the speech ensures that the listeners can visualize the process. Nada, the character who at the beginning of the play seemed to be the love interest in a tale of ambitious scientists, is now pictured as a corpse with its skull sawn open and the brain exposed. The description not only creates the scene in the listeners' imaginations, it also builds up to an example of a *Hermit's Cave* sound effect — the "CLUNK" may have been created by a box lid or coconut, neither of which is "grisly" unless the audience is sustaining an image of trepanation in their minds. The scene is made even eerier for the acute imagination of the ideal listener when the demented man throws himself against his electrified cage and the whole laboratory is cast into darkness. Court fumbles for a candle, and we hear the deep, rasping breathing of Nada as she returns to life before the operation has been completed, and the scraping metal of the cage as it creaks open. The plot device of the power short circuit and the candle means that the listeners now picture the scene in the light of the flame. In the classic André de Lorde and Alfred Binet Grand-Guignol horror play *L'Horrible Expérience* (1909) we witness a similar attempt at resurrection, albeit with more compassionate motivation (a devastated Docteur Charrier attempts to revive his dead daughter). At the same moment in the experiment there is also a power cut, and the scientists have to use an oil lamp. In the French stage play this shift in the source and degree of lighting is a great demonstration of the use of stage technology in the creation of theatrical suspense (Hand and Wilson, 2002, 62–64). "The Search for Life" proves that the imagination of the audience is all that is required to achieve the same effect: the listener can depict and hold the image of the concept, and be, as it were, the play's own lighting technician.

Like Docteur Charrier, Doctor Frankenstein and almost every other scientist who dares to play at being God and manipulate the natural order of things, Browson and

Court do not receive half measures regarding their just desserts. The reanimated Nada speaks in a clear but monotonous voice and commands the "man from the past" liberated from the cell to seize Browson and bring him to her. In another wonderful example of a grisly sound effect, Browson shrieks manically as he is put to death by his two specimens: "They're crushing my head ... my head ... *my head*...! (SPLITTING CRUNCH)." Another fate is reserved for Court. After the demented man is shot and killed in order to liberate him from his miserable and unnatural existence, Nada takes the shotgun and executes Court, delivering the type of line one expects in a tale of the abuse of science—"This is the end of the world ... you created"—before she expires.

"The Search for Life" is a lurid tale, but not one without genuine surprises. By the end of the play all four principal characters are dead; the cold-hearted scientists at the heart of the story have no pangs of remorse nor morality, and not only kill the female lead for being a "career woman," but subject her corpse to brain surgery and reanimation. The play makes well-placed and contextualized use of sound effects, whether in conveying a painstaking brain operation, execution by shotgun or skull crushing. The demented "man from the past" may sound exactly like Mel Blanc's "Tasmanian Devil" (Warner Brothers, 1954–79), but is no less disturbing for that. The economy of the script means that scenes are well-established and technically evocative in a work that is a concise but efficient post–*Frankenstein* morality play about the perils of the abuse of science.

Another play about the abuse of science in *The Hermit's Cave*'s repertoire is "Spirit Vengeance," although it resolves its narrative with the supernatural. The play opens in a house during a storm, with the menacing figure of Professor Rommel Santo intimidating with delight his near-hysterical wife Rosa, who hooks the listener when she reveals that "terrible things" have happened in the house during the previous three days. Sound effects are carefully used to escalate the atmosphere and suspense: the dialogue of the conflicting Santos—yet another example of an unhappily married couple in *The Hermit's Cave* (a sure way of creating passionate, dramatic conflict at the heart of a play)—is broken into sections by the rolling thunder outside and the portentous chimes of a clock inside. A few moments later, Rosa reveals that she is thankful for the storm, as it ensures that, "No one will visit this house of murder tonight!" In the dramatic irony that governs the universe of horror radio, this is a cue for a knock at the door. Richard and Bella Kenton are lost tourists who have come to the Santo mansion seeking refuge from the storm. The Kentons are in the area to visit their newlywed daughter Lisa and her husband Charles, who recently moved to a nearby village. The mad professor—who speaks with the stereotypical accent of the evil German, a favorite archetypal villain in this era of war—insists that the Kentons stay overnight, muttering out of their earshot that he would never "turn away specimens." With the Kentons out of the room, the appalled Rosa reveals that it was probably the Kentons' daughter and husband who the Professor murdered two days before. We also receive an insight into Santo's mad science: he dreams of making "the heart beat on forever."

Elsewhere in the house the Kentons are also bickering, but not about such a macabre theme. In their room for the night, Bella is anxious while Richard is blasé and delighted by the grandeur of the surroundings. When he has drifted off to sleep, the insomniac Bella hears the uncanny and disembodied voice of her daughter: "Mother ... It is I, Lisa..." Soon after we hear two piercing screams, at which point the Hermit interrupts.

The Hermit's mid-show interludes always heighten dramatic suspense; although *The Hermit's Cave* was not a series of continuing episodes, returning to the Hermit midway through every episode enabled the creation of a cliff-hanger within each self-contained play. The interludes also allow the Hermit to refresh our grasp of the occasionally convoluted plot. The interludes can also be an expedient moment for dramatic ellipsis, allowing for a smooth transition in location or time ("It is the following morning..."). The midway interruption of "Spirit Vengeance" is interesting in that the Hermit brings it to a close by saying, "It is a few seconds later," a line that takes us back to the piercing screams with no explanation on the part of our omniscient host as to who or what they might be.

After the screams, the Kentons confront the wicked Santo. But before he can subject them to his devilish experiments, a door swings open and Lisa and Charles come into the room and "thrust a knife through the hearts" of Santo and his obligatory evil assistant. Despite the pleas of the Kentons, their daughter and her husband creep away, their feet scraping across the wooden floor (it is ostensibly the revenge of "Spirits," but they sound more like zombies). They are dead, but came "back for revenge" and to save the parents, Santo's desire to make "the heart beat on" ironically fulfilled by the bonds of filial love from beyond the grave. The play is a pedestrian tale of supernatural revenge, and as a story of abused science it lacks the desolation found at the end of "The Search for Life." However, what "Spirit Vengeance" does evoke very well is the setting, a classic horror "Old Dark House." The play is full of creaking timber, wooden floors and an implied faded opulence that impresses Richard but unnerves Bella. To begin the play with a thunderstorm is a well-worn standard even in the 1940s, and even when the storm is over we are given descriptions that may shift us away from horror clichés of "dark and stormy nights" but create another suitably Gothic description of the "moon pushing its way through the clouds" (ostensibly a line about how the weather has improved, but really a line that re-establishes the atmosphere and even the lighting within our imaginations).

The carefully created setting in "Spirit Vengeance" is reminiscent of *The Hermit's Cave*'s "The Vampire's Desire," a play that in all its heightened terror and glorious excess becomes a masterpiece of horror radio. The play opens with a peal of thunder — a cliché, but one that an ideal listener heartily embraces, as it immediately sets the scene for the play and its plot construction. We are introduced to Mr. Winton and his manservant John (there is no indication of the time period, and so the tale belongs to the kind of Gothic no-man's-land that exists in the realm of twentieth-century popular horror). The heroes find themselves desperately seeking refuge in the doorway of an evidently untenanted house. The foreboding house is described in heavy-handed terms as a "tomb of a place." Again this line is a cliché, but such language is welcome for its lack of ambiguity. The opening to the play has thus far been extremely economical in establishing its two central characters, their relationship and their situation. They pound on the door but receive no answer. Just as they are about to force their way in to find sanctuary from the driving rain, the door creaks open and a woman curtly informs them that they are "not welcome," and tries to close the portal. John manages to block the door with his foot, and they force their way inside. Out of the storm, they slam the door behind them and find themselves in utter darkness. The woman who sounded supercilious before is now heard cackling menacingly, causing John to exclaim, "We're in the house of a madwoman!" Refusing to return to the natural perils outside, the men step into the darkness, hoping to find a room where they can wait until the storm has passed.

The play establishes the lightless environment extremely successfully: the two men call across to each other in the dark, informing one another — and the listener — of their progress and ideas. "Feel along the wall for a light switch or a door," commands Winton. They eventually stumble across a bookcase in what seems to be a house of empty and freezing cold rooms. Sensing this item to be important, they attempt to light matches but fail, since all are "sopping wet" from the storm. This dramatic decision ensures that Winton and John continue to talk to each other, and possibly act erratically or perilously given the circumstances, but it also serves as a timely reminder to the audience that the men continue to be in the dark. At this moment the fourth character in the play is introduced to the listener: a man with a commanding voice (and, we assume, very good eyesight) orders the men to, "Stay away from the bookcase." A moment later he repeats the behavior of the first tenant of the house and starts laughing insanely, and is joined by the returning "hideously cackling" woman. Soon afterwards we are given the power of vision again, but only momentarily. Winton and John see an old man with a shaded lantern at the end of a corridor, and they pursue him. He mysteriously disappears, and we are plunged in darkness once more. Moreover, our heroes are trapped in a "hermetically sealed room" that gradually begins to drain of air. John stumbles over something on the floor. "I shall have to feel," he declares and, as it were, makes us reach down with him. It is the corpse of a man, which crumbles to the touch. The air becomes sparser and the performers allow themselves to build slowly to breathlessness and despair. At the last moment, John is slipping into unconscious when Winton, in a flash of aristocratic know-how, finds the spring that releases a door, and the men are able to escape into air — but also into another realm of impenetrable darkness.

In another sequence that reiterates the sense of environment, the men knock against the wooden panels of the wall, listening for "any hollow sounds." Eventually, they find one and we hear distant and indistinct voices beyond the wall. John says he cannot hear them, and when invited to press his ear against the wall he — and the listeners with him — can hear a man and woman talking in angry tones. Another switch reveals a secret staircase, and although it is a tight space, Winton and John descend. As they do so the strange voices become clearer and clearer. When they arrive at the bottom (in the final third of the play), we at last are given light again in a play so dominated and dependent upon an evocation of pitch dark. The vision we receive is redolent of Gothic cliché: a coffin lies in the middle of the room, with a lighted candle at each corner. In the coffin lies a man who we hear talking and laughing viciously, although his lips do not move. A woman is present in the room, and when the heroes force the coffin lid shut, she at last breaks out of a trance. She is Lydia, a lady who has been at the mercy of her "brother Garnet," who has been dead for eight years but continues to hold a power over her. He was always a wicked man, she declares, who continues to exercise his evil will after his death. The siblings had fiercely contested their father's will during Garnet's lifetime, and now in death he forces Lydia to bring him animals regularly so that he may suck on their blood and regain the energy to leave his coffin for a while. Brother Garnet starts speaking telepathically again, and Winton decides to put the vampire to death by using the heavy candlesticks in place of the more familiar stakes. Winton declares that he is "ridding the face of the earth of a vampire" who has long been dead but whose "soul has been held in bondage by the result of his evil practices in life." After Garnet is destroyed, a quick search of the bookcase reveals the late father's will. It is at this point that "The Vampire's Desire" comes to an end.

There are no twists and no surprises in "The Vampire's Desire," and neither is there much ingenuity to the plot. Nevertheless, the play is a paradigmatic example of how to create atmosphere, location and a sense of space. The story is extremely simple — a Gothic sketch more than a developed narrative — but the play remains a very profound work for its attention to detail in constructing the storm outside, and the sound and feel of the ultimate "Old Dark House" and its various rooms, corridors and staircases. It is so dark, in fact, that only a fraction of the play is to be imagined in light. In addition, all of the light sources chosen for the listener to imagine are infused with a connotation of horror: the lightning of a storm; the ghostly image of a shaded lantern; and the candles surrounding a coffin. The terse dialogue offers clichés appropriate for the intensity of the story, and is also capable of fully conveying the environment: the protagonists call out to each other in the impenetrable darkness; they gasp and despair as they seem to be suffocating; and they resolutely solve the mystery and destroy the vampire. The economy and efficiency make it as hermetically sealed as the room with the crumbling corpse; it is a horror play that is entirely dependent upon the construction of atmosphere and in the facilitation of the audience's suspense as they imagine the mystery and terror of the benighted house. So strong is the establishment and purely experiential journey through the house that the play becomes very traditional and very contemporary at the same time: on one hand, it is like an early nineteenth-century "Shilling Shocker," which in their short, sensational tales would sacrifice plot for a simple conveyance of atmosphere; on the other hand, it is curiously like a precursor to "survival horror" computer games, such as *Resident Evil* or *Silent Hill,* in which plot is not as important as a careful and convincing creation of environment and the development of different locations, zones and levels in a journey with "no going back" that leads inexorably towards an encounter with an ultimate horror (in this case, brother Garnet). In this way, although "The Vampire's Desire" may be clichéd and unadventurous in plot, its technical achievement makes it an excellent example of the establishment of space and environment in horror radio of the golden age.

John Dunning writes, "'The Mummers' co-titled their show 'The Little Theater of the Air,' a rather literary moniker for such a blood-and-thunder spook show" (Dunning, 1998, 319). However, I would argue that "The Mummers" was an appropriate name for the ensemble. In the history of popular theater, "Mummers" were amateur actors who specialized in the performance of folk plays, which is apt given the formulaic and fabulous feel to many of *The Hermit's Cave* plays. Nevertheless, it was also a wide-ranging series in terms of genre that would offer gruesome stories with explicit violence one week, and lyrical tales of beautiful horror the next. As for being "The Little Theater of the Air," this may allude to the Little Theatre in the West End of London which had, during the early 1920s, offered some successful and celebrated seasons of Grand-Guignol horror plays. Indeed, the Parisian Théâtre du Grand-Guignol that the London experiment modeled itself after was famously, despite the ironic "Grand" in its title, a very small theater.

The Hermit's Cave plays that remain as recordings are frequently passionately acted, not least because the series was a springboard for an up and coming generation of radio actors. As we have seen, some of the episodes also demonstrate an impressive exploration of radio form and genre in creating a sense of environment and atmosphere. Above all, the aged Hermit and his baying pack of wolves remain a successful host and framing device that is a paradigmatic example of the portrayal and function of the horror host in popular culture, as well as evoking a specific era in golden age radio.

7

The Paradigm of Horror Radio: Himan Brown and *Inner Sanctum Mysteries* (1941–1952)

Inner Sanctum Mysteries was the creation of Himan Brown, one of the major figures in American broadcasting history and one who occupies a special place in radio drama. For Allison McCracken, Brown is "one of radio's most prolific showmen" (Sterling and Keith, 2003, 746). Brown first worked on radio as a teenager, and consolidated his career with astonishing industriousness, sometimes "working on as many as 20 programs on the networks each week" (Grams, 2002, 5). Brown started as a performer but soon discovered that his forte was in the area of directing and producing. His output spanned a diverse range of genres, including, as well as the horror of *Inner Sanctum Mysteries*, comedy and crime. In a career that spanned "eight decades (1920s–90s)" (Sterling and Keith, 2003, 250), Brown was involved with, and often the driving force behind, programs as diverse as *The Goldbergs, The Gumps, Bulldog Drummond, The Adventures of the Thin Man, The Adventures of Nero Wolfe* and the great revival of horror radio in the 1970–80s, *The CBS Radio Mystery Theater*. Himan Brown was not a writer, but, in his own words, he edited "every story I've ever broadcast," and was the director and producer of every episode of *Inner Sanctum Mysteries* throughout its long and successful run. As Grams puts it:

> [Brown] created ideas, outlined them and collaborated on the writing with his staff of writers, peddled and sold the products to sponsors and did the casting and directing [Grams, 2002, 7].

Brown secured many of the greatest actors of radio for *Inner Sanctum Mysteries,* including stars ranging from Boris Karloff and Peter Lorre to Agnes Moorehead (who had begun her radio career thanks to Brown). Although not a writer himself, Brown secured excellent scriptwriters for the show, and Brown himself edited the works into exemplary radio. Grams reveals that, "*Inner Sanctum* featured scripts penned by more than twenty authors during the twelve years on radio" (Grams, 2002, 58). Brown was a creative entrepreneur of radio, with formidable talents in developing concepts, programs and scripts. The title of *Inner Sanctum Mysteries* alluded to the Simon and Schuster series of thriller books: Brown struck a mutually beneficial deal with the publishers in order to use the name for his brand new series, an arrangement which demonstrates Brown's business acumen.

Inner Sanctum Mysteries was an extremely popular show that always enjoyed very high ratings. This success demonstrates how Brown understood what would appeal to the mass audience of radio; it was not the first horror show but he knew how to shape the genre to achieve enormous popularity. This popularity was not simply in terms of listener ratings: in April 1949 it received the Edgar Allan Poe award for Best Mystery Radio Show of 1948, with Poe busts presented to Himan Brown, principal writer John Roeburt and CBS. For John Dunning, *Inner Sanctum Mysteries* will always be the "epitome of radio melodrama" (Dunning, 1998, 347). Himan Brown makes even grander claims for the significance of his creation:

> If anything is a standard in our business it's the *Inner Sanctum*. When anyone talks about remembering radio they remember as a kid getting under the covers on Sunday night and listening to *Inner Sanctum Mysteries*. And it'll always work [Bob Morgan interview with Himan Brown, April 9, 1984].

Brown may not have been the greatest innovator — an honor we may choose to lavish on Wyllis Cooper or Orson Welles — but his brilliance lay in his understanding and consolidation of the potential of radio drama, especially in the area of mystery and horror. By the same token, *Inner Sanctum Mysteries* may not be as original or groundbreaking as our other case studies in horror radio, but what it does achieve quite brilliantly is an assimilation of the form. *Inner Sanctum Mysteries* did not invent the horror host, but it nonetheless created one of the most memorable. Likewise, the program did not even exist when the signature sounds of *Lights Out* (the portentous chimes and gongs) were first heard, but its own signature sound is the single most famous sound from the era of live radio drama. The *Inner Sanctum Mysteries*' signature sound effect of a "creaking door" has entered radio folklore. Indeed, it was an instant classic. Let us consider Norman DeMarco's "On the Air: Writing the Radio Play," an article on the techniques of radio drama written for *Players Magazine* (October 1947):

> A script may employ the "shock" technique and open "cold" using any of the following methods: a dialogue, a pistol shot, a shriek, an off-mike voice calling, a ringing phone, a door bell, or a door knock, a crash, etc. The obvious purpose of such an opening is to create immediate attention through emotional appeal. Often such a technique helps create a mood of suspense, or mystery, as, for instance, the creaking door of *Inner Sanctum*.

DeMarco uses numerous *generic* examples to demonstrate how to open a radio play, but only one of them is *specific*: the creaking door of *Inner Sanctum Mysteries*. Himan Brown used the actual door in a studio at NBC because it had rusty hinges and was badly sprung. Brown made it a radio star. The importance of this signature sound is demonstrated in the fact that, as Grams informs us, "in the history of the United States, only two sounds have ever been copyrighted and trademarked: the three NBC chimes and the creaking door" (Grams, 2002, 9).

One could be forgiven for expecting that such a brilliant opening device would have taken a long time to develop, but the concept of the creaking door was evidently Brown's starting point for the program before he had even decided on the title of *Inner Sanctum Mysteries*. In fact, his working title for the series was *The Creaking Door*:

> I had this thing called *The Creaking Door* because I felt there was a sound that didn't need anything more. The door creaking open set the scene for your imagination to take over. And I was gonna go hog-wild with suspense, horror, macabre, just that kind of show for just once a week [Bob Morgan interview with Himan Brown, April 9, 1984].

The commissioning producers were concerned that using *The Creaking Door* as a title threatened to make it sound like a home improvement show. Even if Brown changed the title, he was nevertheless determined to retain the sound of a creaking door as a signature, knowing how effective it would be on the imagination of the listener. Anecdotal evidence of this is provided by Stephen King, who recalls when *Inner Sanctum Mysteries* made the shift onto television and the creaking door could finally be seen:

> And visible, it certainly was horrible enough — slightly askew, festooned with cobwebs — but it was something of a relief, just the same. Nothing could have looked as horrible as that door *sounded* [King, 1982, 132].

From behind the terrifying door of *Inner Sanctum Mysteries* loomed the host. The show had a superb host, predominantly in the guise of Raymond Edward Johnson (page 24) — known simply as "Raymond" — from 1941 until 1945, and Paul McGrath as the nameless "Host" from 1945 until the program's demise in the early 1950s. John Dunning argues that Paul McGrath had "a lighter, brighter demeanor, losing a bit of Johnson's underlying menace" (Dunning, 1998, 347). This is a fair comment, but it is important to note that both the principal hosts of *Inner Sanctum Mysteries* struck a deliberate and exquisite balance between humor and horror. The host's opening narrative would be macabre and even ghoulish, but it would nonetheless be riddled with puns and the host's languid giggle, a sound almost as familiar as the creaking door itself. The cackles of Old Nancy and the Hermit reveal that they had sense of humor long before Raymond came on the scene, but the elaborate framing narratives of *Inner Sanctum Mysteries* — especially in the Paul McGrath era — abound with puns and humorous conceits. In the words of Allison McCracken, *Inner Sanctum Mysteries* is characterized by a "tongue-in-rotting-cheek humor" (Sterling and Keith, 2003, 747).

Between the opening of the creaking door and the host's sardonically menacing "pleasant dreams, hmmm?" at the end of the show, the listener experiences masterful examples of horror drama. Part of the success of *Inner Sanctum Mysteries* was the strong performances given by its actors. Himan Brown would always celebrate the quality of the actors who entered the uncanny world of the Inner Sanctum:

> They were very good: there was Boris Karloff, and there was Claude Rains, there was Vincent Price, and there was Paul Lukas, and Peter Lorre.... We really did incredible things [Bob Morgan interview with Himan Brown, April 9, 1984].

It was a generation of actors that "all really and truly loved radio" (Bob Morgan interview with Himan Brown, April 9, 1984), but at the same time they responded to the conditions of the medium:

> The wonderful things was that these men, these women, they were professionals to their fingertips.... There was no nonsense, no do it and re-do it, or one take and fifty takes, and makeup and costumes and all the paraphernalia that went with film making and television. They just got in there, sat down at a table, they got the script, and they had to make magic [quoted in Grams, 2002, 20].

The intensity of radio drama means that all the accoutrements of stage and screen used to enhance realism are redundant, so that all energies are focused on the voice, pace and rhythm of the performer's speech. This was a demand that most actors on *Inner Sanctum Mysteries* responded to with commitment. Although the hosts had the most unabashed opportunity to play their role for laughs, the ironic humor found in much of the repertoire was probably not lost on any of the actors given the opportunity to perform behind the creaking door. A photograph of occasional guest Peter Lorre and *Inner Sanctum* regular Elspeth Eric in rehearsal for the show superbly captures the drama and hilarity of *Inner Sanctum Mysteries*.

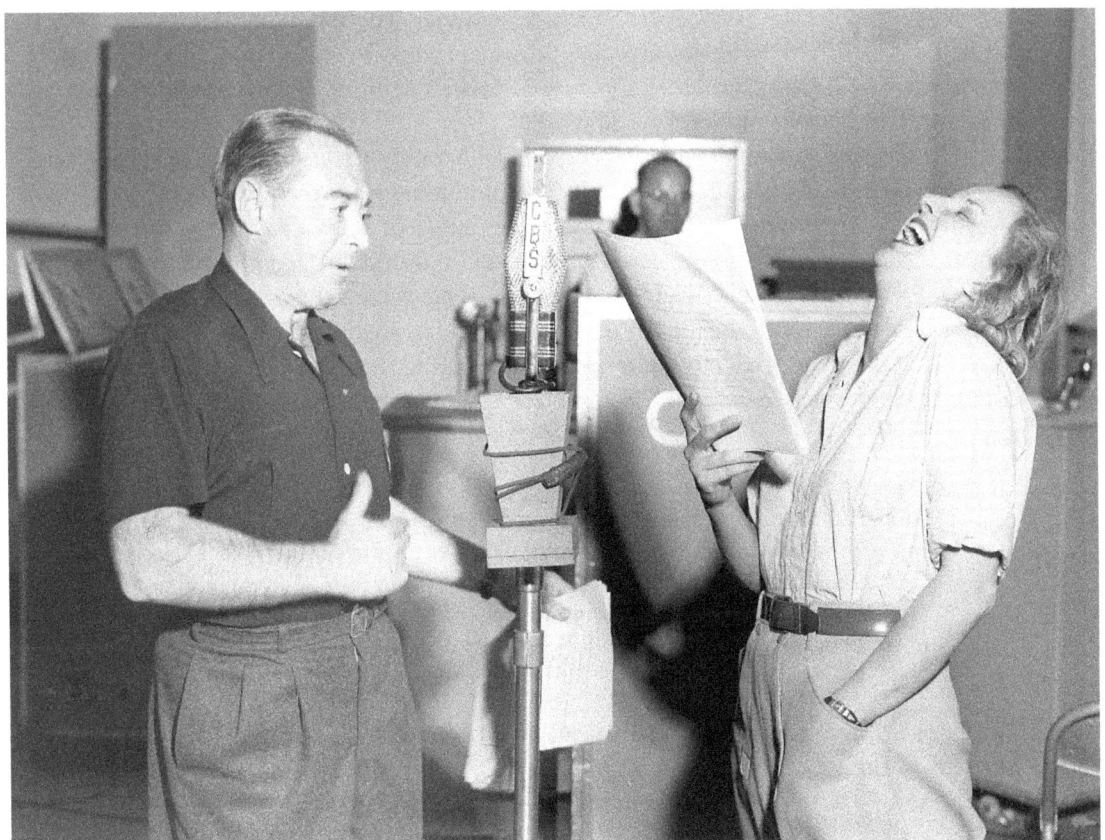

Peter Lorre and Elspeth Eric rehearsing for *Inner Sanctum Mysteries* (Photofest).

Brown understood the technicalities of radio drama, cleverly employing sound effects and the brooding organ music of Lew White (used as a sound effect or atmospheric creation as opposed to "music" per se, which Brown strove to resist). For Allison McCracken, the full exploration of sound was *Inner Sanctum Mysteries*' great contribution to the form of radio drama:

> Brown balanced the program's macabre humor with carefully chosen organ sounds, blood-curdling screams, and other effects, creating some of the most unsettling soundscapes ever heard on radio [Sterling and Keith, 2003, 746].

Through the use of musical effects, realistic sound effects and vocal utterances (speech, gasps, screams, etc.), Brown recognized the limitless potential of radio to generate atmospheres and locations in the creation of a genuinely intense experience:

> I could put you on top of Kilimanjaro by just putting wind noises on and saying "It's cold—this is Kilimanjaro," and you sat at home and you shivered with me because you heard the wind noises and the actors were acting in a way that said cold [Bob Morgan interview with Himan Brown, April 9, 1984].

The repertoire of the *Inner Sanctum Mysteries* presents highly disciplined examples of formulaic writing and production. Brown mastered a "horror" modus operandi in each 30-minute broadcast of *Inner Sanctum Mysteries*. There is a question as to how to define *Inner Sanctum Mysteries*, especially as we are considering it as an example of horror drama. For Grams, the *Inner Sanctum Mysteries*' defining characteristic was that it was "awash in buckets of blood" (Grams, 2002, 8).

The framing narrative was always cast in deliberately stark contrast to the gruesome and bleak horrors within the story itself. The individual plays themselves tended to shy away from the supernatural, preferring to present real (or at least possible) horrors. Psychopaths, killers on the loose, grotesque misfortune and mistaken identity were all favorite themes. Frequently, if a play seems to be taking a supernatural twist, the ghosts haunting the guilty turn out to be the hallucinations of collapsing sanity or the actions of vindictive—and very much alive—acquaintances exacting their just revenge. Although she correctly stresses that *Inner Sanctum Mysteries* was not unique in this, Allison McCracken argues that:

> *Inner Sanctum* stories were a counterpoint (some might even say antidote) to the suburban ideal of the postwar period. Husbands and wives did not get along well in *Inner Sanctum* stories, which were replete with film noir–type characters (including a healthy number of femme fatales) who murdered each other at terrific rates. [...The host] took great glee in the violent disintegration of the postwar family and the impossibility of happy coupling... [Sterling and Keith, 2003, 747].

Even the host's framing narrative can be socially/sexually disruptive. At the end of one play ("The Corridor of Doom," October 23, 1945), the host sells the listener next week's show in terms that now seem startling in their misogyny:

> Next week's story is about ... *women*. Yes, two women who like to be treated rough. Choke 'em to death, shoot 'em, murder 'em. They'll love you for it. And

who do you think is going to be their boyfriend? Mmm? Ha, ha, ha. That's right. Boris Karloff. Boris Karloff will be with us again next week. Because who else could love such women? So if you're in a tender mood, tune in next Tuesday.

Delivered with the host's usual mordant humor, the above speech is infused with social disruption: not only does it playfully reveal extreme sadomasochism as a latent desire, it also breaks convention with the sense of a *menage à trois*, a man with two girlfriends.

The everyday situations and domestic relationships of *Inner Sanctum Mysteries* would usually commence on a realistic basis before rapidly turning sinister. Happy homes would betray macabre secrets; devoted spouses would actually be seething with jealousy and suspicion; lovers in conventionally romantic situations would prove to be warped by profiteering or psychotic motivations; generous strangers or trustworthy old friends would reveal themselves to be driven by the basest physical lust or financial greed. The starting point for all these plays was designed to be something that all listeners could relate to or identify with. Moreover, the subsequent trajectory into ruthlessness and morbidity was intended to follow the lines of what might believably happen, and, possibly, what the more sensationalistic press had claimed had definitely happened in real life. However, although the listener may be swept along by the fast-moving tales within the broadcast that seem to take place in a familiar world, the plots were, as Allison McCracken stresses, "driven by contrivances and coincidences that were highly implausible" (Sterling and Keith, 2003, 746). This is not just a quality that becomes evident with the benefit of hindsight, as is clear in Max Wylie's detailed analysis of one of the plays from *Inner Sanctum Mysteries* (Wylie, 1950, 360–78).

Max Wylie's chosen example is Robert Newman's "Death Across the Board" (June 5, 1945), starring Raymond Massey in the lead role of Dr. Strand. The play begins with Strand going into a pawn shop and admiring an antique chess set. The pawn shop owner, Raphael, speaks with a stereotypical mysteriousness that immediately signposts him as the villain of the play in opposition to the sterling qualities of the protagonist. Raphael, who expresses an interest in challenging Strand to a game of chess, sends him to a nearby address to see a particularly rare chess set. The atmosphere may have been ominous, but on arrival at the address the play shifts into horror, with Strand killing a man in self-defence. Raphael telephones Strand and it becomes evident that Raphael is orchestrating a real-life chess game, with himself as the "black king" and Strand cast as the "white knight." Strand meets other characters in the neighborhood, including Alice (the white queen) and Adams, the chief of police (the white king), with the police officers as white pawns. Strand soon realizes that all the events are occurring in a district that is eight blocks by eight blocks. Strand decides that Raphael is none other than Raphael Norbert, "one of the greatest chess players the world has ever known," who disappeared five years before and is now playing "the maddest game that ever was." Adams is seriously injured by a bomb blast, and Strand and Alice rush him to the hospital where Raphael, in the guise of a doctor, attempts to kill the ailing white king. Strand throws formaldehyde into Raphael's eyes and announces that the white knight, white queen and white king have achieved checkmate. Ever the ungracious loser, Raphael throws himself to his death out the window, and Strand has the final words: "I think that's game, match and … tournament!"

In a play that has, excluding Raymond's framing narrative, 221 lines of dialogue, Wylie identifies over 25 improbabilities ranging from the blatant to the subtle, but all with a profound impact on the plot's "realism." Even the succinct description furnished above makes it clear that the story borders on the ridiculous. However, even if the play rapidly launches from the simple and believable — a man browsing in a pawn shop is a realistic context and opening — into the utterly implausible, it nonetheless lends the tale an impressive quality. On one level, "Death Across the Board" is a bizarre (and maybe refreshing) take on the conventional crime thriller, but it also has a startlingly abstract quality to its plot, with its characters forced into the roles of chess pieces, and its chessboard-like territory. However, we are not supposed to listen to *Inner Sanctum Mysteries* for a reflection of reality: we listen to the program for the experience of thrills and suspense. Max Wylie may point out all the *improbabilities* in the play, but they are not *inconsistencies*: the world of the play is consistently authentic to its own fictional and abstract parameters. Indeed, Wylie devotes more space in his analysis to a celebration of the success of the play in terms of its economy, its clarity, its mood, its gripping narrative and its highly proficient exposition. Although primarily celebrating the play as an example of radio scriptwriting, Wylie also praises the contribution of the music, sound effects and actors, such as when he describes "good screaming ... as the body hurtles down these lethal stairs, with a fine thud at the end" (Wylie, 1950, 374).

Inner Sanctum Mysteries features a repertoire governed by realistic contexts but improbable plots. The plays in the repertoire explore the perceived fault lines of American society: male and female; young and old; haves and have-nots; decency and corruption; good and evil. Looked at like this, *Inner Sanctum Mysteries* belongs to a tradition of melodrama, a dramatic system that functions and exists through the investigation of a system of binary oppositions. Once the "true colors" of the cast of characters have been revealed, we are within an unproblematic black-and-white moral universe where we witness a conflict to the point of inevitable — but not always entirely predictable — resolution. The issue of character is extremely important here. The brevity of the actual play within each broadcast (in an essay for would-be radio mystery writers, Himan Brown is adamant that, "your mystery story must be told in about twenty-one or twenty-two minutes" [Brown, 1950, 358]) makes extreme demands on characterization. Although the actors on *Inner Sanctum Mysteries* would perform with vivacity and passion, the roles they played were two-dimensional archetypes or stereotypes. Typically, the psychology of the characters is simple and clear cut, or if there is any ambiguity it is rapidly resolved so that the character's driving force and moral and ethical standpoints become crystal clear and unalterable.

We will now examine some other examples from the *Inner Sanctum Mysteries* repertoire. A minority of the plays inhabit the supernatural. "The Undead" (December 18, 1945) is a story in which a woman believes she is married to a vampire: the ending is ambiguous (it may be an elaborate hoax), but what is interesting is that, far from being a Transylvanian or heavily Gothic tale, the play is distinguished by being set in a contemporary domestic setting. As such, it's a precursor to the classics "The House in Cypress Canyon" (*Suspense*, December 5, 1946) and "My Son John" (*Quiet, Please*, November 28, 1948). "Judas Clock" (April 17, 1945) is an effective tale of a clock repairman who has searched 30 years for the cursed clock of the title, which will only work when weighted with Judas

Iscariot's 30 pieces of silver (which the repairman owns). This play walks a line between the real and the supernatural. The curse is real (at least if we trust our earnest first-person narrator who mediates the tale): when a man purchased the clock, "his face drained white and his eyes bulged" before he collapsed dead. The repairman's father is crushed to death when the heavy marble clock topples over on top of him. Several other victims are crushed or decapitated by the diabolical timepiece. Although the curse may be genuine, it nonetheless fuels the very human fallibilities and psychoses of the characters that come into contact with it.

Even if the truly paranormal arises only infrequently on *Inner Sanctum Mysteries,* a favorite motif is the *seemingly* supernatural. Time and again we find supernatural phenomenon explained as the actions to drive a victim insane or, conversely, trap the guilty. In "The Voice on the Wire" (November 29, 1944) a guilty woman who killed her husband and his dog is haunted by them. Inevitably, it is revealed as a hoax: the apparitions that secure her confession are really her dead husband's identical twin brother accompanied by an identical breed of dog. The plot may be infuriating, but it is delivered with customary verve and concision.

Some plays succeed in mixing the supernatural with the hoax. "Elixir Number Four" (February 12, 1946) is an intense vehicle for Richard Widmark in the lead role of Alex Gregory. It is a work of scientific speculation in the H. G. Wells tradition. The story, told from the perspective of a first-person narrative, recounts how Gregory steals the formula of a scientist — his girlfriend's father, no less — and murders him. The scientist has developed, in the tradition of alchemy, an elixir of eternal life which Gregory injects into himself. A séance seems to summon the voice of the dead scientist, who denounces Gregory. After Gregory confesses, it becomes clear that the voice was not from beyond the grave but a recording made as Elaine's father died. In this instance, *Inner Sanctum Mysteries* resists the supernatural of the occult, and yet the pseudo-scientific supernaturalism persists: the play ends with the genuinely immortal Gregory laughing hysterically as he is condemned to prison for the rest of his "natural" life.

As Allison McCracken notes, the plays on *Inner Sanctum Mysteries* were generally original, although Edgar Allan Poe was a favorite choice for adaptation (Sterling and Keith, 2003, 746). In fact, Poe is a popular choice throughout horror radio. As Jim Harmon says, Poe would not have known it, but in "The Tell-Tale Heart" he had written "a beautiful radio script" (Harmon, 1967, 75). This particular short story enjoyed numerous dramatizations in horror radio. *The Weird Circle*'s mid–1940s version of "The Tell-Tale Heart" is a conventional dramatization, but offers some points of technical interest. This version features Charles living with his uncle. At the beginning, the sound of his uncle's footsteps upstairs merges with the sound of his heartbeat, which Charles tells us we cannot hear, but we can. The disembodied voices that haunt the mind of Charles are one woman and one man, each telling him to kill his uncle. They variously egg him on or reflect his anxieties and represent a way of putting the listener inside the protagonist's head. Though a relatively loyal adaptation, Richard Thorne's version of "The Tell-Tale Heart" for *The Hall of Fantasy* (June 1, 1953) makes some major changes. In this version, David Crowther arrives at the house of the infirm Mr. Lawrence to offer himself as a care assistant, although he has no references. The listener is made aware at the beginning that Crowther has a history of mental illness and has only recently been discharged from a hospital. The adaptation also adds a housekeeper to the Lawrence home called Mrs. Gorman, a device that allows opportunities for dialogue, in addition to the narrative of Crowther. Additionally, a significant section of dialogue has Crowther expressing his horror of Lawrence's "vulture eye" to none other than the old man himself. Thorne's adaptation decisions allow for a more obviously "dramatic" tension between the three central characters than what would arise from a predominantly monologic approach, which would instantly feel like a reading rather than a drama. Nevertheless, Crowther's framing narrative captures the style of the Poe original, and includes well-placed bursts of increasingly insane laughter as Crowther recounts his descent into murder and madness. "The Tell-Tale Heart" continued to be a favorite for radio adaptation beyond the end of the golden age, with noteworthy dramatizations for *The CBS Radio Mystery Theater* (January 11, 1975) and *Nightfall* (August 1, 1980).

Robert Newman's version of "The Tell-Tale Heart" (*Inner Sanctum Mysteries*, August 3, 1941)—a vehicle for Boris Karloff—is a bold interpretation. The original Poe story forms just a few minutes of the radio play, apart from which it strays into a plot reminiscent of Maurice Level's "Night and Silence" (1920), a horror story about a deaf man and his blind brother. In the play, Simon (Boris Karloff) is a deaf musician who undergoes an operation that gives him superhuman hearing: he can hear the grass growing and the stars moving. He meets Oliver (Everett Sloane), a man who was once blind but now has a similarly superhuman vision. The men live together in an old watermill, but eventually the seemingly gentle Simon descends into madness and murders what he perceives as his increasingly sadistic companion (with his "hawk's eyes") and buries him beneath the floorboards. After this, the play follows the familiar Poe plot to the end. The play creates an effective soundscape which captures Simon's acute hearing: footsteps on the floorboards and staircases, knocking on doors, the groan of furniture, and the creaking watermill. The pounding of Oliver's heart emerges gradually and subtly, effectively underpinning the dialogue of Simon and the police constable (Santos Ortega). The twist at the end of the play comes with the revelation that Simon was not cured by the operation: the sounds that he—and we—can hear so acutely are the delusions of his madness. This version of "The Tell-Tale Heart" is remarkably adventurous in its interpretation of Poe's original, but the same short story was clearly a paradigm for *Inner Sanctum Mysteries*, as it appears as an influence throughout the repertoire. In "The Dead Walk at Night" (September 20, 1942; revived January 29, 1944, and September 28, 1952) a man murders his blind, billionaire uncle and is haunted by the tapping of the dead man's walking stick. "The Deadly Dummy" (January 24, 1949), about a man who murders a ventriloquist and is haunted by the voice of the victim's dummy, owes something to both "The Tell-Tale Heart" and the ventriloquist dummy episode from the film *Dead of Night* (Cavalcanti et al., 1945).

Poe's "The Tell-Tale Heart" is a tale of subjective madness, but some of the *Inner Sanctum Mysteries*' homages to it venture more into the Patrick Hamilton *Gaslight* (1938) territory of someone else attempting to drive their victim insane. Examples include "The Creeping Wall" (January 8, 1946) and "The Corridor of Doom" (October 23, 1945). The latter play is a remarkable triumph of atmosphere. John Clay (Boris Karloff) awakens from an operation in a pristine white room. In the corridor outside the room are a row of doors, each of which has a name emblazoned on it. After collapsing, Clay finds himself back in the white room. Rather than an experience of the afterlife, this turns out to be a plot by his son-in-law to scare Clay to death to secure his fortune. The story may be predictable and melodramatic, but the evocation of the white room and the seemingly endless corridor of doom makes for powerful radio.

One of *Inner Sanctum Mysteries*' most frequently revived plays is "Strange Passenger" (October 14, 1946; revived May 23, 1949, and August 31, 1952). In this play, an effective example of the horror subgenre of the hitchhiker tale, the first-person narrator is John Thompson, a man who recounts a nighttime experience in which he picks up a female hitchhiker called Anne. They listen to the radio, and "Stardust"—requested by a woman called Anne, no less—is played. John remains our point of focus, stepping in and out of narratorial monologue and dramatic dialogue. However, he becomes increasingly uncomfortable listening to "Stardust" and demands that it be switched off: "This is my car! This is my radio!" Soon afterwards the car crashes, and John informs us that he was aware of Anne's neck breaking even before the car stopped. Coming out his daze after the crash, John is puzzled by the fact that Anne's body has disappeared, and can only assume she was thrown far from the vehicle on impact. John's car is still roadworthy and so he continues his journey. "Stardust" begins to haunt him, such as when he hears it at a roadside diner, and eventually he sees Anne thumbing for a lift once more. At the end of the play, John, in custody, reveals that he had murdered his wife—Anne Thompson—in their apartment and taken flight. "Stardust" was on the radio as he murdered her. The plot has therefore taken us back to "The Tell-Tale Heart" homage, with the protagonist's guilt leading to delusions and confession.

All hitchhiker plays in horror radio, however, owe a debt to Lucille Fletcher's "The Hitch-Hiker" (*Suspense*, September 2, 1944). In Fletcher's play the protagonist (Orson Welles) is haunted by a mysterious hitchhiker and attempts to flee from him, becoming increasingly more desperate. The classic twist at the end shares the irony of Ambrose Bierce's "An Occurrence at Owl Creek Bridge"; in other words, the protagonist has been dead from the start. We have empathized with the driver but experience a moment of abjection as we realize that we have been sharing the journey with a dead man in denial. In contrast, the adventurous twist to "Strange Passenger" comes when we learn that the protagonist—who has similarly won our empathy and confidence—is a killer. In addition, the use of "Stardust," the sound of the car, and other soundscapes evocative of the agoraphobic loneliness of the open highway are extremely well-handled structural, atmospheric and technical devices.

"The Corpse That Nobody Loved" (March 3, 1947; revived September 21, 1952) is another effective story of the road, although more of a crime thriller. The play uses devices similar to those in "Strange Passenger," but in this one the protagonist is a woman who takes a taxi and finds herself next to a corpse. The play later explores a more claustrophobic sense of horror when the woman manages to return to the safety of her home only to discover the same corpse in her apartment.

Although fans of *Inner Sanctum Mysteries* evidently liked their hosts' ghoulish puns and the unsubtle melodrama and implausibility of its plots, some plays in the repertoire can be seen as a more complex dramatic experience. For example, "Skeleton Bay" (February 5, 1946; revived January 30, 1950) takes the typical *Inner Sanctum Mysteries* recipe to a more profound stylistic and thematic level. In this play, scripted by Emile C. Tepperman, mystery novelist Carola Winter (Betty Lou Gerson in 1946; Charlotte Holland in 1950) takes a seaside vacation on the "storm-swept, rock-bound coast" of the title. Carola narrates her story, which unfurls in imitation — if not complex pastiche — of the mood and language of the pulp mystery and romance prose of the period. There is a distinctly satirical feel to the script, with the sub–Gothic resonance of Carola being haunted by the name "Skeleton Bay" ("hammering, hammering, hammering inside of my brain ... like the voice of implacable fate commanding, commanding") after having seen the destination in an advertisement some months before. Much of the play is accompanied by the whistling of the sea breeze, which Carola describes as "howling like a hungry beast across the shores." Swiftly, Carola finds herself in a situation much like the plot of one of her own novels: she witnesses a murder. The crime is brutal, Carola seeing "the blade plunge wholly into the throat" of the victim. The event is not a cause for concern for Carola, but rather a cause for ecstasy: "I felt a sudden surge of wild elation!" Rather than run or call for aid, Carola offers to help the killer, Michael Barrett (Martin Gabel in both productions), dispose of the body. She hides the corpse in her room and murders a maid when she discovers it, this becoming another exultant moment for Carola. The intimacy of the narrative (with the voice of Carola telling us the story, as well as being involved in each dramatic scene), combined with the madness of Carola, lends the story a Poe-like quality. Moreover, the narrative of the articulate, lightly-spoken heroine as she leads us into the world of her madness makes the play feel like Charlotte Perkins Gilman's *The Yellow Wallpaper* or Henry James' *Turn of the Screw*. Carola's madness is sexualized and perversely "romantic"— seeing a throat cut open is a moment of love at first sight for her, and her unrequited love causes her to track down and kill not just Michael but also a woman she discovers he has incarcerated for ten years. After her sadistic homicidal spree, the play ends with Carola having completed a confessional novel and awaiting arrest by Detective Sergeant Smith. Carola has already met Smith, and he is evidently another object of desire who will lead this demure, sadistic murderer to a climax of ultimate masochism: the execution chamber.

Despite the gory horror of its early days, *Inner Sanctum Mysteries* did, as Grams writes, begin to lean "toward straight mystery instead of horror tales during the program's later years" (Grams, 2002, 37). Writing on the subject of taboos while the series was still thriving, Himan Brown implies that the only censorial pressure came from him and his creative team: during the Second World War for example, they intended to set a play in a city morgue but abandoned the idea because "We thought that would be in bad taste at that particular time" (Brown, 1950, 354). After all, *Inner Sanctum Mysteries*, like most other drama programs, was not interested in demoralizing the listener, but in boosting morale, and did so with numerous plays that featured Nazi spies as villains.

The issue of "taste" would also be taken into account when preparing programs during periods such as Christmas. Brown describes, and advises, how the issue can dictate a storyline's horror content:

> As to extremes of horror — that, too, is a question of taste. I have found that I can kill fifteen people in one script and not get a rise out of the listeners. But if in the same script I kill a puppy or a bird or any pet, we'll be flooded with thousands of letters. The same principle applies to the use of children — as victims— in the macabre murder story. I have found that where we used a child as the receiving point in a horror plot — and it's terribly effective — the listener gets just as thoroughly upset and not only refuses to listen but floods the station with mail. So

don't kill any children and don't fool around with domestic animals! I can go even further: we never have actually killed a child on any of the programs I have done; the mere fact, though, of putting a child in jeopardy is enough to send the listener into howls of rage and unhealthful tension [Brown, 1950, 354].

But Brown stresses that "there is one segment of the audience" for whom "nothing can be too horrible" (Brown, 1950, 354)—and this is his intended audience. Brown had this ideal audience in mind while producing *Inner Sanctum Mysteries,* and even if he had to alter or self-censor the content to keep the marginals content, he was still going to provide experiential thrills and gore.

As well as the taboos of children and pets, Brown felt obliged to conceal the actual techniques of violence, even if the show wallowed in the gruesome end results. As Jim Harmon explains:

> Brown's biggest trouble was in his methods of killing people. The Federal Communications Commission objected if he got too specific. "The problem," Brown has said, "was not to reveal actual murder methods with such clarity and definition as to give the listener a good idea of how to erase someone he could do without, or even a half-complete knowledge of a known and effective method of killing with only a small chance of being caught" [Harmon, 1967, 79].

This problem should not be taken lightly. If we can trust newspaper reports, it would seem that copycat criminals used *Inner Sanctum Mysteries* as inspiration and education. Grams cites such examples as how four hours after "The Candlestick Murders" (October 23, 1943) broadcast, a real life victim was bludgeoned to death with a candlestick; and two weeks after "Murder in the Museum" (September 2, 1944) hit the airwaves, a murder occurred near the Museum of Natural History in New York (Grams, 2002, 27). Whether coincidental or not, it is clear that such events were another excuse to place the horror and suspense drama under scrutiny. Whatever the reasons, and (as we shall see in the concluding chapter to this book) they are many, *Inner Sanctum Mysteries* made its final broadcast on October 5, 1952.

Brown remained passionate about radio drama, and his indefatigable efforts led to the creation of another magnificent achievement in horror and suspense radio, albeit produced years after the official demise of the golden age of American radio drama. *The CBS Radio Mystery Theater* (1974–82) was, in John Dunning's words, "the most ambitious comeback attempt" in the history of radio (Dunning, 1998, 143). Though the plays on the program were recorded on tape and offered in repeat broadcasts, the five-plays-per-week schedule (each broadcast lasting over 50 minutes) meant that Brown had the formidable task of producing "a show from scratch every 1.9 days" (Dunning, 1998, 143). Brown was therefore obliged to use the rehearsal and production methods familiar from the era of live radio. The account of a *CBS Radio Mystery Theater* rehearsal provided by Gordon Payton and Martin Grams, Jr., reveals that the process was intense, vivacious and convivial (Payton and Grams, 1999, 5–7). The actors would enjoy an initial read-through—which included "considerable horseplay" (Payton and Grams, 1999, 5)—and after a short break would perform the script, along with live sound effects. There were sometimes brief pauses and repeat sound effects, which would be edited later, but over all it is clear that in *The CBS Radio Mystery Theater* Himan Brown was attempting to revive not only the genre but the mood and methods of old-time radio drama. Reviews of the program were mixed — obviously some critics were troubled by the return of a supposedly obsolete form — and yet the series won a number of prestigious awards (Payton and Grams, 1999, 8). For Himan Brown the greatest honor came from individual listeners, such as the person who wrote to him saying, "Thank you for giving my family back the world of fantasy" (Bob Morgan interview with Himan Brown, April 9, 1984).

Unmistakably and inescapably, the influence of *Inner Sanctum Mysteries* looms large over *The CBS Radio Mystery Theater*. *Inner Sanctum Mysteries* was the most successful of the horror radio shows of the golden age. As it did with its rival programs, the rise of television took its toll, not to mention the pressure of censorship. Concerns about violence and "moral" standards on radio meant that, as Grams puts it, "*Inner Sanctum Mystery* was starting to take a bath, and not in blood" (Grams, 2002, 57), and the radio show eventually disappeared in October 1952, after well over 500 broadcasts.

Inner Sanctum Mysteries had already spawned a series of six Universal films in the 1940s featuring Lon Chaney, Jr. In 1954 Brown himself put the *Inner Sanctum Mysteries* on the (small) screen when he produced 39 half-hour television plays. The creaking door remained the signature of the show, but as Stephen King reminded us at the beginning of the chapter, nothing could look as horrific as that dreadful door sounded. The television show would never enjoy a success like its radio parent.

Inner Sanctum Mysteries was one of the flagships of old-time radio. The sound of the creaking door was the trademark of the show, and even now it remains undiminished as an evocative and arresting horror effect. The creaking door also abounds with symbolic value: not only is it a defining sound of old-time radio, it is perhaps the epitome of horror radio, the door to the imagination that threatens or promises to lead us into the presence of terror. With *Inner Sanctum Mysteries* Himan Brown managed to create a program with high production values that, between the opening and closing of its eerie door, presented the listener with evocative effects, well-paced and impassioned performances, morbid humor and disturbing moments of violence and horror. The scripts and productions on *Inner Sanctum Mysteries* are rigorously formulaic: perhaps this is why, arguably, the program does not have any "stand-out" episodes such as "Sorry, Wrong Number" (*Suspense*), "The Thing on the Fourble Board" (*Quiet, Please*) or "Behind the Locked Door" (one of the crowning achievements of our next case study, *The Mysterious Traveler*). However, it does mean that the *Inner Sanctum Mysteries* "package" was of an ubiquitously high standard, with a repertoire that is predominantly consummate and professional in its quality and execution. *Inner Sanctum Mysteries* was the most successful and legendary production in Himan Brown's long career. For Brown, *Inner Sanctum Mysteries* represented an exploration and exploitation of a superb and timeless genre — mystery/horror — that he helped develop to its creative apogee on radio, its "highest form":

> [Mystery/horror will] always work because there's a timelessness to Edgar Allan Poe and to Hawthorne and to Henry James and to Stevenson — they all wrote mysteries. It's a wonderful thing — you look around — today, of course, it's Stephen King and people like that — but the mystery as an art form, as a literary form, is fantastic. And I think I helped develop it through the ear and your imagination to its highest form because I could create horror with your help, with your imagination [Bob Morgan interview with Himan Brown, April 9, 1984].

8

The Eclectic Horrors of Robert A. Arthur and David Kogan: *The Mysterious Traveler* (1943–1952)

Robert A. Arthur and David Kogan were both talented writers in their own right who, when they decided to collaborate as writer-producers, formed a formidable creative team that left an indelible impression on horror radio. In the area of horror radio they were behind the Mutual series *The Sealed Book* (1945) and *The Strange Doctor Weird* (1944–45). John Dunning incorrectly cites *The Strange Doctor Weird* as written solely by Robert A. Arthur (Dunning, 1998, 643) but as David Kogan makes clear, "*The Strange Doctor Weird* was a collaboration" (letter to Richard J. Hand, September 18, 2004), another jewel in their remarkably prolific and successful collaboration. Dr. Weird, the host of *The Strange Doctor Weird*, was played by Maurice Tarplin, who also acted as the eponymous host of *The Mysterious Traveler* (1943–52), Arthur and Kogan's longest running and most successful series. An eclectic series, *The Mysterious Traveler* embraced a wide range of genres. Listeners would experience hardboiled crime one week, a whodunit the next, and science fiction the week after that. But horror had a special place in the program, and its most acclaimed broadcast, "Behind the Locked Door" (May 24, 1949; revived November 6, 1951), remains a masterpiece of the horror genre.

Before working for radio, Robert A. Arthur had had considerable experience in the 1930s writing for pulp fantasy magazines such as *Amazing Stories*, *Wonder Stories* and *Unknown Worlds*. During the same period, he had an even more prominent career writing pulp detective stories for many magazines, including some of Street and Smith's detective titles—*The Illustrated Detective Magazine*, *Detective Fiction Weekly* and *The Shadow*. A portentous event for the history of radio drama occurred in 1940 when Arthur opted to study radio writing under Erik Barnouw at Columbia University; in the same class he met David Kogan, another young writer. Unlike Arthur, Kogan had already established a radio career for himself writing a script for *Bulldog Drummond*, and had followed this with work for *The Shadow* and *The Adventures of the Thin Man*. It appears that it was Kogan who persuaded Arthur to collaborate on radio drama, and together they produced *Dark Destiny* (1942–43), later reusing some of these early scripts for episodes of *The Mysterious Traveler*. Arthur and Kogan also co-wrote the 1944 summer season of *Nick Carter, Master Detective* (1943–55), a series that had previously featured Kogan as scriptwriter. During this period, Arthur managed to maintain his pulp fiction career, with numerous short stories appearing in magazines such as *Weird Tales*, *Astounding Science Fiction* and *Household Magazine*. Arthur also became Copy Editor and, subsequently, Head Writer for *Parade*. As well as collaborating on *Dark Destiny*, *Nick Carter* and *The Mysterious Traveler*, Arthur and Kogan also wrote and produced *Murder by Experts* (1949–51), a series that featured notable icons of mystery such as John Dickson Carr, Dorothy L. Sayers and, in its final year, Alfred Hitchcock as hosts. John Dunning describes *Murder by Experts* as "a better series than most of its counterparts" (Dunning, 1998, 470). As an example of a *Murder by Experts* play, "Dig Your Own Grave" (August 15, 1949) is an effective tale of suspense (indeed, it is very much in the *Suspense* style) in which a nagging wife drives her innocent husband to adultery and, ironically, murder when his suicide bid fails and he accidentally kills his wife in the process. This play, like other examples from the *Murder by Experts* repertoire, is a crime drama on the border of horror in its manipulation of suspense, and its portrayal of psychosis and gruesome murders. Likewise, another play in the series, "Conspiracy" (April 24, 1950), takes horror-genre delight in a prolonged sequence of drowning.

Arthur and Kogan's magnum opus, *The Mysterious Traveler*, was merely a "sustainer" for Mutual that did not enjoy commercial sponsorship but fulfilled the network's obligations to provide programs for its affiliate stations. In an interview with Anthony Tollin, Kogan explains that mystery programs were the most popular genre for sustainers, as "they didn't require high-priced comedy or musical talent" (Tollin, 20). However, we should not let Kogan's self-effacement deceive us regarding the quality of *The Mysterious Traveler,* or, for that matter, *The Sealed Book* and other Arthur-Kogan productions. In retrospect, many of their plays are finely tuned paradigmatic examples of golden age broadcasting across a number of separate but linked genres.

All drama is a collaborative art form, and radio drama is no exception. However, it usually seems to be a case that each collaborator finds his or her niche in the dramatic process. For instance, in the case of *Quiet, Please* there is the consistent triangular formation of writer-producer Wyllis Cooper, lead actor Ernest Chappell, and musician Albert Buhrmann: it is a strong collaboration, with each person contributing their expertise. This formation in *Quiet, Please* is only rarely challenged, such as on the broadcast in which Cooper plays himself accosted by a drunk in a bar—"Where Do You Get Your Ideas?" (February 20, 1949). The resulting drama is almost post-modern in its playful self-reference and irony.

Much horror radio seems, in hindsight, to be dominated by individual figures, such as Alonzo Deen Cole or Arch Oboler, with the Arthur-Kogan collaboration seeming a conspicuously successful exception. However, in terms of creative, collaborative practice, Kogan provides an interesting insight when he describes their working methodology in the Foreword to this book, and in an interview with Anthony Tollin:

> We developed the plots together and then one or the other of us would go off and write it. Bob Arthur didn't really care for directing so he usually left that for me [Tollin, 2001, 35].

So it would seem that they shared the writing, but Kogan specialized in directing. However, there was a clear demarcation in expertise when it came to genres:

> I've always loved science fiction stories so I tended to write the scripts in that genre.... Bob Arthur was a former *Weird Tales* pulp writer so he generally handled the horror scripts [Tollin, 2001, 20].

So it would seem that Robert A. Arthur is the creative force behind the horror works. However, it is of central importance that they developed the plots together, and it is probably the case that Arthur gives the science fiction and crime plays on *The Mysterious Traveler* their distinctive horror twist. Whatever the genesis of the scripts through plot development, scriptwriting and production, their working methodology obviously provides a template for successful collaboration in radio drama of the time. Moreover, given Kogan's penchant for directing, he is clearly a figure who understood the potential and discipline of horror performance.

We will begin our analysis with the most famous play from *The Mysterious Traveler*: "Behind the Locked Door." The reputation of "Behind the Locked Door" is one that has grown with time. It is worth noting, however, that if the impact of a show can be gauged on listener response, then "Death Comes to Adolph Hitler" (March 24, 1945; revived as "Death at Fifty Fathoms," on April 18, 1950) was the most "successful" because it generated more listener mail than any other epidsode during the run of the series, with "Behind the Locked Door" in second place. "Death Comes to Adolph Hitler" was remarkably topical for its context of broadcast towards the end of the Second World War: in this play, outlined by Arthur and scripted by Kogan, Adolf Hitler attempts to escape to Argentina in a submarine. As David Kogan writes, at the time of broadcast the fate of Hitler was "uppermost in a great many minds" (letter to Richard J. Hand, September 18, 2004). In contrast, "Behind the Locked Door" was not topical, but it created a scenario that proved as timeless as it was original. The play begins in the mountains of Arizona, with Kathy visiting her fiancé Martin at a mountain lodge. He is unkempt and distressed, and in hiding from the authorities regarding the disappearance of a Professor Stephens. This is the opening narrative frame before the extended flashback that forms the principal section of the play. The archaeologist Professor Stephens invites Martin to join him on a ten-day exploration along a section of the Colorado River, with a view to discover Aztec relics. Martin is momentarily hesitant because of Kathy, but soon opts to join the Professor. In studying the rocks and cliffs they discover a cave and decide to blast the rocks away. Sam, their Indian guide, warns them of a sleeping evil within the blocked cavern. The constant references to the Aztecs seems to be paving the way for a tale of modern man cast into arcane myth, rather like the curse of the Roman sarcophagus in *Lights Out*'s "He Dug It Up" (February 9, 1943), or the curse the hero discovers in the Egyptian tomb in *Quiet, Please*'s "Whence Came You" (February 16, 1948). But Arthur and Kogan have a major surprise in store for their listeners.

Once inside the cave, a number of conventional devices are used to establish the atmosphere of the location: Martin and Stephens' heavy footsteps and voices resonate as we are told that the ceiling is some 200 feet high. We then hear rats scurrying around, followed by the description of huge bats on the ceiling. Incidentally, the suspenseful potential of this setting had already been exploited by Arthur and Kogan in "The Devil's

Cavern" (*The Strange Doctor Weird*, April 3, 1945), which also features cave exploration and a similar technical progression and establishment of atmosphere through the use of squeaking rats, bats on the ceiling and the ominous echo, but is a crime tale of two money-hungry nephews who follow their wealthy uncle into the deep cavern of the title and then cast him to his death. In contrast, "Behind the Locked Door" leads us not into a crime scenario but into horror.

As well as the rats and bats, the explorers stumble across human skeletons. Immediately after this comes Arthur and Kogan's distinctive coup, a genuine surprise for the listener: the explorers discover a wagon train consisting of some 30 or 40 wagons. Some of the numerous skeletons of humans and horses have been pierced by Navajo arrows. We were beginning to anticipate a tale of Aztec curses, but now, about a third of the way into the play, we are presented with a tale of lost pioneers of the mid-nineteenth century—a startling twist. The archaeologists rummage through the boxes and luggage and learn that the wagon train was heading west for the gold of California in 1849. True to horror form, the explorers head deeper and deeper into the linked caverns. Sam panics about the "evil" in the cavern and flees. But it soon becomes clear that the peril in the cave is not supernatural: there are fish bones near an underground river, and the explorers hear Sam "fighting" in the distance. When they discover his body, he has been clawed to death. At this point—halfway through the play—the Professor realizes that the descendants of the pioneers may have survived for a century behind the blocked entrance to the cavern. The men speculate about this "nightmare you can't awaken from," imagining what this underground race of humans would have evolved into over a few generations. It is a conjecture that places the play not in the realm of ancient curses but in the tradition of speculative fiction: "Behind the Locked Door" evidently owes something to H. G. Wells' *The Time Machine: An Invention* (1895), in which, in another subterranean realm, the hero of the novella discovers the troglodytic Morlocks that half the human race has evolved into. Arthur and Kogan's take on the theme, however, presents something not futuristic but horrific in the hills of a contemporary, paranoid America.

Martin sees the Professor struggling with "a huge, dark figure." The Professor dies, and Martin—his narrative voice steadily mounting in anxiety and emotion (very successfully achieved by Lyle Sudrow in the 1951 revival)—struggles to find his way out of the intricate caverns. The final third of the play begins with Martin being attacked by something in the dark that produces a sound like a roaring hog before Martin slips into unconsciousness. When he awakens he becomes aware of "a heavy, calloused hand" bathing his wounds, and when he addresses his helper in the dark it brays gutturally. Martin discovers that his "savior" is also his "jailer," and he loses track of time while being nursed back to health but confined to an existence beside the bank of the subterranean river. Falling into the river, Martin and the monster of the cavern are washed out onto the banks of the Colorado River. After this, Martin's narrative closes and we are back in the present. Martin insists that the creature is still with him, inside the bedroom. Kathy claims that he is deluded, and when she tries the bedroom door she asks, "Why is the door locked?" We suddenly realize that the "Locked Door" of the title is not the blocked cave opening, but a literal door in the mountain lodge. The phrase "locked door" carries a connotation of the taboo. It is also possibly a mischievous allusion to *Inner Sanctum Mysteries*: in the latter series, Raymond opens the creaking door at the start to admit us into a world of terror; in "Behind the Locked Door," the door is too terrifying to open until the very end.

When Kathy (Ann Shepherd in the 1951 production) opens the door to prove there is nothing there, she utters the kind of blood-curdling scream most appropriate for the horror genre, and this concludes the play. If the locked door hides a taboo, then what is it? Martin has stated that he is reciprocating the kindness of the female monster that nursed him back to health and protected him in the cavern. This reciprocation of kindness, his demands that Kathy leave him, and the fact that the creature is locked in his *bedroom* comes together to suggest that Martin is now in a relationship with a creature not described beyond its callous hands, claw-like fingers and guttural noises: it implies that the engagement with Kathy is off, and Martin has found himself a new partner. If we return to parallels with Wells' *The Time Machine*, it is as if the Traveller abandons his romance with the attractive Eloi Weena for one of the Morlocks.

The shocking sexual twist at the end of "Behind the Locked Door" is obviously reminiscent of the ending to *Quiet, Please*'s "The Thing on the Fourble Board" (August 9, 1948), broadcast less than a year before. The sexualized shock ending of both plays, in which the "normal" hero encounters a terrifying female monstrosity but ends up marrying her, is a fascinating shared theme, especially in the historical context of their broadcasts. Both plays were produced just a few years after the end of the Second World War, and arguably reveal the zeitgeist of social and gender anxieties of the period. It was a period of unprecedented economic growth and international influence for the United States, and yet in terms of masculine identity there was a sense of postwar trauma and crisis in the process of readjustment to the demands and responsibilities of peacetime society. The respective heroes—*Quiet, Please*'s Porky, an oil engineer (securing the resources for America's future), and *The Mysterious Traveler*'s Martin, an archaeological explorer (uncovering the heritage of America's past)—are ideal examples of the US male: responsible and pioneering. Porky's domestic situation is unclear, but Martin is engaged to be married to the "attractive" Kathy Evans: an ideal family is in prospect. By the end of the plays both men are "married," but although their chosen marriages may be domestically conformist, they are essentially monstrous. This shared theme also reflects the disquiet of an America entering an age of anxiety and paranoia: marriage and the family unit should be a cornerstone of society, yet these two particular units are morally repugnant and socially dangerous.

Such challenges to the sanctity and paradigm of domesticity are to be found elsewhere in golden age horror radio. Both "The House in Cypress Canyon" (*Suspense*, December 5, 1946) and "Stranger in the House" (*The Mysterious Traveler*, January 29, 1952) begin with young married couples buying new houses, reflecting the postwar context of new beginnings and the establishment of homes and economic stability. The home the young married couple, James (Robert Taylor) and Ellen (Cathy Lewis), buy in "The House in Cypress Canyon" seems to be plagued by a werewolf (although the word is never explicitly uttered in the dialogue, the howling makes it unambiguous for the listener). It does, however, become clear that, far from an external peril, it is Ellen who transforms into the monster; although when she bites through the flesh of his arm, James describes her merely as baring her teeth like an animal rather than literally transforming into one (while such metamorphoses are easy for radio to achieve, the play's basis in realism makes it all the more frightening). The fact that it is the wife who is dangerous and monstrous makes the play, as Allison McCracken argues, a remarkable treatment of the sexual deviancy of women and its potential for social disruption (McCracken, 2002, 201). The play ends with the annihilation of what were the beginnings of a family unit ideal for postwar America: James kills Ellen and then himself.

A similar theme is pursued in "Stranger in the House," wherein the husband plans and ultimately succeeds in killing his wife after falling passionately in love with the ghost of a woman who used to live in their new home. Both works show the disruption of new homes and the destruction of the young couples that have bought them. In both plays the disruptive force is female (a werewolf and a ghost, respectively), just as in the other plays we have analyzed the men descend into "abnormal" relationships with an ancient female being from the depths of the earth, or with a female example of an "unnatural" evolution from the depths of a sealed cavern. In all these works, the deviancy of the female corrupts, changes, or kills the male protagonist.

To return to the implications of intertextuality in *The Mysterious Traveler*, "The Thing on the Fourble Board" is not the only *Quiet, Please* play that shares a theme with one of *The Mysterious Traveler* plays: "Behind the Locked Door" was first broadcast during the same week as *Quiet, Please*'s "The Oldest Man in the World" (May 22, 1949), another tale of prehistoric human life uncovered in the depths of the earth. A number of *The Mysterious Traveler* programs seem derivative, which raises issues of intertextuality in popular culture, but also perhaps reveals Arthur and Kogan's research and inspiration in their mastery of the formula of horror radio. There may even be a knowing degree of playful allusion at work. However, even if "Behind the Locked Door" owes something to "The Thing on the Fourble Board," it nevertheless has a distinctive quality in its story (the evocative idea of the lost wagon train), and excellent performances that distinguish it as an individual achievement.

Another example worthy of comparison with a precursor is "The Visiting Corpse" (January 9, 1944), which, like the *Lights Out* episode "Knock at the Door" (December 15, 1942), is a play about the murder of a mother-in-law. The highly effective "Knock at the Door" has a resentful wife murder her interfering mother-in-law, to whom her "mommy's boy" husband had always been beholden. The dead woman returns from the grave, knocking on the door of the basement where she was cast into a disused well. Her son, perturbed by his mother's disappearance, is delighted when she returns, and does not seem to notice that his reanimated mother is an undead corpse dripping water on the floor. He does, however, notice how cold she is, and insists that his wife lay in bed with his mother to warm her up. The extraordinary situation of a killer sharing the bed with her living dead victim is a profound moment of sexual horror similar to the climax of J. Sheridan Le Fanu's "Strange Event in the Life of Schalken the Painter" (1851)—an unjustly neglected horror story (*The Weird Circle*'s "The Wooden Ghost" [December 3, 1944] being a rare adaptation) in which the eponymous hero ventures into a crypt and sees his former sweetheart in bed with a demonic, undead man. "Knock at the Door" similarly uses sexualized horror to shocking effect, but it also functions as a powerful study of guilt (the reappearance of the mother may be a manifestation of the guilt that leads the killer to her gruesome suicide). The play also serves as a complex metaphor for the dysfunctional American family. Of course, the play is sardonically humorous, being perhaps the ultimate mother-in-law joke. Arch Oboler is aware of this when he takes the opportunity in his introduction to plead with any mothers-in-law that may be listening not to send him poison pen letters saying, "I'm really not responsible for what happens in the twisted brains of my characters, am I?"

In *The Mysterious Traveler*'s "The Visiting Corpse," it is not a wife but a husband who murders his mother-in-law. Albert (Mason Adams) is driven to despair by the fact that his mother-in-law (Connie Lumke) constantly comes to stay. In a fit of rage he murders her and stuffs her body into the large trunk she always brings with her. While his wife Louise (Adelaide Klein) descends into depression because of the disappearance of her mother, Albert's attempts to dispose of the trunk prove futile. The baggage always seems to find its way back to him, at which point he invariably hears the disembodied voice of the dead woman: "You've always wanted to get rid of me, Albert, to keep me away from my only child. But I refuse to give her up. I've come back, Albert, and I'm staying for good." Albert also refuses to give up, and eventually seems to have succeeded until, after a year has passed, a locked trunk appears at an auction that Albert and Louise attend. Even though the trunk has no name or initials on it, Albert becomes increasingly paranoid, as he believes he recognizes it. He is frantic in his bidding, and, once he has bought it, drags the trunk away in a furious panic. In his haste to depart, he falls down the stairs and is crushed to death by his acquisition. When opened, it is found to contain nothing but books.

The constantly reappearing trunk has itself become a central character in the play, and this uncanny item of luggage is reminiscent of the mysterious and homicidal chest bought at an auction in another *Lights Out* play, "The Story of Mr. Maggs" (December 1, 1942). However, "The Visiting Corpse" is more aptly compared to "Knock at the Door" because of its depiction of resentment and murder within a family. Although "The Visiting Corpse" does not exploit the bold sexualized horror of its *Lights Out* precursor, its strength lies in the central performance of Mason Adams and his guilty descent into paranoid delusion. "Knock at the Door" kept the same issue of crime and guilt at a certain level of ambiguity (like Shakespeare's *Macbeth*, one could argue), not only with the son interacting with his undead mother, but when, after the killer's suicide, we hear the dead mother-in-law laughing; if it had been pure delusion, there should be permanent silence. "The Visiting Corpse" functions as a more straightforward exploration of guilt and fatal delusion unquestionably within Albert's mind.

"The Visiting Corpse" is a simple but well-crafted play which is carried by Mason Adams' compelling performance. We find a similar phenomenon elsewhere in *The Mysterious Traveler* repertoire. "Death Has a Thousand Faces" (September 21, 1948; revived September 4, 1951), for example, is essentially a melodrama about a husband killing his wife. At first the husband, Horace, seems to be nothing but "a small, mild-mannered man in his late forties," the play opening with him receiving gifts in recognition of 25 years of service as parole officer at the state prison commission. Horace appears to be gentle and generous, and, professionally, on the side of law and order. However, the listener is offered an ominous signpost when told that Horace's wife Millie is 20 years younger than him. In the conventions of crime drama, such an age gap in a marriage usually sets the scene for adultery and/or murder. This is reinforced when one of Horace's gifts turns out to be a bomb, assumed to have been sent by a bitter former convict. The second scene opens in Horace's home, where the couple are heard bickering and Millie seems to have an unsettling interest in Horace's life insurance policy. The plot develops, with Horace drinking poisoned beer and suffering a heart attack. Horace's police colleagues begin to suspect Millie, to Horace's outrage. In the climactic scene, Horace and Millie, on vacation, explore a gigantic cavern (a location reminiscent of the cave in "Behind the Locked Door"). In this atmospheric setting Horace reveals his true character and intentions: it has all been an elaborate plan in which Horace has set up Millie to look like a murderer. He kills her, but confesses all while delirious. Over all, "Death Has a Thousand Faces" is a conventional melodrama of wife-murder, but the focus on Horace — he is in every scene, but we are very much "listening in" and are not privy to his confidence — makes it an intriguing example of a character endeavoring to achieve that ever-elusive "perfect crime."

Many of the offerings that lean toward the crime genre on *The Mysterious Traveler* have a mood, narrative and plot similar to the contemporaneous output of the cinema of film noir. There are tales of criminal expediency, such as "Christmas Story" (December 25, 1951), in which a man impersonates a car crash victim for financial gain; and tales of victims of circumstance, like "The Man Who Knew Everything" (October 9, 1951), about a man with a photographic memory embroiled in a world of crime. However, *The Mysterious Traveler* crime plays typically concern crimes within the family: "Survival of the Fittest" (January 10, 1950) is the melodramatic tale of the return of a long lost brother; "No One on the Line" (September 1, 1946) is about a jealous husband who kills the man he mistakenly believes is his wife's lover. Both "The Case of Charles Foster" (March 10, 1945) and "Change of Address" (January 22, 1952) are concerned with the vengeful actions of henpecked husbands; while "The Good Die Young" (February 27, 1944) is a surprisingly violent portrayal of a dysfunctional family, the play concerning a girl who attempts to kill her stepmother but is poisoned herself in the process.

If a number of plays in *The Mysterious Traveler* repertoire fit comfortably into the crime genre, other memorable works clearly belong to the area of science fiction. "Fire in the Sky" (August 28, 1951) is an apocalyptic tale in which a seemingly mad professor abducts a young family and traps them in a mine. He has, in fact, saved them from a comet which will wipe out the human race. The intention is that they will be the foundations of the reestablishment of human life on earth (although, this being *The Mysterious Traveler*, the listener is obliged to hope that in the 15 to 20 years before they are permitted to return to the surface they have not evolved into the creatures from "Behind the Locked Door"!). The play includes some deliberate allusions to *The Mercury Theater on the Air*'s "War of the Worlds" when the family tune into the radio and hear the unfurling catastrophe caused by the radioactive comet.

"The Green Plague" (June 17, 1952) is another science fiction piece in the repertoire that locates itself somewhere between *Mercury Theater*'s "War of the Worlds" and *Lights Out*'s "Chicken Heart." The story concerns a scientist who invents a growth formula for plants which proves so potent that the earth is overwhelmed with vegetation. The play uses radio news bulletins as a method of plot exposition, and at the end the protagonist is trapped in a radio station broadcasting to a dying human race on its ironically never-so-verdant planet.

Such overreaching scientists are inevitably punished. "The Man the Insects Hated" (October 7, 1944; revived July 27, 1947) presents the inventor of a pesticide who descends into madness when he comes to believe that insects have a vendetta against him. It is an atmospheric and unnerving play, predating the celebrated "Leiningen Versus the Ants" (*Escape*, January 14, 1948), a masterpiece of radio in which a hero battles against a swarm of ants.

One of *The Mysterious Traveler*'s finest science fiction offerings is "Strange New World" (February 19, 1952). In this play, the British submarine *Valiant* rescues Daniel Walker (Clifford Carpenter), an American co-pilot, from a life raft. Daniel recounts how the pilot, Pete (Lawson Zerbe), and he were flying a plane from Honolulu when a severe storm caused the plane to crash into the ocean. The men were then washed up on a seemingly uncharted island. The opening section of the play has already signposted the narrative journey of the story, with Pete reading a newspaper report of a recent nuclear test, and reacting less than enthusiastically, having been on one of the planes accompanying *Enola Gay* when the atomic bomb was dropped on Hiroshima. It comes as no surprise that after a few moments on the mysterious island, they discover a monster:

> It was like a nightmare. A nightmare you can't escape from, try as you will. There, fifty yards away in a clearing in the underbrush was a monster. A monster that baffled the eye and brain for a moment then began to come into focus and take shape. What I saw before me was a water crab, only a *hundred times larger* than the crabs that scurried along the beach. The monster crab in the clearing stood fully twenty feet high ... with legs the thickness of palm tree trunks ... the antennae on its frightening head was yards long ... and its eyes were unbearably evil, even from a distance ... its twelve legs carried it slowly but lightly through the underbrush...

This key section of exposition in "Strange New World" demonstrates Arthur and Kogan's skill with suspense narrative. The speech is enhanced by Clifford Carpenter's rather understated delivery, effectively accompanied by a cyclical looping flute refrain. The pilots discover they have landed on Bikini Atoll, and mutant sea life crawls from the Pacific. Pete is crushed by one of the ever-increasing number of monster crabs, and dies with an apocalyptic vision of monstrous sea creatures, inadvertently spawned by atomic testing, destroying the world. The title alludes to the "brave new world" (V:i.183) in Shakespeare's mysterious island play *The Tempest* (1611), but also the vision of dystopia in Aldous Huxley's *Brave New World* (1932), another dire projection of the world the human race might be making for itself. The British submarine crew regards Daniel as insane, but the play ends with the *Valiant* narrowly escaping from an attack by some mysterious "creature from the deep."

Tales of monsters from the depths of the sea surface in many of human civilization's ancient legends and continue to represent one of humanity's most fundamental fears. In its context, Arthur and Kogan's play reflects the radioactive monstrosity so familiar in the movies and popular fictions of 1950s science fiction. Nevertheless, "Strange New World" has a refreshing concision, and its lack of closure (the sea monsters are not even confronted, let alone destroyed) lends the work a sense of understated and enigmatic realism — quite an achievement given the excesses of its theme. The play is also interesting for what could be seen as its anti-nuclear skepticism at the start of the atomic weapons race, and is an oblique indication of the paranoid political context that the series itself will fall victim to.

"Murder in 2952" (April 29, 1952) is another play with monstrous animal life, albeit not created through human negligence but in a futuristic existence where distant planets have been colonized. The play has a decidedly surrealistic register, with its hallucinogenic dream apples and the hideous "surgeon birds" that speak English and delight in operating on earthlings, adjusting their senses and rearranging or adding to their limbs. John (Chris Carpenter), unjustly under arrest in a spaceship, is seriously injured when the vehicle crashes. The surgeon birds, finding the experiment "irresistible," do not give him four legs (like they have done with other "subjects"), but instead insert John's brain in the skull of the corrupt lieutenant who framed him before they scamper away, squeaking "Earthmen get angry so easily." The brain transplant theme had already featured in an episode of the sister series, *The Strange Doctor Weird*—"The Man Who Lived Twice" (January 30, 1945), in which a criminal has his brain transplanted after execution, only to be arrested for a capital offence a second time. As Dr. Weird concludes, he "has two graves and is buried in both of them."

For six months in 1945 (March through September), Robert A. Arthur and David Kogan were the writers on *The Sealed Book*, another horror series for Mutual. This show was consciously different from *The Mysterious Traveler* in that it tended to revel in the heightened melodrama of plot and performance, rather than focus on the "straight" and generally understated journeys the listeners shared with the Mysterious Traveler. Dunning describes *The Sealed Book* as "a corny takeoff on *The Witch's Tale*" (Dunning, 1998, 602), to which we could add that the cackling keeper of the sealed book is unmistakably similar to the host of *The Hermit's Cave*. *The Sealed Book* is characterized by its emphasized (some would say excessive) use of the Hammond organ.

"The Hands of Death" (March 18, 1945) is a typically heightened tale of horror which is "real" until the supernatural denouement. A rich gentleman in San Francisco, Edward Morlock, collects artifacts of infamous murders, such as a fifteenth-century headsman's axe and the dress of one of Jack the Ripper's victims. His brother Cain has returned to San Francisco, and in the first scene of the play we hear Cain strangle an innocent victim with his hideously distorted, immensely powerful hands. Edward sets up his brother to murder his butler and then contacts the police. After Cain's execution, Edward acquires the ultimate exhibits in his collection: the killer's severed hands and his butler's ashes, "the murderer and his victim." At the climax to the play, Edward fondles the severed hands, and, like the fate Peter Lorre suffers in *The Beast with Five Fingers* (Robert Florey, 1946), the dismembered items strangle their final—and for once deserving—victim to death. The play is full of extremely melodramatic characterization—the two brothers above all, who, both as irredeemably wicked as each other, giggle, groan and growl through their sadistic dialogue.

The Sealed Book also made use of science fiction as well as horror, but the results take just as much delight in exploiting the melodramatic potential of the speculative story. In "King of the World" (March 25, 1945), for example, a criminal acquires a serum that makes him superhuman, but it means, as it does for the protagonist (Ray Milland) of *X— The Man with X-Ray Eyes* (Roger Corman, 1963), his senses develop to such a phenomenal degree that even the sound of his heartbeat is agony. This affords the play and performers many opportunities for melodramatic effects.

"Broadway Here I Come" (June 17, 1945) is a tale marginally less melodramatic in characterization, but not in plot. The story presents a classic love triangle in which an adulterous couple murder the woman's husband. However, far from allowing the guilty to get away with the crime, the play follows a favorite plot in modern horror, traceable back to Ambrose Bierce's "An Occurrence at Owl Creek Bridge" (1891): the "shock" ending reveals that the killers did not survive the car crash they were involved in after committing the crime. Bierce's story may be the original instance of this plot device, and before "Broadway Here I Come" it was used to great effect on radio in Lucille Fletcher's "The Hitch-Hiker" (*Suspense*, September 2, 1942) and elsewhere in golden age horror radio.

A different but decidedly linked plot device has a play ending where it began. This occurs in *The Mysterious Traveler* story "New Year's Nightmare" (January 5, 1947), in which an amnesiac awakens in a hospital after having been involved in a car accident; the story ends with him awaking once again. It is a precursor to *Groundhog Day* (Harold Ramis, 1993), yet the fact that the protagonist himself is unaware makes the play derivative of the neverending nightmare that frames the narrative of the British horror film *Dead of Night* (Cavalcanti et al., 1945). Such nightmares of being caught in an endless cycle are, of course, a mainstay in traditional horror, as they explore the individual's fundamental fear of a lack or loss of control, as well as exploiting the apprehension, and even uncanny sensations, associated with an experience of *déjà vu*.

Another instance of the use of the endless cycle in golden age horror radio comes in "The House in Cypress Canyon." However, in this example the device seems almost redundant next to the genuine horror and social resonance of the central story. Perhaps the endless cycle in the play serves to expand and transform the violence and sexual deviancy of the story from an isolated incident (or "legend") into a phenomenon that will recur and repeat in an ever-developing America.

Hopefully, the analysis in this chapter has demonstrated how rich and eclectic was the repertoire of *The Mysterious Traveler* (and even *The Sealed Book*); certainly listeners cannot have been sure what genre they would enter when they tuned in. It is also evident that the plays did adhere to the formulae of various genres: this was not a series like *Quiet, Please* (but, then again, very little was ever like the subject of our next chapter). One exception is perhaps *The Mysterious Traveler* horror play entitled the "The Haunted Trailer" (June 3, 1952), a remarkable play in concept, even if it conceals its complexity in a consciously humorous execution. The story concerns Melvin (James Stevens), who goes on vacation in his new trailer. Stopping near a haunted railroad station, Melvin is visited by the plain-speaking ghost of a man called Spike Higgins (Larry Haines), who Melvin describes as looking like "a disreputable old man carved out of a chunk of London fog." Melvin is a rational man who does not believe in ghosts, which Spike takes as an invitation to demonstrate a variety of different voices and sounds—what he calls his "whole bag of ghostly tricks":

> SPIKE: Okay, I'll run through my repertory for ya: the ghostly groan, the dying scream, the scream of the banshee, the hollow footsteps, the squeaking door…
> MELVIN: No, no, anything but that…

The play offers the listener a delightful example of metadrama in golden age radio: radio drama that is self-referential. When the ghost demonstrates his repertoire of ghostly noises it is also an opportunity for radio to demonstrate, sequentially, its repertoire of eerie sound effects. It is also possibly satirical: one cannot help interpreting the "squeaking door" that Melvin so readily dismisses as a playful allusion to the creaking door of *Inner Sanctum Mysteries*. But "The Haunted Trailer" is even bolder in its post-modernist playfulness and narrative game-playing. Halfway through the play, Spike declares that he wants to listen to the radio program that all ghosts listen to. We then find ourselves listening to *The Mysterious Traveler* alongside Melvin, Spike and another ghost. "Sometimes he even scares *us*!" Spike declares. The second half of the play is a more conventional farce in the tradition of Noël Coward's *Blithe Spirit* (1941), with Louise (Shirley Blanc), Melvin's fiancée, unable to see the ghost. She becomes increasingly confused by Melvin's behavior, and ultimately breaks off the engagement. The play draws to a close with a return to self-reference:

> I can't get a job. Oh, look. Do any of the radio stations carrying my story need a good sound effects man for mystery programs? Oh, with me and Spike Higgins' ghost working together, we can guarantee authentic effects!

After this, the play concludes with Melvin and Spike demonstrating their eerie sound effects. It is not the most profound play in the history of horror radio, but its experiments in metadrama make it an inventive and satirical horror play *about* horror radio.

In tandem with their work on *The Mysterious Traveler*, Robert A. Arthur and David Kogan wrote *The Strange Doctor Weird* (1944–45), which also used Maurice Tarplin in the role of the host. Dunning describes the series as "a poor man's *Mysterious Traveler*" (Dunning, 1998, 643), not least because each program was only 15 minutes in duration. However, *The Strange Doctor Weird* proves an enlightening series to analyze, as one can see that in producing a 15-minute drama the formula remains the same as it does for the 30-minute format. Many of the stories are very similar, with *The Strange Doctor Weird* merely reducing the amount of exposition, and having fewer obligations to develop characterization or atmosphere. For example, "The House Where Death Lived" (November 7, 1944) concerns a bungled attempt to rob a wealthy recluse, the crooks ending up trapped in a room with the emaciated corpses of other failed criminals.

There is a parallel between this and other golden age horror plays where people are trapped in the isolated houses of lonely and eccentric men. *Lights Out*'s "Valse Triste" and *The Sealed Book*'s "Design for Death" (June 3, 1945) use roughly the same formula, but differ in that they both include a consciously sexual theme (whereas "The House Where Death Lived" is simply a tale of just desserts for criminals). "Beezer's Cellar" (*Quiet, Please*, October 10, 1948) is also similar, although this latter example develops the theme into the legendary, with the unfortunate burglars trapped in a cellar that proves to be a gateway to Hell. *The Strange Doctor Weird* itself revisits the same plot in "The Secret Room" (February 13, 1945) with a theme topical for a Second World War context, in which two escaping German prisoners-of-war find themselves stuck inside a room from which it is impossible to escape.

The Strange Doctor Weird demonstrates that a complete radio drama can easily fit into a 15-minute slot; but we should not think that even this is a minimal limit for a radio play of this genre. For instance, *The Strange Doctor Weird*'s "Beauty and the Beast" (January 16, 1945) seems to be a simple tale of a beautiful woman married to an unattractive older man who displays all the quirks and behavior that would seem to link him to a series of recent murders; it turns out, of course, that he is nobly protecting his schizophrenic wife. It is a tale so simple it would not only work comfortably on another 15-minute mystery program *The Unexpected* (1948), but could even be easily adapted into the 60-second format of *Ellery Queen's Minute Mysteries*.

Although "Beauty and the Beast" is typical of *The Strange Doctor Weird* repertoire in that it is a simple and/or simplified story, there are exceptions. In "Tiger Cat" (January 2, 1945), Arthur and Kogan are almost audacious. This 15-minute play is a tale of growth experimentation combined with a story of a pet's vengeance on the people who murdered its owner — enough material for a full hour's worth.

The Mysterious Traveler enjoyed enormous popularity in its heyday, which encouraged the further collaborative efforts of Arthur and Kogan. From 1948 to 1951 they co-produced a television version of *Dark Destiny*, while in November 1951 they launched the first of five issues of *The Mysterious Traveler Magazine*, a vehicle for stories by Arthur and other notable mystery writers. As for the radio show itself, in April 1952 the Mystery Writers of America awarded the Edgar Allan Poe award to *The Mysterious Traveler* for Best Mystery Radio Show. It is supremely ironic that later in the same year — September 1952 — *The Mysterious Traveler* made its last broadcast before being canceled. In fact, its own demise was almost as quick as that of many of the unfortunate victims it had luridly dispatched in its nearly decade-long repertoire of plays. In June 1950 the American Business Consultants published *Red Channels: the Report of Communist Influence in Radio and Television*. As Howard Blue explains, this "215-page report listed 151 performers, editors, and writers with 'subversive' views whom it accused of furthering the Communist cause" (Blue, 2002, 349). The work accused everyone from Norman Corwin to Burgess Meredith and Edward G. Robinson, and it also attacked Robert A. Arthur and David Kogan. As Blue clarifies, "Many of the accusations against the alleged subversives were totally inaccurate" (Blue, 2002, 350). Arthur and Kogan were members of the Radio Writers Guild, the leadership of which had strongly denounced the McCarthyite witch-hunts, only to see a blacklist of its own "pro-communist individuals" published by a faction within the Guild itself (Blue, 2002, 360). Welbourn E. Kelley of the Radio Writers Guild wrote a confidential report about pro-communism within the Guild that was made public. In the *New York Times*, Kelley is quoted as having "the greatest respect" for writers such as Kogan and many others who had been unfairly denounced:

> I have no doubt that these people will be harmed, an intention furthest from my mind. Therefore I respectfully ask that the statements made by me which somehow were omitted from the records now be made part of the record — namely, that I cannot say of my own knowledge that any member of the Guild is a communist [*New York Times*, August 28, 1952].

Although Arthur and Kogan cleared their names, the damage had been done, and *The Mysterious Traveler* made its last broadcast less than three weeks later. In the wake of this turmoil and bitterness, Robert A. Arthur did not write for radio again, although he did work for a while as co-producer for the radio show *Mystery Time*, and later enjoyed a modest career in television. In the 1960s he returned with a vengeance to his first love — popular fiction — ghost-editing many "Alfred Hitchcock" anthologies for adults and children. In the last few years of his life (he died in 1969) he was the creator of a hugely successful phenomenon in the history of popular culture: "The Three Investigators" series of detective novels for children. David Kogan became a portfolio manager, and although his creative writing career was tragically curtailed, he continued writing articles for financial publications.

9

The Unsettling Universe of Wyllis Cooper and Ernest Chappell: *Quiet, Please* (1947–1949)

We have already seen in an earlier chapter that although Arch Oboler made *Lights Out* indelibly his own, it was created by Wyllis Cooper and was promoted to national syndication under his lead. Oboler was genuine in 1951 when he argued that Cooper's *Lights Out* signified the beginning of radio drama as an original form. In *Oboler Omnibus* (1945), Oboler takes the opportunity to sing the praises of Cooper:

> Wyllis Cooper ... is the unsung pioneer of radio dramatic techniques; his mind was the first in American radio broadcasting which sought, in a sustained series of plays, to make use of the spoken word and the subtlety of sound effects, not in imitation of the theater, but with the wonderful intimacy of approach that is unique to "blind" broadcasting [Oboler, 1945, 21–22].

Oboler's praise was published two years before Cooper created *Quiet, Please*, which was similarly successful in its radio dramatic techniques, and which, in its stories and narration, created works of astonishing originality. *Quiet, Please* represents Cooper's return to horror and fantasy radio in the *Lights Out* mold, although any attempt to categorize the series feels like diminishing the scope of its achievement.

Wyllis Cooper had been an oilfield and railroad worker before becoming a newspaper reporter. From there, he broke into radio, working as a continuity editor for the NBC in Chicago, where he became a writer on various soap operas and created *Lights Out*. Cooper left *Lights Out* for Hollywood, where he wrote (usually as "Willis Cooper") *The Phantom Creeps* (Ford Beebe and Saul Goodkind, 1939), a 12-part serial in which the mad scientist Dr. Zorka (Bela Lugosi) invents a giant robot and turns entire armies into zombies; *Son of Frankenstein* (Rowland V. Lee, 1939), the final chapter in Universal's great trilogy of Frankenstein movies; and a number of the popular *Mr. Moto* movies featuring Peter Lorre. For the status Oboler attributes to Cooper, his Hollywood career is somewhat low-key, especially if we compare it to the impact of Hollywood's poaching of Orson Welles. Interestingly, around the same time Welles left radio for film, Cooper returned to the airwaves as the writer on the final, Welles-less season of *The Campbell Playhouse* (formerly *The Mercury Theater on the Air*), where he worked for Welles' erstwhile partner John Houseman. During the Second World War, Cooper made a contribution to the war effort. While Oboler continued his horror radio plays on *Lights Out* or *Arch Oboler's Plays* (but with stories or contextualization that alluded to or emphasized the war), Cooper was writer/producer of *The Army Hour* (NBC, 1942–45), a remarkable series of reality radio broadcasts that included live link-ups with soldiers in the battlefield.

Wyllis Cooper (courtesy Library of American Broadcasting, University of Maryland).

The first broadcast of *Quiet, Please* came on June 8, 1947, on Mutual. The series ran on a weekly basis, broadcast out of WOR on Mondays and Mutual on Wednesdays until September 1948, when it shifted to ABC until the series ended permanently with its last broadcast on June 25, 1949. Interestingly, before ABC acquired *Quiet, Please*, there existed a CBS memorandum (dated March 26, 1948) from the prominent CBS executive Davidson Taylor accompanying a number of recordings of the WOR *Quiet, Please* stating: "I like this show a lot and I believe we could get it if we want it." In total there were 106 thirty-minute broadcasts. Some 89 episodes exist as recordings, and recently all 106 scripts (the personal studio copies of Wyllis Cooper) have been brought to public light.

As much as *Quiet, Please* is a brilliant achievement in scriptwriting, a major part of the success of the series came from the contribution of its lead actor Ernest Chappell, the supporting cast, and the understated but supremely effective musical accompaniment of Albert Buhrmann. Ernest Chappell was a well-established radio announcer (and sometimes production manager) working on CBS programs such as *The Campbell Playhouse* during Orson Welles' final seasons (1938–40) and *The Adventures of Ellery Queen* (1942–44). He was also the question master on the children's quiz show *Are You a Genius?* (1942–43). With *Quiet, Please,* Cooper gave Ernest Chappell the chance to act, and the result was a revelation. Chappell proved himself to be versatile in accent and delivery. He was able to play an East European immigrant one week ("Tap the Heat, Bogdan," February 6, 1949) and a drunken barfly two weeks later ("Where Do You Get Your Ideas?" February 20, 1949); while he could create a comic persona ("Thirteen

Ernest Chappell performing on *Quiet, Please*, March 1949 (Photofest).

and Eight," April 26, 1948) as effectively as he could create the tremulous voice of "unutterable loneliness" ("My Son John," November 28, 1948). The versatile Chappell played everyone from a two-foot, three-inch midget ("Little Fellow," December 15, 1947) to the angel Azrael ("Shadow of the Wings," April 17, 1949).

In many of the *Quiet, Please* plays, the opening tone is conversational and disarming, with Chappell establishing a distinctive personality that attempts to hook the listener's attention immediately and comfortably, even if the play may build to a terrifying crescendo. According to Dunning, "The actors were told to play it straight: Cooper's pet hate was 'acting,' and he wanted [each story to be] related with a deadpan sense of 'here's how it happened'" (Dunning, 1998, 559). It is worth commenting that the deadpan mood has already been established before Chappell opens his mouth by the languid tones of the program's signature tune, Cesar Franck's *Symphony in D Minor*.

Cooper was a master of the opening line. Almost every episode of *Quiet, Please* begins with a sentence or two that hooks the listeners, commanding their attention and their curiosity. "Good Ghost" (October 24, 1948) opens thus: "I never did anything wrong in my life. That's why I was so upset when Schuster murdered me." The listener already knows from the title of the episode that the tale is probably about the supernatural, and the speaker confirms this. Consequently, the listener wants to know what happened and why. Also, the issue of blamelessness—the ghost declaring that he never did anything wrong in mortal life—raises the inherent drama of conflict in terms of justice or lack of it, and it also signals the issue of morality, a theme that is never far from any of Cooper's work.

As another example of the opening to a *Quiet, Please* play, let us consider "There Are Shadows Here" (May 10, 1948): "Look at my hands. They're trembling like a leaf. And there's nothing I can do to stop it either. Well, if you'd been through what I've been through ... [Pause] Last week, last Wednesday..." This is another exemplary demonstration of storytelling. The listener is drawn in by these simple and physical words, and wants to know the background to the story: what makes the speaker tremble uncontrollably, and would we agree that we also would be equally terrified if we experienced the same thing?

Cooper constantly experiments with the potential of the radio listener. As much as

Cooper creates distinct and disparate roles for Ernest Chappell, he also enjoys creating roles for the audience: passive listener, surreptitious eavesdropper, or even someone implicated in the action and story itself. At one extreme, "Pathetic Fallacy" (February 2, 1948) opens with Mr. Quinn, a computer scientist, holding a press conference and never making any direct link to the audience; whereas Porky in "The Thing on the Fourble Board" talks to each of us as individuals invited in "for dinner." Some episodes even include an acknowledgement that we are listening to the radio, and Cooper and Chappell enjoy the playfulness involved in referencing the form they are utilizing. A fine example of this comes at the start of "Anonymous" (September 19, 1948), when we are told to "Sit still and listen. Well, you've got nothing better to do, you're listening to the radio anyway." Chappell, in whatever fictional guise, addresses us at the other end of the wireless in what is sometimes a confessional relationship, which brings us back to the theme of morality.

In a contemporary review, Harriet Cannon reveals that, "Although in no sense a 'religious' show, [*Quiet, Please*] has some of its strongest supporters among the clergy" (*Writer's Digest*, May 1949). Certainly a number of *Quiet, Please* plays have a directly religious theme. The listeners heard tales imbued with Christian faith, such as "Rede Me This Riddle" (December 12, 1948), an evocative account of the gathering of the three magi before they commence their journey to Bethlehem. Two weeks later, *Quiet, Please* broadcast "Berlin, 1945" (December 26, 1948), a play in which a group of American troops in the ruins of Berlin are visited by Jesus Christ in the guise of a quiet, hungry soldier. Both of these plays are ingenious, meditative and somewhat gentle, but Cooper also produced plays with a quasi-religious morality as unsettling as the aforementioned plays were comforting. For example, "Good Ghost" may be humorous, but it is nonetheless a haunting depiction of the soul of an unjustly murdered man in limbo; while "Three Sides to a Story" (September 8, 1947) is a compelling and frightening tale of three lost souls walking along a desolate road recounting their lives for the final time as they approach, we gradually realize, the fires of hell on the horizon.

"Three Sides to a Story" is supremely well-structured. With regard to this, it is an interesting example in the *Quiet, Please* canon, for, although Ernest Chappell, as the character of Clyde, has the first and last word, the play strikes an exquisite balance between Chappell and the two other actors, Ralph Morgan (Victor) and Claudia Morgan (Frances). The story they recount is a tale of adultery and premeditated crime, and as such is very film noir in terms of plot: one is reminded of the more or less contemporaneous movies *Double Indemnity* (Billy Wilder, 1944) and *The Postman Always Rings Twice* (Tay Garnett, 1946). But it is, to an extent, a hybrid of film noir and Existentialism, inasmuch as it is reminiscent of another classic work from the same time period: Jean-Paul Sartre's *Huis Clos* (1944), often translated as *No Exit*. The three central characters in *Huis Clos* are, like Cooper's, trapped in the afterlife. Each of them is condemned to endlessly recount their lives of corruption and moral cowardice, and eternally judge each other. Yet in Sartre's brand of Existential philosophy it is clear that the three souls are *self-condemned* in a Hell of their own devising, to the extent that when they are offered a genuine chance to escape they refuse to take it, thus remaining in a Hell of "other people" for eternity. In contrast, the three characters in "Three Sides to a Story" have evidently been judged and condemned, with no chance of reprieve. Even more frightening, their respective crimes were foiled, so they were not even condemned for their actions but for their *intentions*:

> I guess you don't actually have to commit murder to be guilty of it. If you think about it, and plot and plan it, well, that's enough. You get punished anyway. You know what that big fire we're walking into is? We know.

With that final speech of the play, we realize that we have been privy to their final 30 minutes of purgatory before they step into eternal, fiery damnation. In "Three Sides to a Story," Cooper, like Sartre, takes a literal interpretation of an arcane concept of Hell and places contemporary people into it. The subject was treated similarly by May Sinclair over 20 years before in her short story "Where Their Fire Is Not Quenched" (1923), in which a tale of adultery and realistic detail startlingly evolves into a disturbing depiction of damnation in the afterlife. While this formula may be an isolated instance in the works of Sinclair and Sartre, it is one of Cooper's characteristic devices. In "Beezer's Cellar" (October 10, 1948), one of the most *Lights Out*–style tales in the series, a gang of burglars find themselves trapped in a cellar that seems to come alive and opens up into the pits of hell. It is worth noting that in these examples evil is punished. In fact, Cooper merely adheres to the approved resolution in crime and mystery drama: crime does not pay, and criminals always get their just desserts. It just so happens that rather than being apprehended *Dragnet*-style, some of Cooper's wrongdoers find themselves condemned to an even more inescapable fate: hell itself or simply utter oblivion. In "Nothing Behind the Door" (June 8, 1947), the first *Quiet, Please* broadcast, a gang of bank robbers break into an astronomy laboratory to hide their loot and are abnegated when they step inside a vault of pure "nothingness."

As well as exploring the concepts of hell and antimatter, *Quiet, Please* also presents horror stories that draw on the more conventional traditions of popular horror and science fiction: vampires, Egyptian tombs, monsters from the deep, time travel, and so on. But the stories, more often than not, feature an ingenious twist. In "Let the Lilies Consider" (June 28, 1948), flowers start to speak, but they are not like the monstrous plant that imitates humans in "Green Splotches" (*Suspense*, March 31, 1950). Cooper's lilies acquire the human emotion of love, erotically wailing "love you, love you" as they bewitch and eventually abduct the man who planted them. In "Gem of the Purest Ray" (May 17, 1948), the lost city of Atlantis does not merely exist, but is inhabited by gill-necked citizens who conspire to reclaim the earth. In "Take Me Out to the Graveyard" (November 3, 1947), we spend an evening with a taxi driver bemused by the number of requests made for the cemetery. The driver — some 50 years after Ambrose Bierce's "An Occurrence at Owl Creek Bridge" (1891), but 50 years before *The Sixth Sense* (M. Night Shyamalan, 1999) — does not realize until the end of the story that he himself is dead. *Quiet, Please* is a universe where a man can discover a model of the earth in a Mexican temple, affect the climate of the whole planet when he handles it, and destroy the world when the model is dropped to the ground ("The Man Who Stole a Planet," July 26, 1948). The last broadcast of *Quiet, Please* ("Quiet, Please," June 25, 1949) is similarly apocalyptic, but in a style more earnest: it is a tale from Mars, warning Earth of the perils of self-destruction. But Cooper also wrote plays that are sentimental and lyrical. The narrator of "In the House Where I Was Born" (May 24, 1948) is a dead soldier wandering through his memories in a stream-of-consciousness as poetical as Oboler's "Johnny Got His Gun" is polemical.

In contrast to most of the other programs we have so far studied, *Quiet, Please* cannot be classified simply as a horror show. John Dunning describes it as "outstanding dark fantasy" (Dunning, 1998, 559), which is perhaps a satisfactory description, although some of its more sentimental and humorous examples are not particularly "dark." For example, the title of "It Is Later Than You Think" (August 2, 1948) clearly alludes to the opening catchphrase of *Lights Out* that Oboler added to Cooper's "Lights out, everybody!" when he took over the show, and is therefore quite possibly a playful jibe. The story takes the phrase at face value, and far from the foreboding *momento mori* of the *Lights Out* preamble, it is an amusing tale of a soldier who discovers he can travel in time by adjusting his wristwatch. Without doubt, the fact that the listener may never know what kind of story they are about to hear enhances the experience of listening to *Quiet, Please*. In a way, this aspect of suspense means that the performance begins before the broadcast has commenced, when the listeners are waiting for the wireless to warm up or are retuning the dial in anticipation.

For the sake of this study, we will concentrate on the episodes of *Quiet, Please* that fall within the broad domain of horror. In some instances, Cooper takes classic horror themes such as lycanthropy, or the use of locales such as Egypt, and proceeds to give them a singular and sophisticated treatment. Lycanthropy can work very well on radio—just consider *Suspense*'s "The House in Cypress Canyon" (December 5, 1946)—and *Quiet, Please* makes effective use of it. In "Be a Good Dog, Darling" (September 22, 1947), a misogynist encyclopedia salesman discovers how to turn his wives into dogs by reading the section on "Magical Formulas" in Volume Six of the encyclopedia he sells. Cooper delights in adding an element of satire to the tale, with Grover, the salesman, declaring, "I suppose that I am probably the only encyclopedia salesman in the world who reads his product." There is also an undertone of sexual satire, as Grover marries serially and keeps his female "dogs" on a leash before being transformed into a "nasty, squalling little mongrel" himself when his final wife discovers the incantation for lycanthropic transformation.

Less humorous but no less effective is "My Son John" (November 28, 1948). In this play, Chappell plays the father of a young man who was killed in the war. His despair sends him to a mystic who explains that he can, if he wishes, summon his dead son back to life. In a pitch-black room, the voice of John (Warren Stephens) is heard, regretting his resurrection and urging his father to keep the lights off, as he did not know how he died. So far the tale seems to be a reworking of W. W. Jacobs' classic short story "The Monkey's Paw" (1902), a favorite for dramatization, while the only direct intertextual reference has been to Shakespeare, the play opening with a direct quote from *Henry IV Part I* (III.1.53): "I can call spirits from the vasty deep." However, the play's next literary reference surprises the listener. When the father switches on the light, his son is revealed as a large, gray wolf. His son John was not killed as a consequence of battle, but by a ravenous wolf who was, in fact, none other than Count Dracula: "Most people think that Bram Stoker invented him. That he's fiction. But he isn't." John—variously transforming into a wolf, a bat or a cat—preys on the people of New York City. After considering exterminating his undead son, the father allows himself to be vampirized and joins John as a Great Dane, ending the play by threatening the listener: "Maybe my son John and I will come hunting you some night." In this story Cooper takes a mainstay of horror and gives it a twist: the first half of the play functions as an occult tale in the W. W. Jacobs style, exploiting the desperation of a man who has lost all that he loved. After this establishment, the surprising Dracula twist — occurring at the midway point of the play — does not take the story into the typical realm of Transylvanian cliché, but into the contemporary world outside the window of the urban listener.

"Whence Came You" (February 16, 1948) functions in a similar way, although rather than updating a horror myth for the contemporary world, its contemporary protagonist is ultimately trapped in the arcane realm of legend. The play uses a locale ideal for a tale of horror, as it is set in Egypt among Egyptologists. Chappell plays an archaeologist called Austin who visits his friend, Abe Feldman (Murray Forbes), who is about to excavate an ancient tomb. One might expect a simple tale of reanimated mummies, but Cooper gives us one of his most remarkable and unsettling achievements. Austin is stalked by a mysterious Egyptian woman, "the one most beautiful woman I have ever seen in all my life," whom Abe describes as "Cleopatra." He is also haunted by the odors of myrrh, spikenard and cinnamon, spices used in ancient Egyptian funeral rites. Eventually, after a meticulous establishment and consolidation of atmosphere and suspense, Austin is trapped in the opened tomb, where he finds the mummified corpse of a man with a giant hawk's head: the body of the god Osiris. On the wall is a picture of the daughter of Osiris and Isis; it is, of course, the woman pursuing Austin. With the exit blocked, Austin goes deeper into the excavated tomb and finds himself next to a sarcophagus on which is inscribed: "I have freed you, Austin. Now free me." Above it is a picture of the mysterious woman, but this time with the head of a hawk; the monstrous god is alive beneath the stone lid. The play ends in a haunting stasis, with Austin terminally trapped, in dying lamp light, but afraid to open the sarcophagus. "Whence Came You" ends on the cusp of reanimation, and is all the more effective because Cooper mixes aspects of Egyptian mythology with the grotesquely erotic: when Austin first sees the woman, he is so sexually attracted to her that his knees tremble. Ultimately, however, she becomes a mortifying image of abjection stirring into life beneath the coffin lid. One of Cooper's best devices is to combine the mythic or arcane with the real and familiar. In "My Son John," Dracula's "children" are placed in New York City, while in the Egyptian play an American archaeologist finds his name carved into a sarcophagus thousands of years old, his dreadful fate being to love an incarnation of ancient myth.

Cooper employs excellent structuring devices in creating 30-minute radio drama. We have already considered the structural balance in "Three Sides to a Story," and have seen how in "My Son John" Cooper implements a twist exactly halfway through the play. In "Whence Came You" he develops suspense in a number of ways. Early on, Austin cautions the listener not to expect an eerie apparition when Austin returns to his hotel room after seeing the enigmatic woman in the bar, because this "isn't a ghost story." The recurrent description of the odor of spices, and the final half of the play, set within the dark and musty tomb, are evocative instances that demonstrate "theater of the imagination" at its most effective. Meanwhile, the piercing death scream of Abe, and the various accents and emphases of Albert Buhrmann's music provide classic moments of horror radio melodrama. Cooper strengthens the script of "Whence Came You" with a technical knowledge of archaeology and Egyptian mythology. Throughout the *Quiet, Please* oeuvre, Cooper lends an authenticity to his stories through an evidently researched contextualization. As in the best science fiction, the succinct explanations of the computer in "Pathetic Fallacy" (February 2, 1948), the electron microscope in "One Hundred Thousand Diameters" (June 7, 1948), and oil drilling technology in "The Thing on the Fourble Board" (August 9, 1948) are enough to let you believe in Chappell's portrayal of scientists or engineers. Similarly, the systematic ridiculing of the jargon of hard-boiled detective fiction in the opening of "Never Send to Know" (March 8, 1948) strengthens the authenticity of the private investigator protagonist, while the irritating quoting/misquoting of Shakespeare in "The Hat, the Bed and John J. Catherine" (June 11, 1949) makes you accept the self-important and pretentious wannabe actor of the title. The latter is often cited as one of Cooper's weakest plays, while "The Thing on the Fourble Board" is frequently regarded as the supreme achievement of horror radio as a whole. I would argue that "One Hundred Thousand Diameters" is also worthy of note, although no recording exists. I would like to analyze the script of this play before providing a close reading of "The Thing on the Fourble Board," which Dunning describes as "a classic shocker, as terrifying as anything the medium has produced." (Dunning, 1998, 559)

In "One Hundred Thousand Diameters" (June 7, 1948), the histologist and bacteriologist Verne Judd (the name is probably a playful allusion to Jules Verne, pioneer of science fiction) is the active narrator in a tale of the abuse of science. The play opens with a fine example of a horror "hook" speech that involves the listener:

> Just sit perfectly still. Better keep your hands in your lap, there. And don't move your feet. Just be still. (A PAUSE) It'll go away in a second: all you have to do is play dead! And don't look at it! Just sit stiiiiilllll ... (A PAUSE) It's fascinatin'... you look at it and you see all kinds ... hasn't got any eyes but it sees you — it hears you — wiggles along the floor toward you...

The program, like every week, has already requested us to be "Quiet, please," and now we are asked to remain totally still. The implication is that we are in mortal danger, but the opening also serves to create an ideal, attentive radio listener. Our interest — "fascination" even — is also engaged when we wonder what this lethal, eyeless entity wiggling towards us is. Soon afterwards, Judd introduces himself and makes it clear that he is "not a doctor, not a mad scientist," but merely a man who looks through microscopes. Be that as it may, Judd's friend Kurt certainly *is* a mad scientist. Before we meet him, Verne provides a concise explanation of lens microscope and electron microscope technology. The combination of the experiential horror opening and the knowledge conveyed in Judd's succinct lecture sufficiently equips the listener to enter Kurt's laboratory. After some convivial dialogue and gin and tonic, Judd describes Kurt's invention:

> An electron microscope takes up a good part of a small room. It looks like a modernistic drill-press, or one of those super-science instruments you see in *Stupefying Stories*, or something. The power unit takes up a lot of room, too, and the microscope itself stands taller than a man. This was the biggest one I'd ever seen — and it was different. Usually, there's a bulge in the middle of the tube, about table height, with a number of holes through which you look down at the magnified image on the fluorescent screen. That part was missing on this one. Instead, there

was a thing built into it that looked ... well, something like a strange sort of coffin, and there was only one eyepiece leading into the coffin.

This example of narration serves a number of functions. It continues the scientific aspect of the story — a tale told by a histologist — while simultaneously developing the story as horror. The reference to "*Stupefying Stories*" is ironic, as this particular *Quiet, Please* play falls precisely into the pulp science fiction tradition, albeit given the Wyllis Cooper treatment. It is the addition of the strange "coffin" that signals that Kurt's invention is an abuse of science. Furthermore, the coffin is an evocative icon of horror, and Cooper's choice therefore consolidates the play as horror drama. The listeners know that no good can come from that coffin, and they are proved right.

Kurt's invention, it turns out, does not enlarge the image of the specimen beneath the electron microscope; within a mysterious fluid inside the coffin, it enlarges the specimen itself. Kurt demonstrates with a minuscule section of mosquito wing, enlarging it into something "a foot thick and tough as Plexiglass." Like the best of mad scientists, Kurt dreams of assisting humankind by building indestructible ships from the chitin of gigantic beetles, and rearing massive bees for honey production. But, this being 30 minutes of horror radio, the negative consequences are immediately forthcoming: something living is lurking inside the coffin — Kurt has unwittingly released gargantuan viruses into the world. The idea of growth experimentation and/or massive animal life was well-established in science fiction by this time, in novels like H. G. Wells' *The Food of the Gods* (1904), and in explorations on *Lights Out* in "Chicken Heart" (March 10, 1938), "Spider" (May 18, 1943) and Cooper's own "Amoeba" (December 4, 1935). *Quiet, Please* itself will go on to produce "Tanglefoot" (June 4, 1949), a tale of two plumbers' encounter with increasingly larger generations of flies, culminating in a fly "bigger than a Shetland pony" they call Louise (despite it being male), to which they feed the listener, trapped on "manpaper." "Tanglefoot" is an effective tale of the ironic grotesque, but the global implications at the end of "One Hundred Thousand Diameters" and "Chicken Heart" mark them as explorations of a science fiction sub-genre in a style that makes the works precursors to the nuclear age/Cold War anxieties of *Tarantula* (Jack Arnold, 1955), *The Incredible Shrinking Man* (Jack Arnold, 1957) and *The Blob* (Irvin S. Yeaworth, Jr., 1958).

Whenever *Quiet, Please* is discussed, the one play mentioned time and again is "The Thing on the Fourble Board." What is more, it is often cited when pollsters are looking for the greatest examples of horror radio, or even radio drama as a whole. This play came just over halfway through the *Quiet, Please* run, being the sixtieth effort of the 106-play series. It is many things at the same time, and exemplary in many ways. It possesses a faultless structure, and presents Chappell and the supporting cast at the height of their powers. Chappell plays Porky, an affable former oilfield worker who invites the listener to sit down and meet his wife Maxine (who prefers to be called Mike). Mike is busy in the kitchen, so Porky begins to tell us his story instead. Porky's tale has a quality shared by many of the best horror offerings in popular culture: it is, at one and the same time, fresh and familiar. The narrative the play presents feels as original as its somewhat puzzling title (at least puzzling for listeners not familiar with oilfield engineering), and yet the story is really a take on the pan-cultural "monster from the depths" legend. Traditionally, these would be associated with the sea: the legendary kraken. But Cooper's version initially aligns the story with modern engineering, with a discussion of the three-mile-deep drill-hole plumbed by Pure Oil in Wyoming. Cooper's use of modern drilling technology in the oil industry fulfils the function of establishing authenticity. This foundation serves as a rational way to take the listener into the secret depths of the earth, and to lead the story into the supernatural. Porky reflects, "I don't think there's an oilman in the world that don't wonder one time or another what's down there besides rock and oil and gas." Cooper's own experience working on oilfields obviously became a useful creative inspiration; like the oilmen in Porky's narration, the experience set him "wondering" about the depths of the earth. "A Mile High, a Mile Deep" (August 17, 1947) is about a deep shaft miner who discovers Mother Earth herself; and in "The Oldest Man in the World" (May 22, 1949) a living Neanderthal caveman is discovered deep inside a cave in France. But the Thing Porky and his work associate Billy discover is far more abstract and chilling than either of these.

After the opening mixture of technology and speculation, the play proceeds in what is almost classic ghost story mode. It is night and Porky sits alone by the drill site frying pork chops on a fire. Billy (Dan Sutter), a geologist, joins him, and their exchange of dialogue establishes the atmosphere of an isolated drill site in the middle of the night, enhanced by the mental picture and sound of the frying pork chops. As in the classic horror or ghost story formula, Billy thinks he hears something that Porky, inevitably, cannot. The exchange also continues to establish authenticity with some technical discussion of the drilling. But, true to horror form, there is something decidedly unusual about the particular hole they are working on. The drill hole breaks the rules of normality, as it has water at the bottom of it. We are about to dive into the supernatural. The fact that the water is like that from "the bottom of the ocean" signifies that whatever has been released from the depths is in the kraken tradition. This early section of dialogue also contains ironic sign-posting: Billy bewails his "tough luck"; and his following line, "I'm dead," may mean that he is tired and hungry, but will shortly prove horribly prophetic.

In an ingenious marriage of form and content, the narrative develops in the same way as drilling for oil — gradually more and more is revealed as we get deeper and deeper into the horror. It becomes clear that there is something on the fourble board (which Porky explains is a platform on the derrick or drilling tower) 80 feet above the ground. Billy was the first person to hear a noise, but now Porky and the radio listener can hear the scrape of metal. Then Billy discovers a gold ring in the core dug up from thousands of feet beneath the earth, taking the listener into the fantastic. The next development — the next turn of the drill, as it were — takes the listener into the horrific. In fact, it was enough to make Porky "pretty near jump out of my pants." The two men find a severed finger covered in mud. It is heavy, like stone, and when they rub it clean it is invisible. The two men, profoundly unnerved, down a pint of gin. Porky falls asleep and is troubled by "awful dreams — black widow spiders crawling all over me with gold rings on their legs." Awakened by the sound of Billy falling to his death from the fourble board, Porky sees his friend lying next to him with a broken neck and his little finger missing.

The narrative then offers us a respite as Cooper releases the tension before returning with the terrifying denouement. The sun rises, and the rest of the drilling crew return, followed by a policeman investigating Billy's death, who summarily labels it "another accident." The men return to work, but the respite from horror proves short lived, as Ted, the foreman, is crushed by the two-ton travelling block, the cable of which Porky sees snap like a piece of string between invisible fingers. The oil rig is abandoned, but Porky, driven by curiosity and undaunted by danger (like any stereotypical horror hero), equips himself with a revolver and returns to the site two days later to solve the mystery. By this point in the narrative the need for authenticity has passed, as we are into the fourth and final stage of the story. Consequently, the location of the story is now described purely in terms appertaining to Gothic horror, with the abandoned oil well looking as desolate and dismal as a "skeleton."

Up on the fourble board Porky encounters the "thing" made of invisible stone, and vainly fires at it. It is only when he throws paint (blood red, of course) onto it that all is revealed, and Porky's description represents the climax of the tale:

> The face of a little girl, frightened. Crying with hunger and terror. Hands like a human being. And a finger ... missing from the left hand. And a body ... Well, I'll not tell you about that. I told you how I'm scared of spiders. But I knew where it came from. It'd come from the bowels of the earth, come riding up on the drill pipe as we yanked it out of the well. Come to an alien world. And was lost. It stood there dripping with red paint, blood red from head to foot, like some horrible dream. And it put its hand on my arm. Its hand was stone. Living, moving stone. And it looked into my eyes. And mewed like a lost kitten.

This may be the climax to the tale, but it is not the ending. Cooper provides an audacious twist. When someone beholds one of the Great Old Ones in H. P. Lovecraft's Cthulhu mythos they are driven insane. When a man looked at the Medusa of Greek legend he is turned to stone. When the stone Thing in Cooper's play puts its hand on Porky's arm and looks plaintively into his eyes we are witnessing not ultimate horror but love — mad love, certainly, but nonetheless love at first sight. Porky confides his feelings to the listener, although some of the ellipses he includes significantly leave shocking details unsaid:

> I didn't want to see its body — I can see that in my nightmares. But its face ... I can't help wanting to see that pathetic, little girl face. I'm afraid maybe I've fallen ... Ah, but it's very beautiful. And when it's well made-up, it's ... But making it up, rubbing greasepaint on a stone face that looks at you and smiles and it makes sounds like a lost kitten ... I can disguise the body in long dresses. She can't hear very well and when she's hungry, I have to stay out of her way.

At the end, Porky commands us to sit still: it is obviously dinnertime, and "I want you to meet my wife. Or rather ... my wife wants to meet you." The listener — each and every one of us — will be the next victim. It's a twist ending Cooper uses in other plays, but never so effectively as here.

"The Thing on the Fourble Board" is an amalgamation of many things. Partly the play takes its place in the traditions of myth and horror: Maxine is a monster from the depths, but her living stone body makes her a modern Golem. The oil drilling team unleashes a Pandora's box of evil and are what Noël Carroll would term horror "overreachers" (Carroll, 1990, 118), using science and technology to explore realms that should be left alone. The play is also a precursor to subsequent works of horror and science fiction. Like "One Hundred Thousand Diameters," it is the creature-feature territory of alien monstrosity, although the narrative emphasizes that we are alien to this million-year-old species of earthling. Moreover, its part-human, part-spider appearance reminds us of one of the most chilling incarnations of the monster in *The Thing* (John Carpenter, 1982), another monster unleashed — as in the original film version (Christian Nyby, 1951) — from ancient depths (the polar ice of Antarctica).

Such examples aside, there is a unique and unsettling stamp on Cooper's play. Maxine is a hybrid of the vulnerable and the fatal: Porky's "marriage" to it implies a sexual union even though it has the face (and disembodied voice) of a "pathetic little girl" and the body of a spider, which presents to the listener a hideous mixture of pedophilia and bestiality. Porky has already told us of his arachnophobia, and so he hides the spider body beneath "long dresses." Maxine is not just a femme fatale, but what Barbara Creed in her Kristevan analysis of horror would call a *femme castratice,* or abject woman (Creed, 2000, 64–70). Beneath Maxine's skirts lurks the ultimate *vagina dentata,* which Porky knows is there but conceals in his love affair with her upper body. The fact that he sees the lower body in his "nightmares" perhaps suggests a semiconscious or nighttime connection: they have been married for 20 years, and one assumes there must have been an attempt at consummation. The spider-human hybrid is reminiscent of the spider Anansi trickster of African and Caribbean folklore; but evidently Porky is the trickster, having lured the listener into his home. Porky tells us that he has to avoid Maxine when she's hungry (enter the listener), otherwise Porky would become like one of his pork chops. The names are interesting here: in the story we hear Porky's pork chops sizzling, and at the end we realize that we are destined to be Mike's meat. Not only do we have the porcine living with the arachnid, but there is a curious ambivalence in the Thing's names. She is called Maxine but prefers the male nomenclature of Mike. Cooper employs the same device in "Tanglefoot" when the listener is fed to a giant male fly called Louise. Cooper uses sexual ambivalence for the purposes of horror, in a similar way to the sexual schizophrenia of the sheriff in David Mamet's *Prairie du Chien* (1985), or Norman Bates in the novel *Psycho* (Robert Bloch, 1959) is used to enhance the horror of the respective tales (Bloch's novel would not work if Norman became, say, Mr. Bates the elder). Transgression of gendered identity is perceived as inherently horrific. Rather like Alfred Hitchcock's film version of *Psycho* (1960), "The Thing on the Fourble Board" is something of a gruesome joke when the full picture becomes clear. Norman Bates dresses up as his mother while living with her mummified corpse, and Porky — another affable lunatic — marries a monster and finds victims to feed to her. Both Bates and Porky are delusional madmen who attempt to turn their nightmarish existences into the semblance of American domestic normality.

"The Thing on the Fourble Board" makes exquisite use of an oppositional structure: Maxine/Mike is both beautiful and hideous to Porky, who pities and fears her at the same time. Over all, the story demonstrates a perfectly executed oscillation between the horrific and the comic, the rational and ridiculous. The script also demonstrates masterful structure and storytelling in the development of character, establishment of locale and the subtle use of ironic lines ("Everybody's scared of somethin'. Me, spiders scare the tar out of me," Porky reveals early in the play). It is interesting to note that Cooper's directing copy of the script indicates that he added a line at the last minute (i.e. during final rehearsal): after scribbling the 19 minute 30 second mark on the script, Cooper adds, "I told you how I'm scared of spiders." The line, in fact, contradicts Porky's previous line —

"And a body ... I'll not tell you about that"—but becomes an effective moment of horror, as the line suggests and disturbs by inference more than it describes or illustrates. The play also makes excellent use of radio: this absurd monster—an invisible girl-spider made of living stone—can easily be brought to life in the listener's imagination through radio. Moreover, as John Dunning observes, when Cecil Roy finally gives the creature a voice—crying like a small child or mewing like a cat—"the blood chills" (Dunning, 1998, 559). "The Thing on the Fourble Board" was only broadcast once, and it remains a moment of radio brilliance. Wyllis Cooper would rehearse each *Quiet, Please* play on Friday and again on Sunday before broadcasting the performance in the evening. This means that the plays are fresh and sharp but not over-rehearsed. But the plays are unmistakably "live": the sound of Ernest Chappell quietly giggling at the end of "The Thing on the Fourble Board" merely enhances what will always remain a vivid, theatrical experience.

Wyllis Cooper's scripts for *Quiet, Please* demonstrate excellence in the area of structure, even if Cooper himself prefers to highlight the importance of his "twists": "Plot should consist of a twist rather than a formalized structure" (*Writer's Digest*, May 1949). Despite the ingenuity of some of his stories, Cooper also emphasizes that character is even more important than narrative: "I don't believe in too strong a story line because it's apt to be too hard for the listener to keep in mind.... The charm in radio consists of good characterization" (*Writer's Digest*, May 1949). With the talent of Ernest Chappell and the supporting casts, Cooper's *dramatis personae* are given outstanding characterization, and his terse lines and dialogue are delivered in a highly effective fashion. The best of his work seems highly complex. This is especially the case with the works that are philosophically playful, where Cooper takes an idea and extrapolates it, whether it be a scientific invention, or in plays such as "Bring Me to Life" (which explores scriptwriting) and "Where Do You Get Your Ideas?" (which features Cooper playing himself). Additionally, Cooper ensures that the principal characters in each episode almost always enjoy a technical knowledge or an experiential reality. However, despite the complexity of the plays, the best of them have an underlying simplicity. Cooper is a master of radio form who understands and develops his own approach to the 30-minute radio play structure. Even when he demonstrates his skill at using scientific knowledge, he does so in order to imbue his characters with authenticity. Aside from this, many of the plays adhere to the genre of horror radio and its structural formality; the suspense, the moments of shock and spine-tingling revelation, the opening line and closing line, and everything in between are all carefully deployed and manipulated.

Wyllis Cooper brought his mastery of the craft of radio drama to bear on *Whitehall 1212* (NBC, 1951–52), a series of factual plays revolving around the infamous "Black Museum" of New Scotland Yard, and arguably a more compelling series than the contemporaneous vehicle for Orson Welles, *The Black Museum* (BBC, 1951). But, as John Dunning argues, tying Cooper to "a set of facts" (Dunning, 1998, 721) could not do anything other than restrict the creativity of the man who created *Quiet, Please*. Cooper ventured into television as the writer/narrator of *Stage 13* (1949) and *Volume One* (1950), which were in the area of horror and mystery but were both short-lived. One suspects that the limitations of early television—and the visual medium as a whole—compromised Cooper's creativity differently but just as critically as *Whitehall 1212* had done.

Also, in the 1950s Cooper began to do battle with failing eyesight, which did not affect his creativity but probably did compromise his confidence and, unfortunately, his image as an aspiring television writer.

The extraordinary body of work that is *Quiet, Please* would never be far from Cooper's mind. Many radio programs made the shift to television, and those that did not aspired to. *Quiet, Please* was no exception. In 1953, Cooper and Chappell discussed the possibility of turning *Quiet, Please* into a television series. In a letter to Chappell, Cooper wrote:

> I don't believe we should do much pictures on it at all: mostly your voice and the others as in radio, with a few shots of the people as needed, and nice closeup shots of things that are important to the story... [April 10, 1953].

Chappell responded positively: "Makes a lot of sense. Instead of putting the voice to the picture, put the picture to the voice" (letter to Wyllis Cooper, April 14, 1953). Despite their mutual enthusiasm about the possibilities of television adaptation, an objective reading of these letters merely reveals that *Quiet, Please* is quintessentially radio; and, even if they did not openly acknowledge it, both men constantly infer it. The draft document (June 2, 1953) that Chappell went on to write as a basis for pitching *Quiet, Please* to television companies cannot help but make the same inference:

> "Quiet, please!" on TV will be a true extension of what has been only heard before. It is believed that the function of television is to *extend* the scope of the stories.... The television viewer will assume the same place formerly occupied by the listener.... The television versions will be interpretations, rather than excursions in a new, untried direction.

One can imagine that the television executives who received the document would have found the suggestions and tone at best backward-looking and, at worst, somewhat insulting. This would have been compounded by Chappell's suggestion that, "whenever feasible, actors previously chosen for the radio version will again be employed," an idea one can imagine most television producers being opposed to, especially when Chappell declares that the old *Quiet, Please* radio actors are most familiar with the program's "philosophy."

However, nothing sums up the problem better than a sentence in Cooper's letter to Chappell where he suggests that the television *Quiet, Please* would have "a screen that is black most of the time while you are talking, and which comes to life only occasionally..." (April 10, 1953). If Cooper had been given the chance to witness *Quiet, Please* produced like this, he might have become as great a television innovator as he was for radio. More likely, however, it would have been a dreadful mistake — an irritating and confusing misuse of new technology, and glaring evidence that *Quiet, Please* was untranslatable into any other medium. Perhaps this reveals that Cooper and Chappell misunderstood television. Certainly there is no question that Cooper underestimated it. In the same letter, Cooper declares that his idea of a mainly black screen would be an immediate success with the American public, who are definitely "getting tired of TV": "I believe it would make QP–TV just as new and exciting as QP radio was, and I am sure that the jaded public would welcome it; they'll welcome anything new on TV!"

Cooper and Chappell's *Quiet, Please* television ambitions did not come to anything, so Cooper continued to attempt to develop and sell other scripts. He wrote to Herbert C. Rice (Mutual Broadcasting System) on August 4, 1953, in a mood of high spirits, saying that, "I got a million [ideas]!" One idea was a radio drama series called *Listen!* which would be a star vehicle for Ernest Chappell. He explained that one script for it had already been bought by the *Tales of Tomorrow* television series, but it would be better on radio, confiding to Rice: "radio is the place for imagination." One can imagine that *Listen!* sounded too much like a return of *Quiet, Please*, not least in its proposed use of Chappell as central performer. On March 23, 1954, Cooper wrote to producer-director Carl Eastman, proposing for radio or television a "series of Bible dramas in modern dress and modern language, the way Shakspere [sic] has been so often so successfully." Cooper argues that with "the resurgence of interest in the Bible, I think it can't fail." Cooper certainly proceeds to reel off plenty of ideas for plays in the series. One cannot help feeling that the premise of the series belongs to the same territory as *Quiet, Please*'s "Berlin, 1945," but, emphatically, Cooper makes no mention of *Quiet, Please* or, for that matter, Ernest Chappell (a fact that probably reflects the lack of success in developing the television or radio plans in 1953).

While Cooper's new proposals may have come to nothing, *Quiet, Please* would not go away. In July 1954, CBS producer Ted Lloyd asked Cooper to send him some of the old *Quiet, Please* scripts in case any could be reworked for *The Whistler*. Cooper declined to send any, writing to Lloyd, "I'm not at all certain that any of these scripts could be adapted for 'The Whistler'" (letter to Ted Lloyd, July 20, 1954). But early the following year, Cooper was desperate for something — anything — to happen with them. We find Cooper keenly responding to the slightest rumor that someone is interested in the *Quiet, Please* scripts. In a letter to Rodney Erickson (February 11, 1955), Cooper jovially asks "what's cooking," but follows it with the sobering lines: "I've been sick and disabled for two years now, and of course completely broke, so I hasten to inquire about whatever may make a buck, you see."

To say that the final months of Wyllis Cooper's life were poignant is a bitter understatement. His last letters are heartbreaking. Cooper was afflicted with poor health and virtually blind. He was unable to sell any scripts. In a letter (March 1, 1955) to the accountant Seymour Schneidman, Cooper writes:

> We are desperately in need of money; and I don't seem to be able to sell any other scripts I create. Part of this is, of course, my inability both physically and financially to get around New York.

In the meantime, Ernest Chappell was continuing his attempt to sell *Quiet, Please* and other possibilities under the guise of "Chappell-Cooper Productions." (In an undated letter to Schneidman, probably during March 1955, Cooper insists, "There is no such organization as 'Chappell-Cooper Productions.' That is merely a name Chappell thought up himself for their [i.e., the *Quiet, Please* scripts] possible sale.") In the March 1, 1955, letter to Schneidman, Cooper bemoans the fact that Chappell quoted "a figure which I thought was more or less ridiculous — and of course I had not been consulted about the price at all." Schneidman, in a collected tone (letter to Cooper, March 16, 1955), sums up the situation as being one of "adverse interests": "It seems that Mr. Chappell earns a considerable amount of money and is interested primarily in capital gains.... Your problem is to get income." He concludes by saying to Cooper: "I'd like to see you make a couple of hundred thousand dollars." Perhaps this figure is similar to the amount that Chappell was suggesting, but either way Cooper wrote to Schneidman the next week:

> It has been a long time since we have had any income, except the grant that the New Jersey state Blind Commission sends us, and a little income would be a genuine windfall. [Meanwhile, all the *Quiet, Please* scripts] sit quietly ... in a filing-cabinet, doing nobody at all any good [March 21, 1955].

It is important to note that despite Schneidman's emphasis on "adverse interests," we should not think that Cooper and Chappell's friendship was in any way compromised. After all, in May 1953, Chappell gave Cooper and his wife Emily tenancy of "Breezy Hill," a house owned by Chappell in New Jersey. Moreover, their letters to each other always seem warm and encouraging. In March 1953, Chappell writes to a despondent Cooper:

> Don't let's ever again hear you say or suspect that you ain't got it in you any more!! I don't know, he says. I'll try, he muttered. They don't come easy any more, he sighed. Nuts!! [...What] is rightfully yours can never be taken from you. And I don't care whether we're talking about your talent or your eye sight or what have you. Bub, you got it, and nobody's ever going to take it away from you — EXCEPT maybe you yourself. But I have a strong hunch maybe you've found out how *not* to dissipate your life; and by your life, I mean your TRUTH [Letter to Cooper, March 31, 1953].

Certainly Cooper was still writing scripts for Chappell as late as March 1955, including a five-minute script for radio. The script, perhaps the last Cooper wrote, is untitled and is reminiscent of the short plays broadcast on *The Unexpected* (1948). Cooper's play concerns a businessman who is interviewed by a man he believes to be a detective, and to whom he confesses having murdered his business associate. The stranger is, in fact, an insurance man who had come to tell the businessman that he was the beneficiary of his late partner's life insurance. Cooper tells Chappell that either role is suitable for him, and "if it's a trifle too long, just use the scissors" (letter to Chappell, March 11, 1955). It is a slight piece — understandable given its length — but it nonetheless shows that Cooper was, until the end, creative and still retained his handle on characterization and story.

Wyllis Cooper died in June 1955 at the age of 56. Despite his death, the wrangling and hopes over the *Quiet, Please* scripts continued. On August 5, 1955, Ernest Chappell wrote to the widowed Emily Cooper regarding the *Quiet, Please* scripts: "I'm sure the future is bright for all concerned." But this optimism proved unfounded, as Emily Cooper was fast discovering. In a letter to her lawyer, Max Alpern, she urged:

> I would be inclined to forget the TV adaptations in connection with the Hitchcock show, in view of the fact that [Bill] Morwood said he was interested only in story material [August 13, 1955].

In other words, selling the *stories* of *Quiet, Please* was not the same as selling the *scripts*. Around this time we also see Emily's frustration at trying to locate or establish details of her late husband's contracts or agreements, as, "Foolishly" (letter to Alpern, August 13, 1955), Wyllis Cooper had kept his own creative files but not his own business files. Alpern seems keen to secure anything for Emily. In February 1956 he updates her, saying that he has tried to sell the *Quiet, Please* scripts to NBC or CBS for "a temporary tag of between $50,000.00 and $60,000.00 on the series, lock, stock and barrel. This tentative offer was turned down," and, despite Emily's misgivings, he is still "waiting for an answer from Hitchcock." (Letter to Emily Cooper, February 17, 1956) Two months later, an announcement from the Notary Public of New Jersey (April 19, 1956) declared that the complete *Quiet, Please* scripts and the six television scripts "Volume 1 to 6" in possession of Emily Cooper are merely worth a total $10,000, as they have not produced any income since their only broadcast, and all attempts to sell them have failed.

A touching coda to this story is that in the mid–1960s Chappell wrote to Emily Cooper, telling her that he has transferred

> [The] entire "quiet, please" library to tape. That is all the shows I have; I am missing eleven records. I have all the records here, safely stored. Naturally, you have a mutual interest in them with me.... If you are interested in having tapes of any particular shows I will be very happy to dubb [sic] them.... It took a lot of hours to make the tape transfers but I got a big thrill out of hearing them all over again and I want to say there were many occasions when my emotions blew up and I just plain bawled. They brought back such wonderful times and so many intimate memories of such a treasured friend [April 26, 1966].

It is tempting to see Cooper as a tragic icon of the end of the golden age horror radio: a writer who goes blind just as television's ascendancy is clearly the inexorable destiny of popular culture. Nevertheless, Oboler always insisted that Cooper was the great innovator of radio drama. Cooper himself had always prided himself on being something of a rebel, having enjoyed considerable prestige as a radio writer, despite being involved with fewer commercial programs than any other writer in his league. Cooper never enjoyed the success or stature of Oboler, Welles or Corwin, but *Quiet, Please* at its best represents the zenith of horror radio of the golden age. All the scripts and most of the recordings survive, and they have all aged well, remaining by turns humorous, thought provoking and deeply unsettling. The *Quiet, Please* opus alone makes it clear that Cooper must be regarded as one of the greatest auteurs of horror radio.

10

Conclusion

Looked at from the perspective of our own time, horror radio in the golden age of American broadcasting seems to have fully explored the aesthetic and technical limits in its presentation of the unexpected and the "impossible." At times, horror radio pushed not just aesthetic and technical parameters, but moral boundaries. However, despite the endless scope of its exciting technical, formal and thematic possibilities, as well as its reworking of the motifs and narratives of traditional horror culture, and despite a regular audience in the millions, the contributions of movie stars, and substantial commercial sponsorship, horror radio went the way of golden age American radio as a whole, and other forms of popular performance culture such as vaudeville and Victorian melodrama: it died. The reasons for its demise are manifold. We saw in the introduction how the National Association of Broadcasters increasingly advocated measures against gore and violence in the light of what they believed were declining moral and ethical standards. "When the Grave Is Open" (*The Shadow*, September 14, 1947) is a particularly significant example. The play features two grave robbers who are unable to obtain the corpse that their scientist contact desires, so they turn on an associate to transform him into the required corpse. The corpse was supposed to be that of a lame man, so the grave robbers use "instruments, blowtorch and a vise" to murder and mutilate their victim so that he has a damaged leg and his face is unrecognizable. In the play, the disfigurement and slaying happen in a gap: we hear three final screams of "No ... No ... No!" in mounting terror, and then the scene fades. Subsequently, Lamont Cranston discovers the butchered and unidentifiable corpse. The National Association of Broadcasters staged a photograph to enact the grotesque scene (page 163). The photograph is intended to make the scene visual and therefore more real in order to shock the reader into supporting demands for increased stringency. They add a saw to the picture as one of the unspecified "instruments." Not only is the National Association of Broadcasters filling in the visual gaps, it is also filling the narrative gaps: the scene in question does not actually "happen" on the air but remains unheard within a narrative ellipsis. More critically, the photograph includes the Shadow himself; it goes without saying that Lamont Cranston would not have tolerated such inhumanity had he been able to prevent it.

10. Conclusion

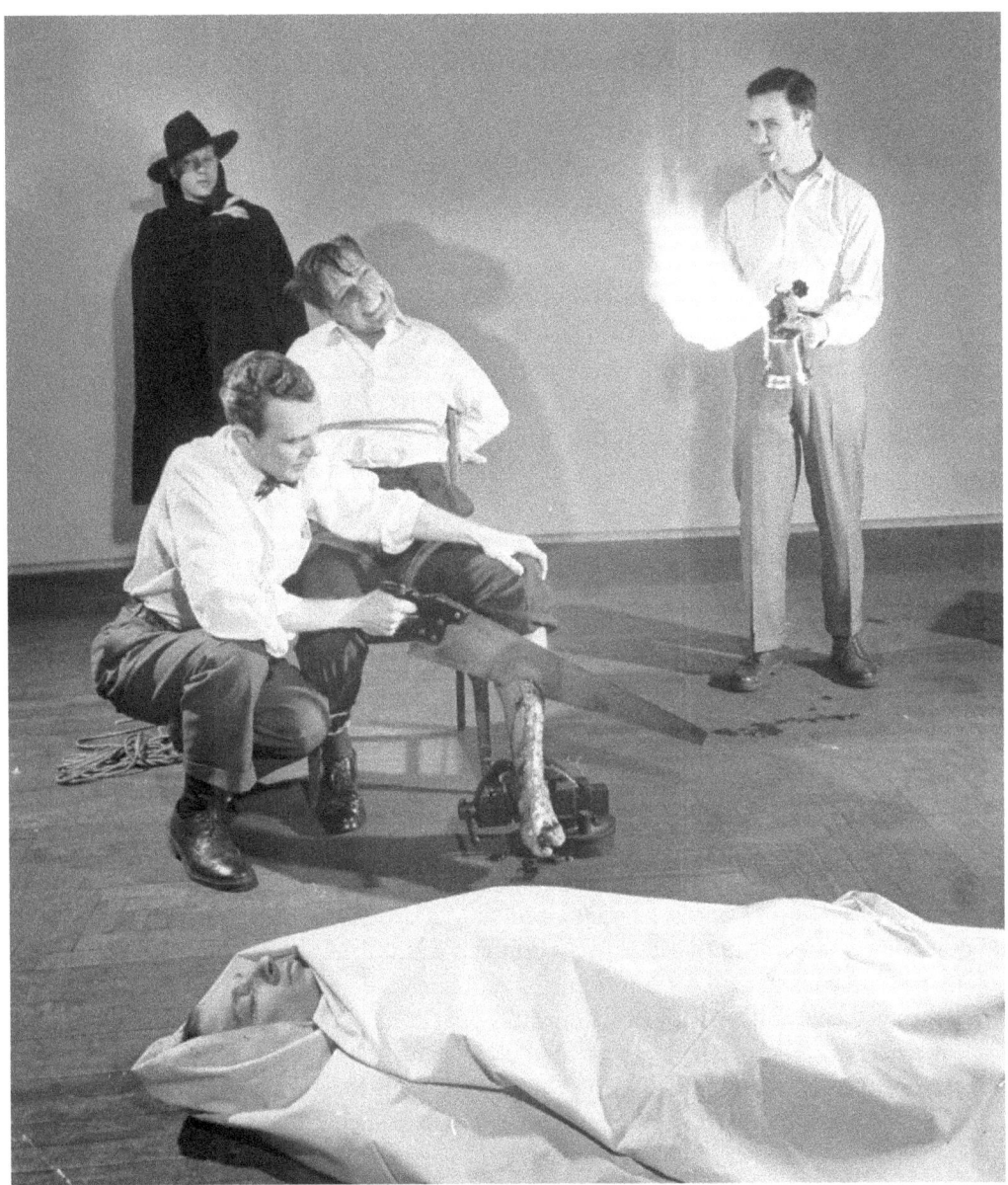

The National Association of Broadcasters reconstructs a scene from "When the Grave Is Open" (*The Shadow*, September 14, 1947) for the camera (Bernard Hoffman, Getty Images.

    The actions of the National Association of Broadcasters reflects the postwar zeitgeist of an America that was concerned with morality and the changing values in the new social and world order. It is the same impetus that enforced the suicide of another form of popular horror — the pre-code horror comic — and, more broadly, would scrutinize television, rock and roll music and other popular forms with similar vigilance. Ostensibly, the concerns were about delinquency and immorality, but it is unquestionably tied in with the spirit of McCarthyism. EC horror and suspense comics, for example, ran full-page advertisements pleading their case that they are not communistic: in fact, "THE GROUP MOST ANXIOUS TO DESTROY COMICS ARE THE COMMUNISTS!" (Von Bernewitz and Geissman, 2000, 27). The introduction of self-regulation in the form of the Comics Code Authority meant that comics that did not adhere to the stringencies of the code would not be distributed, and it ended the golden age of the horror comic. Although these measures effectively destroyed a form of popular horror and forced the creators to adapt their work or abandon the industry, no one in the comic business was subjected to communist witch hunts, per se. Radio, in contrast, was part of the entertainment industry and was thoroughly "examined" by the McCarthyites. The paranoia of the McCarthy period took a heavy toll on American radio. As Gerald Nachman reveals, figures such as Orson Welles and Himan Brown were smeared in the anticommunist witch hunts (Nachman, 1998, 496), but managed to survive. Himan Brown was mentioned three times in *Red Channels*. Laurence Johnson, owner of a supermarket chain and an officer in the National Association of Supermarkets, used his influence to strangle the sponsorship of "un-American" radio:

> In the fall of 1952, when [Himan Brown] heard through the grapevine that Johnson was gunning for him, he went to see Johnson in the latter's New York hotel room. For three hours, Brown, usually a very proud man, argued his case, among other things pointing out as a sign of his patriotism that he had worked for the Treasury Department [Blue, 2002, 351].

Himan Brown continued to enjoy a fruitful career as a producer for radio with successful forays into television and even cinema. He was more fortunate than other radio figures smeared in *Red Channels,* such as David Kogan — the co-creator of *The Mysterious Traveler*—who, as we saw earlier, cleared their names but failed to rebuild their careers in broadcasting. Actors were a favorite target in McCarthyism. Vincent Price was "gray listed"—in other words, he was placed on McCarthy's list of "Premature Anti-Nazi Sympathizers" (Price, 1999, 173). This effectively froze Price's career in the summer of 1953 and forced him into a compromising and coercive move to reactivate his career, signing a personal anticommunist statement for the FBI and the head of CBS. This humiliating gesture was kept quiet by the actor, and his daughter Victoria Price describes how deeply she was "shocked" (Price, 1999, 174) when it came to light after her father's death. The mood of paranoia that resulted in the humiliation, persecution and/or dismissal of many talented radio figures represents a factual scenario far more terrifying than anything the fantasy worlds of horror drama ever created. The anticommunist purges and policies were a tragedy that changed the landscape and spirit of radio, stifling many of the innovative and radical possibilities of the medium.

Another reason for the demise of American radio is cultural and technological determinism. The gradual replacement of live broadcasting with prerecorded material undoubtedly sapped some of the adrenaline, spontaneity and pleasurable danger out of the medium, but far more critical was the rise of television. Sponsors turned away from the radio to invest in television, and many creators and performers attempted to bail out of radio into the new medium. Even if radio figures did not attempt to join the flourishing television industry, they nonetheless had to redefine themselves in relation to it; television simply could not be ignored. Some radio shows tried to make the transition to television. *Inner Sanctum Mysteries* made some 39 broadcasts on NBC television in 1954; *Starring Boris Karloff* (1949) attempted to run radio and television versions of the same stories in the same week; while *Suspense* enjoyed a highly successful run of 260 broadcasts from 1949 through 1954, contemporaneous with, but not outliving, its radio parent, which ran for over 20 years, ending in 1962. More typical is the experience of *Lights Out*, which, having made the transition to television, was soon to disappear. Mike Dann, the NBC program chief responsible for the transfer of *Lights Out* to television, remembers: "We were wiped out quickly.... We never knew what happened, but it happened and happened fast" (Quoted in Nachman, 1998, 491)

Although radio and television are ostensibly linked as media because of their perceived location within the domestic environment, they are radically different from one another. As Jim Harmon observes, "The very stuff of radio was imagination, the very antithesis of television." (Harmon, 1967, 260) This suggests that it was not as easy to shift from a broadcaster's radio offices to its television offices as one might expect. Moreover, there is a sense that television — an exciting, burgeoning medium — was perceived as requiring a new start. Whether it is Wyllis Cooper attempting to pitch ideas for television or William Conrad being made to audition for the lead in the television transfer of *Gunsmoke*, one senses that they may have been perceived as yesterday's men by the new generation of television executives who were searching for original styles, voices, and moods. Above all, they were thinking visually and were endeavoring to build, consciously or otherwise, a vivid iconography for a new medium and its limitless possibilities. However, not everyone believes that television fulfilled its limitless possibilities. Vincent Price, for one, laments that television failed to live up to its aesthetic potential and yet, perversely, succeeded in another aspect: it thoroughly "visualized" the culture of America, and thus destroyed any chance of a renaissance in American radio (Chuck Shaden interview with Vincent Price, Chicago, 1971). The significant radio producer-director William N. Robson concurs:

> You see you have a culture now which is visually oriented — and a whole generation ... they've been babysat by television sets. You cannot get people to sit or listen. I have tested this time and again — somebody will say — oh, you did *Suspense* ... have you got any tapes — put something on — the attention wanders. A whole generation is conditioned to the picture. And they will not make the effort — because radio required an involvement of the individual — or you missed it [Edwin Dunham interview with William N. Robson, April 27, 1967].

When listening to recordings or reading the scripts of horror radio's greatest period — those produced during the golden age in American radio — one is constantly impressed by their inventiveness and originality, but also by their solid contributions to the traditions (and clichés) of horror culture. Moreover, as much as one can detect how horror radio has built on or departs from what came before, its place as a precursor to so much that has followed in the visual forms of popular horror culture — such as television, film and comics — is startling. The influence of horror radio had a massive impact on horror television. Whether it is an in-program host like an earnest Rod Serling on *The Twilight Zone* and *Night Gallery*, the witty undead Cryptkeeper in the television version of *Tales from the Crypt*, or the television horror movie host (from Vampira in the 1950s to the present day), a debt is owed to the structural function and diverse styles of the horror radio host. Although few radio shows survived the metamorphosis into television, classic TV offerings such as *Alfred Hitchcock Presents, The Twilight Zone* and *The Outer Limits* are unthinkable without their mystery, horror and science fiction antecedents on radio.

As for film, the gigantic man-made monsters in "The Revolt of the Worms" (*Lights Out*, October 13, 1942) or the subterranean dinosaur in "Subbasement" (*Lights Out*, August 24, 1943) may remind us of the best of the creature features of the 1950s. Given Arch Oboler's significant contribution to the genre, it is perhaps ironic that in 1967 he should deride movies that present "papier-mâché monsters coming out of the Japanese ocean, a Tyrannosaurus Rex attacking Riverview with the army blasting away — that sort of thing is ridiculous" (Oboler, 1967, 15). Oboler obviously felt that such material works best in the imagination of a listener. For other examples of radio's influence on the horror film, we may consider the tourists' deadly mistake in trusting the locals and entering a remote house in "Valse Triste" (*Lights Out*, March 30, 1938; revived December 29, 1942) — a story not dissimilar to *The Texas Chainsaw Massacre* (Tobe Hooper, 1974) and numerous other movies. In "Papa Benjamin" (*Escape*, January 21, 1948), a jazz musician steals a voodoo tune for his own composition and is destroyed by its curse; the same story returns as an episode within the portmanteau movie *Doctor Terror's House of Horrors* (Freddie Francis, 1965). The film's uncredited source story is "Dark Melody of Madness" by William Irish (a pseudonym of Cornell Woolrich), first published in *Dime Mystery Magazine* (July 1935), but the theme of jazz music lends itself to dramatization extremely well, and it makes a memorable episode of *Escape* (which does credit William Irish as the original author and John Dunkel as adapter). Milton Subotsky, the scriptwriter of the Amicus movie, had worked as a writer on the television version of *Lights Out* in the late 1940s (Bryce, 2000, 17); if Subotsky had not read the original short story, he must have at least been listening to the radio in 1948.

Even one of the most extreme horrors of horror radio — the abject creature with a human head and spider's body in "The Thing on the Fourble Board" (*Quiet, Please*, August 9, 1948) — finally finds credible screen equivalents through the latex and/or computer special effects technology of *The Thing* (John Carpenter, 1982) and *The Faculty* (Robert Rodriguez, 1998).

The influence of horror radio on other cultural forms is also evident: Stephen King's celebration of horror radio demonstrates what lessons it could offer a future writer of fiction. I believe there is even a parallel to be drawn between horror radio and survival horror computer games: both forms offer participants the immediacy of a lived experience, ideally keeping them not passive but engaged, involved and implicated. There are many more parallels, allusions and influences to be uncovered across the broadest range of horror culture, not least because horror radio has been so scandalously overlooked in the ever-proliferating field of horror studies.

One of the most interesting influences and legacies of horror radio is to be found in comics. The pre-code horror comics of the 1950s frequently use the stories and structure of horror radio. Stephen Sennitt cites horror radio as a major influence on horror comics, giving a special mention to *The Witch's Tale*, regarding it as "probably the main influence on the horror comics' conception of having a witch-like 'host' to tell the tales" (Sennitt, 1999, 10).

Just as the use of the host was a standard ingredient in horror comics during the pre-code era and in the renaissance of the horror comic in the 1960s onwards, stories and plots were frequently snatched and resurrected. Let us consider three examples from the most famous horror comic title, EC's *Tales from the Crypt*. In "Spider" (*Lights Out*, May 18, 1943) two men discover and attempt to capture a "natural" monster, a spider the size of a dog. In "Sucker for a Spider" (*Tales from the Crypt* 29, 1952) a man is trapped and devoured by a spider no bigger than his own torso. "Tight Grip" (*Tales from the Crypt* 38, 1953) has features similar to "The Story of Mister Maggs" (*Lights Out*, December 1, 1942), in which a haunted chest murders the occupants of a house one at a time, and "The Visiting Corpse" (*The Mysterious Traveler*, August 10, 1948), in which a man murders his mother-in-law and locks her corpse in a trunk, only to be haunted and eventually crushed to death by it. In "Tight Grip" a man kills his wife and hides her dismembered corpse in a trunk before being forced to hide in the trunk himself, where he is crushed to death. "A Rottin' Trick" (*Tales from the Crypt* 29, April 1952) and "White Pearls of Terror" (*The Strange Doctor Weird*, December 19, 1944) both feature ruthless criminals who take refuge on remote islands only to discover they have disembarked on leper colonies. The parallel is unmistakable, but it is worth noting that both are prefigured by the André de Lorde and Henri Bauche's Grand-Guignol play *Le Château de la mort lente* (1916), in which a burglar discovers that he has broken into an asylum for victims of leprosy. No doubt this French play is itself predated by a similar story: the intertextual framework of horror abounds with archetypal stories and subgenres, and it is as difficult to locate a point of origin as it is to say that a story or motif will not be reworked in the future.

All the above examples come from visual media, but horror radio has continued despite its entropy in the 1950s and supposed demise in the early 1960s. Sporadic examples of American horror radio after the 1962 watershed have attempted to make an impact on the visual-obsessed world of American popular culture. Most ambitiously, there was Himan Brown's *CBS Radio Mystery Theater* (1974–82); but this was predated by works such as *Theater Five* (1964–65), featuring the former host of *Inner Sanctum Mysteries,* Paul McGrath, and *The Zero Hour* (1973–74) with Rod Serling — television's equivalent of Arch Oboler (Nachman, 1998, 312) — as radio host. As noteworthy and frequently excellent as many plays in these programs are, they are but a drop in the ocean compared to the dramatic output during the heyday of American radio.

Outside of the United States, however, the fortunes of the genre have been happier. The Canadian Broadcasting Corporation made exceptional contributions to horror radio in the 1980s with *Nightfall* and *The Vanishing Point*. In Britain, a commitment to radio drama has never diminished, with the BBC continuing to broadcast hundreds of new radio plays each year. In the area of horror, noteworthy BBC contributions include *Appointment with Fear,* which premiered in 1943 and continued into the mid–1950s, hosted by a *Suspense*-style "Man in Black." The series made a return as *Fear on Four* (also known as *The Man in Black*) in 1988, with intermittent revivals ever since. Other BBC horror radio programs which have directly carried on the legacy of American horror radio have included the Vincent Price vehicle *The Price of Fear* (1973–75, 1983). The BBC has also endeavored to lead horror radio into new avenues of technology: Mike Walter's award-winning "interactive drama" *The Dark House* (2003) was a daring experiment that enjoyed critical and popular success. The play featured three separate characters within the same story, and the listeners were able to vote online for which character they wanted to pursue; the character who received the most votes would lead to a shift in the narrative and would become the protagonist until the next democratically selected "shift." The play was really three simultaneous scripts, but on the day of broadcast was crafted into a single, experiential horror drama.

Radio exploits the imagination, and can unsettle and upset the listener as it does so. Sam Boardman-Jacobs describes a play broadcast by the BBC in which someone is tortured with an electric drill. Boardman-Jacobs uses this example as a cautionary tale for the would-be radio writer:

> We are accustomed to visual horror. The very "reality" of the scene adds a distance. In this particular radio play, all that was used was the sound of the drill and the recipient's scream, rapidly faded out. The BBC received a huge number of complaints about this scene. Each listener created their own mind picture of the event. Most of the audience found that image too terrifying to deal with. So, be cautious! Take the listener to the stars, but beware of taking them to their darkest nightmares [Boardman-Jacobs, 2004, 11–12].

Boardman-Jacobs cites this example as a warning to aspiring radio writers of the dangers of the powerful form they are entering. But numerous horror radio plays of the American golden age (many of which we have analyzed here) were evidently written with the deliberate intention of taking the listener into the darkest nightmares imaginable. In bold opposition to the lamentation that our culture has become terminally visualized, Boardman-Jacobs suggests that we are inured to visual horror, a suggestion that perhaps demonstrates not simply the abiding potency of classic horror radio, but also opens up exciting potential for the future of the genre. Radio drama requires a listener with imagination: the ability to imagine is in itself creative, and radio drama can fuel, shape and inspire our fantasies. The creative relationship between radio dramatist, radio performer and radio listener can realize some of the ultimate experiences of performance horror, and there is no reason to believe that horror radio is a form that is redundant or irretrievable.

Bibliography

Books and Journal Articles

Abbot, Waldo. *Handbook of Broadcasting: How to Broadcast Effectively*. New York: McGraw, 1941.
Ashley, Mike. *Who's Who in Horror and Fantasy Fiction*. London: Elm Tree, 1973.
Bannerman, R. LeRoy. *Norman Corwin and Radio: The Golden Years*. Birmingham: University of Alabama Press, 1986.
Barnard, Stephen. *Studying Radio*. London: Arnold, 2000.
Barnouw, Erik. *The Golden Web: A History of Broadcasting in the United States, Volume 2: 1933–53*. New York: Oxford University Press, 1968.
_____. *Handbook of Radio Production: An Outline of the Studio Techniques and Procedures in the United States*. Boston: Little, Brown, 1949.
_____ (ed.). *Radio Drama in Action: Twenty-Five Plays of a Changing World*. New York: Rinehart, 1945.
Baughman, James L. "American Broadcasting History: A comment" in *Historical Journal of Film, Radio and Television* 2:2, 1982, 195–98.
_____. *Republic of Mass Culture* (Second Edition). Baltimore: Johns Hopkins University Press, 1997.
Beck, Calvin Thomas. *Heroes of the Horrors*. New York: Collier Books, 1975.
Belton, John, and James Spellerberg. "Spectator and Screen" in G. A. Waller (ed.) *Moviegoing in America*. Oxford: Blackwell, 2002.
Bierce, Ambrose. *An Occurrence at Owl Creek Bridge*. Harmondsworth: Penguin, 1995.
Blackwood, Algernon. *Tales of Terror and Darkness*. London: Spring, 1977.
Bloch, Robert. *Out of My Head*. Cambridge, Massachusetts: Nesfa, 1986.
Blue, Howard. *Words at War: World War II Era Radio Drama and the Postwar Broadcasting Blacklist*. Lanham, Maryland: Scarecrow Press, 2002.
Boardman-Jacobs, Sam (ed.). *Radio Scriptwriting*. Bridgend, UK: Seren, 2004.
Boggs, Joseph M. *The Art of Watching Films* (Second Edition). Palo Alto, California: Mayfield, 1985.
Britton, Andrew. "Stars and Genre" in Christine Gledhill (ed.). *Stardom: Industry of Desire*. London: Routledge, 1991, 198–206.
Brown, Himan. "The Mystery Show" in Wylie, Max. *Radio and Television Writing*. Rinehart: New York, 1950, 351–59.
Brunvand, Jan Harold. *The Vanishing Hitchhiker: American Urban Legends and Their Meanings*. New York: Norton, 1981.
Bryce, Alan (ed.) *Amicus: The Studio That Dripped Blood*. Liskeard, UK: Stray Cat, 2000.
Cantril, Hadley. *Invasion from Mars*. New York: Harper, 1940.
_____, and Gordon Allport. *The Psychology of Radio*. New York: Harper, 1935.
Carlile, John S. *Production and Direction of Radio Programs*. Prentice-Hall: New York, 1942.
Carmen, Ruth. *Radio Dramatics: Instruction Lectures*. New York: Yorston, 1937.
Carroll, Noël. *The Philosophy of Horror*. London: Routledge, 1990.

Cathcart, Robert S. "From Hero to Celebrity: The Media Connection" in Susan J. Drucker and Robert S. Cathcart (eds.). *American Heroes in a Media Age*. Cresskill, New Jersey: Hampton, 1994, 36–46.
Chester, Giraud, Garnet R. Garrison and Edgar E. Willis. *Television and Radio*. Appleton-Century-Crofts: New York, 1963.
Chibnall, Steve, and Julian Petley (eds.). *British Horror Cinema*. London: Routledge, 2002.
Conrad, Joseph. *Youth, Heart of Darkness, The End of the Tether*. Oxford: Oxford University Press, 1984.
Cox, Michael (ed.). *The Illustrated J. S. Le Fanu*. Wellingborough, UK: Equation, 1988.
Crane, Jonathan Lake. *Terror and Everyday Life: Singular Moments in the History of the Horror Film*. Thousand Oaks, California: Sage, 1994.
Creamer, Joseph, and William B. Hoffman. *Radio Sound Effects*. New York: Ziff-Davis, 1945.
Creed, Barbara. "Kristeva, Femininity, Abjection" in Ken Gelder (ed.). *The Horror Reader*. London: Routledge, 2000, 64–70.
Crews, Albert. *Radio Production Directing*. Boston: Houghton Mifflin, 1944.
Crisell, Andrew. *Understanding Radio* (Second Edition). London: Routledge, 1994.
Crook, Tim. *Radio Drama: Theory and Practice*. London: Routledge, 1999.
Crosby, John. *Out of the Blue: A Book About Radio and Television*. New York: Simon and Shuster, 1952.
Czitrom, Daniel. *Media and the American Mind*. Chapel Hill: University of North Carolina Press, 1982.
Deák, Frantisek. "The Grand Guigrol." *The Drama Review* (March 1974), 34–52.
DeLong, Thomas A. *Radio Stars: An Illustrated Biographical Dictionary of 953 Performers, 1920 through 1960*. Jefferson: McFarland, 1996.
Dirda, Michael. "Prosper Mérimée" in Jack Sullivan (ed.) *The Penguin Encyclopedia of Horror and the Supernatural*. Harmondsworth: Penguin, 1986, 288–89.
Dixon, Peter. *Radio Sketches and How to Write Them*. New York: Stokes, 1936.
Douglas, Susan J. *Listening In*. New York: Times Books, 1999.
Drakakis, John. *British Radio Drama*. Cambridge: Cambridge University Press, 1981.
Drucker, Susan J., and Robert S. Cathcart (eds.). *American Heroes in a Media Age*. Cresskill, New Jersey: Hampton, 1994.
Dunning, John. *On the Air: The Encyclopedia of Old-Time Radio*. Oxford: Oxford University Press, 1998.
Floherty, John J. *On the Air: The Story of Radio*. Doubleday Doran: New York, 1938.
Gelder, Ken (ed.). *The Horror Reader*. London: Routledge, 2000.
Giddings, Robert, and Keith Selby. *The Classic Serial on Television and Radio*. Basingstoke: Palgrave, 2001.
Gifford, Denis. *Karloff: The Man, the Monster, the Movies*. New York: Curtiss, 1973.
Goodstone, Tony. *The Pulps: 50 Years of American Pop Culture*. Chelsea House: New York, 1976.
Gordon, Mel. *The Grand Guignol: Theatre of Fear and Terror*. New York: Amok Press, 1988.
_____. *The Grand Guignol: Theatre of Fear and Terror* (Revised Edition). New York: Da Capo Press, 1997.
Grams, Martin, Jr. *Inner Sanctum Mysteries: Behind the Creaking Door*. Churchville, Maryland: OTR Publishing, 2002.
_____. *Radio Drama: American Programs, 1932–1962*. Jefferson, North Carolina: McFarland, 2000.
_____. *Suspense: Twenty Years of Thrills and Chills*. Kearney, Nebraska: Morris, 1997.
Haining, Peter (ed.). *Dead of Night: Horror Stories from Radio, Television and Films*. New York: Stein and Day, 1981.
_____. *The Shilling Shockers*. London: Gollancz, 1978.
_____. *The Television Late Night Horror Omnibus*. London: Orion, 1993.
Halper, Donna L. *Invisible Stars: A Social History of Women in American Broadcasting*. Armonk, New York: M. E. Sharpe, 2001.
Hamilton, Patrick. *Gaslight*. New York: Constable, 1939.
Hand, Richard J., and Michael Wilson, "The Grand-Guignol: Aspects of Theory and Practice," in *Theatre Research International* (Vol. 25, No.3, 2000), 266–75.
_____. *Grand-Guignol: The French Theatre of Horror*. Exeter: University of Exeter Press, 2002.
Harmon, Jim. *The Great Radio Heroes*. New York: Doubleday, 1967.
_____. *The Great Radio Heroes* (Revised and Expanded Edition). Jefferson, North Carolina: McFarland, 2001.
Hayes, John S., and Horace J. Gardner (eds.). *Both Sides of the Microphone: Training for the Radio*. Philadelphia: Lippincott, 1938.
Hiablum, Isidore. "Radio" in Jack Sullivan (ed.). *The Penguin Encyclopedia of Horror and Supernatural*. Harmondsworth: Penguin, 1986, 346–48.

Hilliard, Robert L. *Radio Broadcasting: An Introduction to the Sound Medium* (Third Edition). New York: Longman, 1985.
Hilmes, Michele. *Hollywood and Broadcasting*. Chicago: University of Illinois Press, 1990.
_____. *Only Connect: A Cultural History of Broadcasting in the United States*. Belmont, California: Wadsworth, 2002.
_____ (ed.). *Radio Reader: Essays in the Cultural History of Radio*. New York: Routledge, 2002.
Hilmes, Michele. *Radio Voices: American Broadcasting 1922–52*. Minneapolis: University of Minnesota Press, 1997.
Huxley, Aldous. *Brave New World*. London: Chatto and Windus, 1952.
James, Henry. *Tales of Henry James*. New York: Norton, 1984.
James, M. R. *A Warning to the Curious and other Ghost Stories*. London: Arnold, 1925.
Jancovich, Mark. *Rational Fears: American Horror in the 1950s*. Manchester: Manchester University Press, 1996.
Jenkins, Henry, Tara McPherson and Jane Shattuc (eds.). *Hop on Pop: The Politics and Pleasures of Popular Culture*. Durham: Duke University Press, 2002.
Jensen, Paul M. *Boris Karloff and His Films*. New York: A. S. Barnes, 1974.
Jones, Carless. *Short Plays for Stage and Radio*. Albuquerque: University of New Mexico, 1939.
Jones, Stephen (ed.). *Clive Barker's A-Z of Horror*. London: BBC Books, 1997.
Kahn, Frank J. (ed.). *Documents of American Broadcasting*. Appleton-Century-Crofts: New York, 1973.
Kendrick, Walter. *The Thrill of Fear*. New York: Grove Press, 1991.
King, Stephen. *Danse Macabre*. London: Futura Press, 1982.
Kingson, Walter Krulevitch, and Rome Cowgill. *Radio Drama Acting and Production: A Handbook* (Revised Edition). New York: Rinehart, 1950.
Lass, A. H., and Earle McGill and Donald Axelrod (eds.). *Plays from Radio*. Houghton Mifflin: Cambridge, Massachusetts, 1948.
Lazarsfeld, Paul F. *Radio and the Printed Page*. Duell, Sloan and Pearce: New York, 1940.
Lehman, Peter, and William Luhr. *Thinking About Movies: Watching, Questioning, Enjoying* (Second Edition). Oxford: Blackwell, 2003.
Lindsay, Cynthia. *Dear Boris: The Life of William Henry Pratt*. New York: Alfred A. Knopf, 1975.
Liss, Joseph. *Radio's Best Plays*. New York: Greenberg, 1947.
MacDonald, J. Fred. *Don't Touch That Dial!* Chicago: Nelson Hall, 1979.
Mackey, David R. *Drama on the Air*. New Jersey: Prentice-Hall, 1951.
Maltin, Leonard. *The Great American Broadcast*. New York: Penguin Putnam, 2000.
Mamet, David. *The Shawl and Prairie du Chien; Two Plays*. New York: Grove, 1985.
Mank, Gregory William. *Karloff and Lugosi: The Story of a Haunting Collaboration*. Jefferson, North Carolina: McFarland, 1990.
McAsh, Iain F. *The Films of Vincent Price*. London: Barnden Castell Williams, 1974.
McCracken, Allison. "Scary Women and Scared Men: *Suspense*, Gender Trouble, and Postwar Change, 1942–1950" in Michele Hilmes (ed.). *Radio Reader: Essays in the Cultural History of Radio*. New York: Routledge, 2002, 183–208.
McGill, Earle. *Radio Directing*. McGraw-Hill: New York, 1940.
McLeish, Robert. *The Technique of Radio Production: A Manual for Broadcasters*. London: Focal, 1988.
Meyrowitz, Joshua. "The Life and Death of Media Friends: New Genres of Intimacy" in Susan J. Drucker and Robert S. Cathcart (eds.). *American Heroes in a Media Age*. Cresskill, NJ: Hampton, 1994, 62–81.
Morton, David. *Off the Record: The Technology and Culture of Sound Recording in America*. New Brunswick: Rutgers University Press, 2000.
Mott, Robert L. *Radio Sound Effects*. Jefferson: McFarland, 1993.
Murray, Mathew "'The Tendency to Deprave and Corrupt Morals': Regulation and Irregular Sexuality in Golden Age Radio Comedy" in Michele Hilmes (ed.). *Radio Reader: Essays in the Cultural History of Radio*. New York: Routledge, 2002, 136–40.
Nachman, Gerald. *Raised on Radio*. Berkeley: University of California Press, 1998.
Naremore, James. *The Magic World of Orson Welles*. Dallas: Southern Methodist University Press, 1989.
Netherwood, Bryan A. (ed.). *Terror! An Anthology of Blood-Curdling Stories*. London: Blackie, 1970.
Newman, Kim (ed.). *The BFI Companion to Horror*. London: Cassell, 1996.
Nollen, S. A. *Boris Karloff*. Jefferson: McFarland, 1991.
Oboler, Arch. "Independent Filmmaker: An Interview with Arch Oboler" in *Focus! Chicago's Movie Journal* 1, Documentary Films at the University of Chicago, 1967, 10–15.
_____. *Night of the Auk*. New York: Horizon, 1958.

_____. *Oboler Omnibus*. New York: Duell, Sloan and Pearce, 1945.
_____. *Plays for Americans*. New York: Farrar and Rinehart, 1942.
O'Donnell, Elliot. *Werewolves*. London: Methuen, 1912.
Parish, James Robert, and Steven Whitney. *Vincent Price Unmasked*. New York: Drake, 1974.
Payton, Gordon, and Martin Grams, Jr. *The CBS Radio Mystery Theater: An Episode Guide and Handbook, 1974–1982*. Jefferson: McFarland, 1999.
Pells, Richard H. *Radical Visions and American Dreams: Culture and Social Thought in the Depression Years*. New York: Harper and Row, 1973.
Perkins Gilmore, Charlotte. *The Yellow Wallpaper*. London: Virago, 1997.
Pierron, Agnès. *Le Grand Guignol: Le théâtre des peurs de la belle époque*. Paris: Robert Laffont, 1995.
Poe, Edgar Allan. *Tales of Mystery and Imagination*. London: Harrap, 1935.
Price, Victoria. *Vincent Price: A Daughter's Biography*. New York: St. Martin Press, 1999.
Price, Vincent. *Vincent Price: His Movies, His Plays, His Life*. New York: Doubleday, 1978.
Richards, Stanley (ed.). *10 Classic Mystery and Suspense Plays of the Modern Theatre*. New York: Dodd Mead, 1973.
Rodger, Ian. *Radio Drama*. London: Macmillan, 1982.
Rubin, Martin. *Thrillers*. Cambridge: Cambridge University Press, 1999.
Sartre, Jean-Paul. *Huis Clos*. Paris: Gallimard, 1947.
Savage, Barbara Dianne. *Broadcasting Freedom: Radio, War, and the Politics of Race, 1938–1948*. Chapel Hill: University of North Carolina Press, 1999.
Sennitt, Stephen. *Ghastly Terror! The Horrible Story of the Horror Comics*. Manchester: Critical Vision, 1999.
Settel, Irving. *A Pictorial History of Radio*. New York: Grosset and Dunlap, 1967.
Shingler, Martin, and Cindy Wieringa. *On Air: Methods and Meanings of Radio*. London: Arnold, 1998.
Siegel, David S. (ed.). *The Witch's Tale*. New York: Dunwich, 1998.
Simsolo, Noel. *Avant-Scène du Cinema 97: Boris Karloff*. Supplement to *Anthologie du Cinema* 49 (November 1969).
Sinclair, May. *Uncanny Stories*. New York: Macmillan, 1923.
Skal, David J. *The Horror Show: A Cultural History of Horror*. London: Plexus, 1993.
Skelton, Scott, and Jim Benson. *Rod Serling's Night Gallery*. Syracuse: Syracuse University Press, 1999.
Slide, Anthony. *Great Radio Personalities in Historic Photographs*. New York: Dover, 1982.
Starkey, Guy. *Radio in Context*. Basingstoke: Palgrave Macmillan, 2004.
Stedman, Raymond William. *The Serials: Suspense and Drama by Installment*. Norman: University of Oklahoma Press, 1971.
Sterling, Christopher, and J. Kittross. *Stay Tuned*. Belmont, California: Wadsworth, 1990.
Sterling, Christopher H., and Michael C. Keith (eds.). *The Museum of Broadcast Communications Encyclopedia of Radio*. New York: Fitzroy Dearborn, 2003.
Sullivan, Jack (ed.). *The Penguin Encyclopedia of Horror and the Supernatural*. Harmondsworth: Penguin, 1986.
Summers, H. B. (ed.). *Radio Censorship*. New York: Wilson, 1939.
Tollin, Anthony. *Old-Time Radio Greatest Mysteries*. Schiller Park, Illinois: Radio Spirits, 1998.
_____. *Old-Time Radio Thrilling Mysteries: The Smithsonian Collection*. Schiller Park, IL: Radio Spirits, 2001.
_____. *Old-Time Radio's Stars on Suspense*. Schiller Park, Illinois: Radio Spirits, 2000.
_____. (ed.). *The Shadow Scrapbook*. New York: Harcourt Brace Jovanovich, 1979.
Turnbull, Robert B. *Radio and Television Sound Effects*. New York: Rinehart, 1951.
Tyler, Kingdon S. *Modern Radio*. New York: Harcourt Brace, 1944.
Underwood, Peter. *Horror Man: The Life of Boris Karloff*. Leslie Frewin: London, 1972.
Van Itallie, Jean-Claude. *I'm Really Here* in Robert J. Schroeder (ed.). *The New Underground Theatre*. New York: Bantam, 1968, 35–44.
Von Bernewitz, Fred, and Grant Geissman. *Tales of Terror! The EC Companion*. Seattle: Fantagraphics, 2000.
Walker, John (ed.). *Halliwell's Film and Video Guide* (Fifteenth Edition). London: Harper Collins, 1999.
_____. *Halliwell's Who's Who in the Movies* (Thirteenth Edition). London: Harper Collins, 1999.
Waller, Gregory A. (ed.). *Moviegoing in America*. Oxford: Blackwell, 2002.
Watson, Elena M. *Television Horror Movie Hosts*. Jefferson: McFarland, 1991.
Weigl, Charles. "Introducing Horror" in Henry Jenkins, Tara McPherson and Jane Shattuc (eds.). *Hop on Pop: The Politics and Pleasures of Popular Culture*. Durham: Duke University Press, 2002, 700–20.

Welles, Orson. "What the Listener Should Expect from Radio Drama" in John S. Hayes and Horace J. Gardner (eds.). *Both Sides of the Microphone: Training for the Radio*. Philadelphia: Lippincott, 1938, 121–22.
Wells, H. G. *The Food of the Gods*. London: Sphere, 1976.
_____. *The Invisible Man*. London: Sphere, 1976.
_____. *The Time Machine*. London: Sphere, 1976.
_____. *The War of the Worlds*. London: Pan, 1975.
Wilby, Pete, and Andy Conroy. *The Radio Handbook*. London: Routledge, 1994.
Williams, Lucy Chase. *The Complete Films of Vincent Price*. New York: Citadel, 1995.
Wilson, Michael. *Performance and Practice: Oral Narrative Traditions Among Teenagers in Britain and Ireland*. Aldershot: Ashgate, 1997.
Wise, Robert. *The Rape of Radio*. New York: Rodin, 1941.
Wolf, Leonard (ed.). *The Essential Phantom of the Opera*. New York: Plume, 1996.
Wylie, Max. *Radio and Television Writing*. Rinehart: New York, 1950.
_____. *Radio Writing*. Farrar and Rinehart: New York, 1939.
_____ (ed.). *Best Broadcasts of 1939*. New York: McGraw-Hill, 1939.
Young, Filson. *Shall I Listen: Studies in the Adventure and Technique of Broadcasting*. London: Constable, 1933.
Young, R. G. *The Encyclopedia of Fantastic Film*. New York: Applause, 2000.
Youngkin, Steven D., James Bigwood and Raymond G. Cabana, Jr. *The Films of Peter Lorre*. New York: Secausus, 1982.
Zicree, Marc Scott. *The Twilight Zone Companion*. Los Angeles: Silman-James, 1992.

Newspapers and Popular Periodicals

Chicago Tribune
Cinema News and Property Gazette
Monthly Film Bulletin of the British Film Institute
New York Herald Tribune
New York Times
Newsweek
Players Magazine
Radio and Television Mirror
Radio Digest
Radio Mirror
Radio Review
Radio Stars
Sponsor
Theatre Arts
Washington Post
Writer's Digest

Cited Radio Programs

The Abbott and Costello Show
The Adventures of Ellery Queen
The Adventures of Nero Wolfe
The Adventures of the Thin Man
Amos n' Andy
Appointment with Fear
Arch Oboler's Plays
Are You a Genius?
The Army Hour
The Black Museum
Boris Karloff's Treasure Chest
Bulldog Drummond
The Campbell Playhouse
Candid Microphone
Casey, Crime Photographer
The CBS Radio Mystery Theater
Chase and Sanborn Hour
Command Performance
Creeps by Night
The Croupier
Dark Destiny
The Dark House
Darling and Dearie
The Dean Martin and Jerry Lewis Show
Detective Story Hour
The Devil and Mr. O
Dragnet
Duffy's Tavern
The Edgar Bergen and Charlie McCarthy Show
Ellery Queen's Minute Mysteries
Escape
Fear on Four
Fleischmann Hour
Four for the Fifth
Futuristics
Gangbusters
The Goldbergs
The Gumps
Gunsmoke
The Hall of Fantasy

The Haunting Hour
Have Gun, Will Travel
The Hermit's Cave
Hollywood Fights Back
Hollywood on the Air
I Love a Mystery
I Was a Communist for the FBI
Information Please
Inner Sanctum Mysteries
The Jack Benny Program
Kay Kyser's Kollege of Musical Knowledge
Lights Out
The Lone Ranger
The Lux Radio Theater
The Man in Black
The Mercury Theater on the Air
The Mollé Mystery Theatre
Murder by Experts
The Mysterious Traveler
Mystery House
Mystery in the Air
Mystery Playhouse
NBC University Theater
Nick Carter, Master Detective
Nightfall
Nightmare
Ozzie and Harriet Show
Philco Radio Time
The Player
The Price of Fear
Quiet, Please
Rudy Vallee Show
The Saint
The Sealed Book
Sealtest Variety Hour
The Shadow
Skippy Hollywood Theater
Sleep No More
Space Patrol
Spotlight Revue
Standard Brands Radio Hour
Starring Boris Karloff
Stay Tuned for Terror
The Strange Dr. Weird
Suspense
Theater Five
Theater Guild on the Air
Theater of Romance
The Thin Man
The Unexpected
The Vanishing Point
The Weird Circle
The Whistler
Whitehall 1212
The Witch's Tale
X Minus One
The Zero Hour

Filmography

The Abominable Dr. Phibes (Robert Fuest, 1971)
Annie (John Huston, 1982)
The Arnelo Affair (Arch Oboler, 1946)
Arsenic and Old Lace (Frank Capra, 1944)
The Beast with Five Fingers (Robert Florey, 1946)
Bewitched (Arch Oboler, 1945)
The Blair Witch Project (Daniel Myrick and Eduardo Sanchez, 1999)
The Blob (Irvin S. Yeaworth, Jr., 1958)
The Bubble (Arch Oboler, 1966)
Bwana Devil (Arch Oboler, 1952)
Cape Fear (J. Lee-Thompson, 1961)
Casablanca (Michael Curtiz, 1942)
Cat People (Jacques Tourneur, 1942)
Crime and Punishment (Josef von Sternberg, 1935)
Dead of Night (Cavalcanti et al, 1945)
Dr. Terror's House of Horrors (Freddie Francis, 1965)
Double Indemnity (Billy Wilder, 1944)
Double Jeopardy (Bruce Beresford, 1999)
Dracula (Tod Browning, 1931)
Dragonwyck (Joseph L. Mankiewicz, 1946)
Ed Wood (Tim Burton, 1994)
The Faculty (Robert Rodriguez, 1998)
Five (Arch Oboler, 1951)
The Five Thousand Fingers of Dr. T (Roy Rowland, 1953)
The Fly (Kurt Neumann, 1958)

Frankenstein (James Whale, 1931)
Groundhog Day (Harold Ramis, 1993)
The Haunting (Robert Wise, 1963)
House of Wax (André de Toth, 1953)
I Walked with a Zombie (Jacques Tourneur, 1943)
The Incredible Shrinking Man (Jack Arnold, 1957)
Kill Bill: Volume 2 (Quentin Tarantino, 2004)
Laura (Otto Preminger, 1946)
M (Fritz Lang, 1931)
Mad Love (Karl Freund, 1935)
The Maltese Falcon (John Huston, 1941)
Mr. Moto series (Norman Foster and others, 1937–39)
Night of the Living Dead (George A. Romero, 1968)
Peter Pan (Wilfred Jackson et al, 1953)
The Phantom Creeps (Ford Beebe and Saul Goodkind, 1939)
Phone (Byeong-hi Ahn, 2002)
Phone Booth (Joel Schumacher, 2002)
Picnic at Hanging Rock (Peter Weir, 1975)
The Postman Always Rings Twice (Tay Garnett, 1946)
Psycho (Alfred Hitchcock, 1960)
Scream (Wes Craven, 1997)
The Sixth Sense (M. Night Shyamalan, 1999)
Snow White and the Seven Dwarfs (Walt Disney, 1937)
Son of Frankenstein (Rowland V. Lee, 1939)
Sorry, Wrong Number (Anatole Litvak, 1948)
Tarantula (Jack Arnold, 1955)
The Texas Chainsaw Massacre (Tobe Hooper, 1974)
Theatre of Blood (Douglas Hickox, 1973)
The Thing (John Carpenter, 1982)
The Vanishing (George Sluizer, 1988)
The Vanishing (George Sluizer, 1993)
The Wizard of Oz (Victor Fleming, 1939)
X— the Man with X-Ray Eyes (Roger Corman, 1963)

Selected Websites

www.quietplease.org
www.radiospirits.com

Recorded Interviews

Dean, Don. Interview with Toby Grimmer (WJR, Detroit, July 6, 1978).
Dunham, Edwin. Unbroadcast interview with William N. Robson (April 27, 1967). Archives of the Library of American Broadcasting, University of Maryland.
Morgan, Bob. Unbroadcast interview with Himan Brown (April 9, 1984). Archives of the Library of American Broadcasting, University of Maryland.
Shaden, Chuck. Interview with Vincent Price (Chicago, 1971).

Personal Correspondence

Letters and/or emails to Richard J. Hand, 2003–05, were received from:
 Martin Grams, Jr.   David Kogan   David S. Siegel
 Corey Klemow   Michael Ross

Index

Numbers in ***bold italics*** represent pages with photographs.
Individual episodes or stories are to be found under the program
name (e.g., "Sorry Wrong Number" is under *Suspense*).

Abbot, Waldo 38–39, 41
Abbott, Bud 9, 53
The Abbott and Costello Show (radio program) 51, 56, 58
The Abominable Dr. Phibes (film) 65
Adams, Mason 137
adaptation, literary 45, 69, 72, 75, 76–77, 80
The Adventures of Ellery Queen (radio program) 146
The Adventures of Nero Wolfe (radio program) 118
The Adventures of the Thin Man (radio program) 118, 131
alchemy 100, 125
Alfred Hitchcock Presents (television program) 166
Alpen, Max 160–61
Les Amants (stage play) 25
Amazing Stories (magazine) 131
Amos n' Andy (radio program) 6, 58; "The Locked Trunk's Secret" 58
Anansi 156
Angel Street see *Gaslight*
animals as victims 128–29
Annie (film) 17
Antigone (Sophocles) 16
Appointment with Fear (radio program) 167
Arch Oboler's Drop Dead (recording) 36, 104
Arch Oboler's Plays (radio program) 84, 146; "Johnny Got His Gun" 19, 99, 100, 101, 102, 146, 150; "The Voice Within Me" 103
Arden, Eve 47
Are You a Genius? (radio program) 146
The Army Hour (radio program) 146
The Arnelo Affair (film) 103
Arsenic and Old Lace (stage play) 53, 55, 56
Arthur, Robert 1–2, 131–44
Astounding Science Fiction (magazine) 132
Au téléphone (stage play) 65, 66
Averback, Hy 64

"The Babysitter" (urban legend) 65
La Baiser dans la nuit (stage play) 96
Ball, Lucille 47–48, ***49***
Bannerman, R. LeRoy 86
Barnouw, Erik 8, 34, 35–36, 83, 85, 86, 99, 101, 102, 131
Barrett Browning, Elizabeth 110
Barrymore, Ethel 48
Bates, Norman 156
Bauche, Henri 167
Baughman, James L. 4
Baxter, Anne 108
The Beast with Five Fingers (film) 56, 140
beautiful horror (genre) 110–11, 116
Belton, John 45
Berton, René 77
Bewitched (film) 103
Bierce, Ambrose 75, 127, 141, 149
Bigwood, James 55, 56, 59
Binet, Alfred 112
"The Black Cat" (short story) 57
The Black Museum (radio program) 157
Blackwood, Algernon 32
The Blair Witch Project (film) 95
Blanc, Mel 113
Blanc, Shirley 142
Blithe Spirit (stage play) 142
The Blob (film) 88, 153
Bloch, Robert 10, 52, 156
Blue, Howard 100–1, 143, 164
Boardman-Jacobs, Sam 168
Boris Karloff's Treasure Chest 53
Brave New World (novel) 139
Brechner, Sidney 111
Brecht, Bertolt 56
British Broadcasting Corporation (BBC) 3, 9, 15, 167
Britton, Andrew 53

177

Brown, Himan 32, 36, 38, 58, 118–22, 124, 128–30, 164, 167
The Bubble (film) 104
Buhrmann, Albert 32, 33, 107, 132, 146, 151
Bulldog Drummond (radio program) 118, 131
Bulwer-Lytton, Edward 75
Buñuel, Luis 6
Burnett, Carol 17
Bwana Devil (film) 104

Cabana, Raymond G., Jr. 55, 56, 59
The Campbell Playhouse (radio program) 146
Canadian Broadcasting Corporation 167
Candid Microphone 51
Cannon 62
Cannon, Harriet 148
Cape Fear (film) 98
Carey, Macdonald 102
Carlile, John S. 41
Carnegie, Dale 94
Carpenter, Chris 140
Carpenter, Clifford 139
Carroll, Noël 10, 31, 155
Casablanca (film) 56
Casey, Crime Photographer (radio program) 81; "The Gentle Stranger" 81
Cat People (film) 73
Cathcart, Robert S. 46
The CBS Radio Mystery Theater (radio program) 118, 126, 129–30, 167; "The Tell-Tale Heart" 126
censorship 16, 18, 19, 20–21, 49–50, 81, 128–29, 130
Chaney, Lon, Jr. 130
Chappell, Ernest 36, 132, 145, 146–**47**, 148–61
The Chase and Sanborn Hour (radio program) 51
Le Château de la mort lente (stage play) 167
children as victims 128–29
"Clarimonde" (short story) 75
Cocoon (film) 100
Cole, Alonzo Deen 9, 10, 69–**70**, 71–82, 97, 132
Collier, John 61
A Comedy of Danger (radio play) 9
Comics Code Authority (CCA) 81, 164
Command Performance (radio program) 64
computer games 166
Connell, Richard 61
Connor, Herbert R. 107
Conrad, Joseph 25, 53
Conrad, William 19, 32, 61–62, 106, 107, 165
Conried, Hans 41, **45**, 47, 60, 61
Cooper, Emily 160
Cooper, Wyllis 9, 10, 14, 23, 28, 33, 83, 84, 86, 87, 88, 89, 102, 103, 119, 132, 145, 146–61, **146**, 165
Corman, Roger 65
Corwin, Norman 84, 85, 89, 101, 143, 161
Cosby, Bill 88
Costello, Lou 9, 53
Cotten, Joseph 47
Coward, Noël 142
Cowgill, Rome 39
Crane, Jonathan Lake 52
The Creaking Door (radio program) 120

creaking door (sound effect) 119–20, 130, 134–35, 141–42
Creed, Barbara 156
Creeps by Night (radio program) 4
Crime and Punishment (film) 57
Crime and Punishment (novel) 57
Crisell, Andrew 15, 36, 37, 50
Croft, Mary Jane 102
Crosby, Bing 6
Crosby, John 22, 49
The Croupier (radio program) 33, 64; "The Roman" 33, 64–65
The Cryptkeeper (television host) 165

Daisy Miller (novel) 93
Dann, Mike 165
Dante 111
Dark Destiny (radio program) 132
Dark Destiny (television program) 132
The Dark House (radio play) 167–68
"Dark Melody of Madness" (short story) 166
Darling and Dearie (radio program) 69
Davis, Joan 64
Dead of Night (film) 17, 126, 141
The Dean Martin and Jerry Lewis Show (radio program) 59
de Beil, Alphonse 51
Dehner, John 106
Deliverance (novel) 94, 96
DeLong, Thomas A. 106
de Lorde, André 65, 66, 112, 167
DeMarco, Norman 119
DeMille, Cecil B. 37
Detective Fiction Weekly (magazine) 131
The Devil and Mr. O (radio program) 83, 91, 94, 97; "Alley Cat" 97; "Going Down" 91; "Gravestone" 94; "Paris Macabre" 94
Devitt, Alan 41, **46**, 70
Dickey, James 94, 96
Dime Mystery Magazine (magazine) 166
Dinelli, Mel 48
Dirda, Michael 75
disembodied voice 21–22, 65, 77, 95, 113, 125, 137, 156
Dixon, Peter 20
Doane, Mary Anne 21
Dr. Terror's House of Horrors (film) 166
Dr. Weird (host) 131, 140
Dostoevsky 57
Double Indemnity (film) 148
Double Jeopardy (film) 15
douche écossaise (stage technique) 24
Douglas, Susan 7
Dracula (film) 50
Dracula (novel) 3, 13, 50, 77, 150, 151
Dragnet (radio program) 149
Dragonwyck (film) 62
Duffy's Tavern (radio program) 59; "The Missing Salami Sandwich" 59
Dunkel, John 166
Dunning, John 3, 7, 21, 32, 35, 55, 60, 66, 69, 81, 84,

85, 89, 97, 101, 101–2, 102, 104, 106, 106–7, 111, 116, 119, 120, 129, 131, 132, 140, 142, 147, 150, 152, 157

Eastman, Carl 159
EC Comics 81, 82, 163–64, 167
Ed Wood (film) 26
The Edgar Allan Poe Award 119, 143
The Edgar Bergen and Charlie McCarthy Show (radio program) 86
Ellery Queen's Minute Mysteries (radio program) 143
Elliott, Geraldine 106
Ellis, Anthony 61
Ellstrom, Sidney 35, 41
The Emperor Jones (stage play) 53
Epic theatre 58
Eric, Elspeth **121**
Escape (radio program) 17, 32, 61, 62, 63, 139; "Bloodbath" 63; "Confession" 32; "Evening Primrose" 61; "Leiningen Versus the Ants" 139; "The Most Dangerous Game" 61; "Papa Benjamin" 166; "Present Tense" 17, 63; "A Study in Wax" 61; "Three Skeleton Key" 63–64, 65
The Evangelist (periodical) 86
Evans, Elwyn 13
"Evening Primrose" (story) 61
"The Evil Eye" (extract of stage play) 51
Existentialism 148

The Faculty (film) 166
Fadiman, Clifton 53
Fantasies from Lights Out (radio program) 83
Fear on Four (radio program) 167
Federal Communications Commission (FCC) 19, 129
femme castratice 156
femme fatale 18, 122, 156
film noir 9, 10, 21, 53, 62, 89, 122, 138, 148
Fitz-Allen, Adelaide 70
Five (film) 103–4
The Five Thousand Fingers of Dr. T (film) 60
The Fleischmann Hour (radio program) 55
Fletcher, Lucille 33, 63, 65, 66, 127, 141
The Fly (film) 63
Foleÿ, Charles 65, 66
The Food of the Gods (novel) 89, 153
Forbes, Murray 151
Forman, Bill 106
Foster, John 111
Four for the Fifth (radio program) 101; "Surrender" 101
Franck, Cesar 32, 33, 147
Frankenstein (film) 16, 26, 43, 51, 53, 76
Frankenstein (novel) 10, 75, 76, 111, 112, 113
Frees, Paul 60, 61
Futuristics (radio play) 85, 86

Gabel, Martin 128
Gang Busters (radio program) 49–50, 81
Garland, Judy 44, 48
Gaslight (stage play) 108, 109, 126

Gautier, Théophile 75
Gein, Ed 97
Gerson, Betty Lou 127
Ghoulardi (TV host) 26, 82
Gifford, Denis 55
Gilman, Charlotte Perkins 32, 108, 128
Goebbels, Joseph 100
The Goldbergs (radio program) 118
Golem 155
Gothic 3, 21, 25, 62, 64, 75, 92, 93, 95, 96, 110, 114, 115, 116, 124, 128, 155
Grams, Martin, Jr. 9, 19, 21, 26, 34, 35, 37, 52, 67, 88, 94–95, 118, 118–19, 119–20, 122, 128, 129, 130
Grand-Guignol 24, 25, 50–51, 77, 93, 96, 112, 116–17, 167
Grimmer, Toby 106
Groundhog Day (film) 141
The Gumps (radio program) 118
Gunsmoke (radio program) 62, 106
Gunsmoke (television program) 165

Haines, Larry 141
The Hall of Fantasy (radio program) 4, 26, 57, 125–26; "Shadow People" 57; "The Tell-Tale Heart" 125–26
Halper, Donna L. 5
Hamilton, Margaret 71
Hamilton, Patrick 108, 109, 126
Hand, Richard J. 65, 112
Hardwicke, Cedric 108
Harmon, Jim 4, 8, 14, 17, 31, 32–33, 37, 125, 129, 165
Harmon Coxe, George 81
The Haunting (film) 14
The Haunting Hour (radio program) 4
Hauser, Dwight 111
Have Gun, Will Travel (radio program) 106
Hawthorne, Nathaniel 130
Hayworth, Rita 41, **45**, 60–61
Heart of Darkness (novel) 25
Henry IV Part One (stage play) 150
The Hermit (radio host) 106, 107, 110, 112, 113–14, 117, 120
The Hermit's Cave (radio program) 11, 26, 61, 106–17; "The Mystery of the Thing" 108–10; "Notebook on Murder" 107–9; "The Search for Life" 111–13, 114; "Spirit Vengeance" 113–14; "The Story Without End" 110–11; "The Vampire's Desire" 114–16
Herrmann, Bernard 32
Heyes, Douglas 67
Hiablum, Isidore 107
Hilliard, Robert L. 8
Hilmes, Michele 3, 7, 20, 21–22
Hindenburg (airship) 6
The History of Mr. Polly (novel) 53
Hitchcock, Alfred 132, 143, 156, 160–61
Hitler, Adolf 7, 100, 101, 133
Holland, Charlotte 127
Hollywood Fights Back (radio program) 59
Hollywood on the Air (radio program) 51

Holmes, Sherlock 43
L'Homme qui a tué la mort (stage play) 77
The Honeymooners (vaudeville routine) 69
"The Horla" (short story) 57, 109
L'Horrible Expérience (stage play) 112
horror comics 81, 82, 163–64, 165, 166, 167
Host (*Inner Sanctum Mysteries* radio program) 26, 31, 120, 167
hosts, comic book 165–67
hosts, radio 9, 23–31, 53, 58, 60–61, 69, 76, 78, 79, 81, 82, 88, 106, 107, 110, 112, 113–14, 117, 119, 120, 131, 140, 165–67
hosts, television 165–66
House of Wax (film) 62
Household Magazine (magazine) 132
Houseman, John 6, 8, 146
How to Win Friends and Influence People (book) 94
Howlett, Eric 106
Hughes, Paul 106
Hughes, Richard 9
Huis Clos (stage play) 148–49
Huston, Lou 107
Huxley, Aldous 139

I Love a Mystery (radio program) 17–18, 26, 33
I Walked with a Zombie (film) 17
I Was a Communist for the FBI (radio program) 21
Ibsen, Henrik 6
The Illustrated Detective Magazine (magazine) 131
I'm Really Here (stage play) 93–94
The Incredible Shrinking Man (film) 153
Information Please (radio program) 53–54
Inner Sanctum Mysteries (book series) 119
Inner Sanctum Mysteries (film series) 130
Inner Sanctum Mysteries (radio program) 4, 11, 24, 25, 26, 28, 30, 31, 32, 37, 52, 57, 58, 67, 82, 104, 118–30, 134, 141, 165, 167; "The Black Seagull" 24, 30; "The Candlestick Murders" 129; "The Corpse Nobody Loved" 127; "The Corridor of Doom" 122–23, 126–27; "The Creeping Wall" 126; "The Dead Walk at Night" 126; "The Deadly Dummy" 126; "Death Across the Board" 123–24; "Elixir Number Four" 125; "The Horla" 57; "The Judas Clock" 124–25; "The Listener" 67; "The Lonely Sleep" 26; "Murder in the Museum" 129; "Skeleton Bay" 127–28; "Strange Passenger" 127; "The Tell-Tale Heart" 126; "The Undead" 124; "The Voice on the Wire" 125
Inner Sanctum Mysteries (television program) 130, 165
The Invisible Man (novel) 100
Irish, William 166

The Jack Benny Program (radio program) 54; "The Fiddler" 54
Jackson, Michael 65
Jacobs, W.W. 150, 151
James, Henry 25, 93, 128, 130
James, M.R. 25, 79
Jensen, Paul M. 52

Johnny Got His Gun (novel) 99
Johnson, Laurence 164
Johnson, Mel 106, 107
Johnson, Raymond Edward **24**, 120
Johnstone, Ted 106
Jones, Jeffrey 26
Jones, Spike 54, 60
Joyce, James 89
"The Judge's House" (short story) 80

Karloff, Boris 10, 16, 43, 50, 51–**54**, 55, 62, 63, 65, 76, 96, 102, 118, 120, 123, 126
Kay Kyser's Kollege of Musical Knowledge (radio program) 51
Keith, Michael C. 104, 118
Kelley, Welbourn E. 143
Kelly, Gene 48
Kent, John 106
Kill Bill: Volume 2 (film) 15
King, Stephen 14, 22, 88, 103, 104–5, 120, 130, 166
Kingson, Walter Krulevitch 39
Kinoy, Ernest 18
Klein, Adelaide 137
Klemow, Corey 14
Koch, Howard 6, 8
Kogan, David 1–2, 131–44, 164
Koury, Rex 107
kraken 153, 154
Kristeva, Julia 156

Lamour, Dorothy 55
Laura (film) 62
La Verne, Lucille 71
Lawes, Lewis E. 53, **54**
Le Fanu, J. Sheridan 136
Leginski 82
Lehman, Peter 14, 15, 34
Lem, Stanislaw 18
LeMond, Bob 28
Leroux, Gaston 92, 93
Let's Pretend (radio program) 70
Level, Maurice 96, 126
Lewis, Cathy 135
Lights Out (radio program) 2, 9, 10, 11, 14, 15, 16, 17, 18, 19, 20, 27, 28, 29, 32, 34, 35–36, 41, 50, 52, 65, 81, 83–105, 106, 145, 146, 149, 150, 153, 165, 166, 167; "Amoeba" 86, 88, 153; "And Adam Begot" 103; "The Author and the Thing" 87–88; "The Ball" 91, 94; "Bon Voyage" 28, 91; "Burial Services" 15–16, 85–86, 99; "Cat Wife" 29, 52, 97; "Chicken Heart" 9, 88, 91, 104, 138, 153; "Coffin in Studio B" 87, 89; "The Dark" 35–36; "Death Robbery" 52, 89; "The Dream" 52; "The Flame" 27; "Gevangenpoort" 91; "Happy Ending" 90; "He Dug It Up" 133; "The Hounds of Weir" 97–99; "It Happened" 16, 89, 91, 91–94, 97; "Knock at the Door" 136–37; "Little Old Lady" 97; "Man in the Middle" 89; "Meteor Man" 101; "Murder in the Script Department" 87; "Neanderthal" 91; "Nobody Died" 99–100; "#90" 86–87, 88; "Organ" 18; "Poltergeist" 28,

94–95, 104; "Revolt of the Worms" 88, 91, 166; "Scoop" 17, 19, 91; "Speed" 100; "Spider" 89, 153, 167; "State Executioner" 89–90; "Story of Mr. Maggs" 137, 167; "Subbasement" 91, 166; "The Thirteenth Corpse" 91; "Valse Triste" 16, 29, 96–97, 101, 142, 166
Lights Out (television program) 84, 103, 165, 166
Lindbergh, Charles 46
Lindsay, Cynthia 51, 53
Listen! (radio program) 159
The Little Theater of the Air 116
Lloyd, Ted 159
The Lone Ranger (radio program) 106
Lord, Phillips H. 49–50
Lorre, Peter 47, 48, 50, 51, 55–60, 62, 63, 65, 118, 120, *121*, 140, 145
Louis, Joe 6
Lovecraft, H.P. 10, 155
Lugosi, Bela 50–51, 56, 62, 145
Luhr, William 14, 15, 34
Lukas, Paul 120
Lumke, Connie 137
Lupino, Ida 64
Lux Radio Theatre (radio program) 44–45, 46

M (film) 48, 56, 56–57
Macbeth (stage play) 64–65, 81–82, 137
Mack, Nick 70
MacLeish, Archibald 101
Mad Love (film) 56
The Maltese Falcon (film) 56
Maltin, Leonard 6, 19, 35, 60
Mamet, David 156
The Man in Black (radio host) 82, 167
The Man in Black (radio program) 167
Martin, Frank 19
Mary (radio host) 30–31
"The Masque of the Red Death" (short story) 94
Massey, Raymond 123
Maupassant, Guy de 57, 109
McCambridge, Mercedes 92
McCarthy, Clem 6
McCarthyism 59, 143, 163–64
McCracken, Allison 21, 21–2, 47, 65, 73, 118, 120, 122, 123, 125, 136
McGrath, Paul 26, 31, 120, 167
McIntosh, J.T. 18
McLeish, Robert 32
Medusa 155
Meet the Murderer! (book) 53
melodrama 25, 28, 33, 39, 43, 51, 63, 65, 66, 69, 72, 76, 78, 82, 90, 91, 92, 93, 95, 96, 97, 98, 99, 101, 104, 108, 109, 119, 124, 127, 137, 138, 140, 151, 162
The Mercury Theater on the Air (radio program) 1, 6–9, 13, 15, 20, 28, 32, 41, *47*, 65, 77, 138, 146; "Dracula" 3, 13, 77; "The Hitch-Hiker" 15; "War of the Worlds" 1, 6–9, 20, 21, 28, 51, 65, 77, 138
Meredith, Burgess 143
Mérimée, Prosper 75–76
Méténier, Oscar 25

Meyrowitz, Joshua 50
Milland, Ray 49, 140
Mirbeau, Octave 25
Mr. Moto (film series) 56, 145
Mitchell, Les 59
modernism 25, 52, 89–90, 91, 93, 99
Mollé Mystery Theater (radio program) 4
"The Monkey's Paw" (short story) 150, 151
Moorehead, Agnes 39, *40*, 41, *42*, 45, 48, 65–68, 118
Morgan, Claudia 148
Morgan, Harry 57
Morgan, Ralph 148
Morrison, Herbert 6
Morse, Carleton E. 17–18
Morton, David 5–6
Morwood, Bill 160
"The Most Dangerous Game" (short story) 61
mothers-in-law 136–37
Mott, Robert L. 34
"Mountain Lullaby" (song) 54
The Mummers (acting ensemble) 106, 116
Murder by Experts (radio program) 132; "Conspiracy" 132; "Dig Your Own Grave" 132
Murray, Mathew 19
music 6, 7, 8, 9, 23, 32–34, 37, 107, 108, 122, 124, 140, 151
Mussorgsky 32
"My Old Flame" (song) 60
The Mysterious Traveller (radio program) 1, 11, 16, 73, 130, 131–44, 164, 167; "Behind the Locked Door" 16, 130, 131, 132, 133–35, 138, "The Case of Charles Foster" 138; "Change of Address" 138; "Christmas Story" 138; "Death at Fifty Fathoms" 133; "Death Comes to Adolph Hitler" 133; "Death Has a Thousand Faces" 137–38; "Fire in the Sky" 138; "The Good Die Young" 138; "The Green Plague" 138; "The Haunted Trailer" 141–42; "The Man the Insects Hated"; 138–39; "The Man Who Knew Everything" 138; "Murder in 2952" 139–40; "New Year's Nightmare" 16, 141; "No One on the Line" 138; "Strange New World" 139; "The Stranger in the House" 135, 136; "Survival of the Fittest" 138; "Visiting Corpse" 136–37, 167
The Mysterious Traveller Magazine (magazine) 143
Mystery House (radio program) 50–51; "Thirsty Death" 51
Mystery in the Air (radio program) 4, 55–58, 60, 65; "The Black Cat" 57; "Crime and Punishment" 57; "The Horla" 57; "The Tell-Tale Heart" 57
Mystery Playhouse (radio program) 31; "Two Men in a Furnished Room" 31
Mystery Time (radio program) 143

Nachman, Gerald 7, 85, 164, 167
Naremore, James 8
National Association of Broadcasters (NAB) 20–21, 162, **163**
National Association of Supermarkets 164

Nazimova, Alla **48**, 102
Neill, John 31
Newman, Kim 3
Newman, Robert 123, 126
Nick Carter, Master Detective (radio program) 132
"Night and Silence" (short story) 126
Night Gallery (television program) 26, 165
Night of the Living Dead (film) 16, 17
Night on Bald Mountain (music by Mussorgsky) 32
Nightfall (radio program) 126, 167; "The Tell-Tale Heart" 126
Nightmare (radio program) 4, 58
Nollen, S.A. 51

Oboler, Arch 2, 5, 9, 13, 15, 16, 17, 19, 27, 28, 29, 30, 34, 35, 36, 41, 51–52, 58, 82, 83, 84–86, 87–88, 89–105, 132, 137, 146, 150, 161, 166, 167
The Oboler Comedy Theater (television program) 103
Oboler Omnibus (book) 100, 145
"An Occurrence at Owl Creek Bridge" (story) 75, 127, 141, 149
Odets, Clifford 90
O'Flynn, Marie 69, 70
Old Nancy (radio host) 9, 24–25, 39–41, 69, 76, 78, 79, 81, 82, 107, 120
O'Neill Eugene 53
"Orgie and the Spirits" (music by Leginski) 82
Ortega, Santos 126
Our Town (Thornton Wilder) 25
The Outer Limits (television program) 166
The Ozzie and Harriet Show (radio program) 51

Parade (magazine) 132
Parish, James Robert 63
Parker, Rolon 106
Payton, Gordon 129–30
Pells, Richard H. 21
Penman, Charles 106
Peter Pan (J.M. Barrie) 53–54, 60
The Phantom Creeps (film) 145
The Phantom of the Opera (novel) 92, 93
Philco Radio Time (radio program) 6
Phone (film) 68
Phone Booth (film) 68
Picnic at Hanging Rock (film) 95
Piscator, Erwin 56
The Player (radio program) 60
Poe, Edgar Allan 3, 16, 32, 57, 65, 94, 99, 125–26, 127, 128, 130
Polidori, John William 75
The Postman Always Rings Twice (film) 148
post-modernism 132, 142
Prairie du Chien (radio play) 156
Price, Victoria 62–63, 164
Price, Vincent 13, 17, 31, 33, 47, 58, **62**–65, 108, 120, 164, 165, 167
The Price of Fear (radio program) 167
Psycho (film) 97, 156
Psycho (novel) 156

Quiet, Please (radio program) 7, 9, 10, 11, 14, 23, 32, 33, 34, 36, 84, 87, 110, 111, 132, 135, 136, 141, 145–61, 166; "And Jeannie Dreams of Me" 111; "Anonymous" 148; "Be a Good Dog, Darling" 150; "Beezer's Cellar" 142, 149; "Berlin 1945" 148, 159; "Bring Me to Life" 157; "Gem of the Purest Ray" 149; "Good Ghost" 147, 148; "The Hat, the Bed and John J. Catherine" 152; "In Memory of Bernadine" 111; "In the House Where I Was Born" 111, 149–50; "It Is Later Than You Think" 150; "Let the Lilies Consider" 149; "Little Fellow" 147; "The Man Who Stole a Planet" 149; "A Mile High, a Mile Deep" 154; "My Son John" 124, 147, 150–51; "Never Send to Know" 152; "Nothing Behind the Door" 149; "The Oldest Man in the World" 136, 154; "One Hundred Thousand Diameters" 152–53, 155; "Pathetic Fallacy" 148, 152; "Quiet, Please" 149; "Rede Me This Riddle" 148; "Shadow of the Wings" 147; "Symphony in D Minor" 33–34; "Take Me Out to the Graveyard" 149; "Tanglefoot" 153; "Tap the Heat, Bogdan" 146; "The Thing on the Fourble Board" 14, 16, 130, 135, 148, 152, 153–57, 166; "Thirteen and Eight" 147; "Three Sides to a Story" 148–49, 151; "Twelve to Five" 7; "Whence Came You" 133, 151–52; "Where Do You Get Your Ideas?" 87, 132, 146, 157

Radio Writers Guild 143
Une rage d'amour (stage play) 51
Rains, Claude 120
Raymond (radio host) 24, **25**, 26, 30, 82, 120, 134–35
Red Channels (book) 143, 164
Reid, Elliot 64
Resident Evil (video game) 116
Rice, Herbert C. 159
Richards, G.A. 106
Robinson, Edward G. 143
Robson, William N. 13, 165
rock and roll 163
Roeburt, John 119
Roosevelt, Franklin D. 6, 20, 90
Ross, Michael 39
Roy, Cecil 157
Rubin, Martin 10
The Rudy Vallee Show (radio program) 55
Ryder, Klock 106

The Saint (radio program) **62**, 63
Sammis, Fred R. 84–85
Sartre, Jean-Paul 148–49
Satan the Cat (radio host) 70, 71
Saunders, Bill 106
Schmeling, Max 6
Schneidman, Seymour 159–60
Schoenberg, Arnold 6
science fiction 4, 8, 10, 15, 21, 74, 91, 99, 100, 104, 131, 133, 138, 139, 140, 149, 152, 153
Scream (film) 68
The Sealed Book (radio program) 27, 32, 131, 132,

140, 141; "Broadway Here I Come" 140–41; "Design for Death" 142; "The Hands of Death" 27, 140; "King of the World" 140
The Sealtest Variety Hour (radio program) 55; "Halloween Special" 55; "The Stranger Arrives" 55
Sennitt, Stephen 81, 166
Serling, Rod 26, 61, 165, 167
sex and sexuality 16, 21, 33, 86, 96, 98, 101, 122–23, 128, 135, 136, 137, 141, 142, 149, 150, 156
The Shadow (magazine) 131
The Shadow (radio program) 1, 10, 41–43, 81, 104, 131, 162–63; "The Gibbering Things" 10; "When the Grave Is Open" 162, **163**
Shakespeare, William 9, 64–5, 81–2, 137, 139, 150, 152, 159
Shay, Dorothy 54
Shepherd, Ann 135
Shilling Shocker (genre of fiction) 95, 116
Shingler, Martin 14, 32, 33
Siegel, David S. 69, 70, 71, 72, 78, 80, 81, 82
Silent Hill (video game) 116
Sinatra, Frank 41, **44**, 48
Sinclair, May 149
The Sixth Sense (film) 149
Skippy Hollywood Theater (radio program) 58–59; "Mr. God Johnson" 59
Sleep No More (radio program) 4
Slide, Anthony 6
Sloane, Everett 126
Smith, Mark 41, **46**, 70
Snow White and the Seven Dwarves (film) 71
Solaris (film) 18
Solaris (novel) 18
Son of Frankenstein (film) 145
Sorry, Wrong Number (film) 65
sound effects 6, 8, 14, 15, 18, 22, 32–33, 34–36, 37, 111, 112, 113, 122, 124, 133–34, 141–42, 145
Space Patrol (radio program) 107
Spellerburg, James 45
spider 156
Spier, William **42**, 66
Spotlight Revue (radio program) 54, 60
Stage 13 (television program) 157
Standard Brands Radio Hour (radio program) 62
"Stardust" (song) 127
Starring Boris Karloff (radio and television program) 53, 165
Stay Tuned for Terror (radio program) 10, 52
Stedman, Raymond William 17–18, 20, 33
Stephens, Warren 150
Sterling, Christopher H. 104, 118
Stevens, James 141
Stevenson, Robert Louis 130
Stoker, Bram 3, 13, 50, 77, 80, 150, 151
storytelling 63, 147, 156
The Strange Doctor Weird (radio program) 131, 140, 142–43, 167; "Beauty and the Beast" 142–43; "The Devil's Cavern" 133–34; "The House Where Death Lived" 142; "The Man Who Lived Twice" 140; "The Secret Room" 142; "Tiger Cat" 143; "White Pearls of Terror" 167

"Strange Event in the Life of Schalken the Painter" (short story) 136
Subotsky, Milton 166
Sudrow, Lyle 134
Surrey, Berne 66
Suspense (radio program) 10, 13, 15, 21, 32, 46–49, 55, 60–61, 62, 63, 82, 132, 165, 167; "Dime a Dance" 47–48; "The Doctor Prescribes Death" 51; "Drive In" 48; "The Dunwich Horror" 10; "Fugue in C-Minor" 33, 63; "Green Splotches" 149; "The Hitch-Hiker" 15, 127, 141; "The House on Cypress Canyon" 73, 74, 124, 135–36, 141, 150; "Night Cry" 49; "Nobody Loves Me" 55; "On a Country Road" 15; "Present Tense" 17; "Sorry, Wrong Number" 39, 65–68, 130; "A Study in Wax" 61; "Three Times Murder" 45, 60; "To Find Help" 44, 48, 66; "The Waxwork" 13
Suspense (television program) 165
Sutter, Dan 154
Symphony in D Minor (music by Cesar Franck) 147

Tales from the Crypt (comic): "A Rottin' Trick" 167; "Sucker for a Spider" 167; "Tight Grip" 167
Tales from the Crypt (television program) 82, 165
Tales of Tomorrow (television program) 159
Tarantula (film) 153
Tarplin, Maurice 131, 142
Tasmanian Devil (cartoon character) 113
Taylor, Davidson 146
Taylor, Robert 135
television, rise of 102, 102–3, 130, 158, 161, 164–65
"The Tell-Tale Heart" (short story) 3, 32, 51, 52, 57, 125–26, 127
The Tempest (stage play) 139
Tepperman, Emile C. 127
Texaco Star Theater (radio program) 103; "Alter Ego" 103
The Texas Chainsaw Massacre (film) 97, 166
Theater Five (radio program) 167
Theater Guild on the Air (radio program) 53
Theater of Blood (film) 65
Theater of Romance (radio program) 107
The Thing (film) 156, 166
Thorne, Richard 125–26
three-dimensional movies 104
The Three Investigators (book series) 144
"Thriller" (song) 65
The Time Machine (novel) 25, 134, 135
Tollin, Anthony 132
Toudouze, George Gustave 64
Tremors (film) 88
Trumbo, Dalton 99
Turn of the Screw (novel) 25, 128, 130
The Twelfth Night (radio version of stage play) 9
The Twilight Zone (television program) 26, 61, 67, 165, 166; "The After Hours" 61; "The Invaders" 67

Underwood, Peter 52
The Unexpected (radio program) 143, 160
Universal Pictures 9, 16, 43, 50, 51, 69, 76, 130, 145

Unknown Worlds (magazine) 131
urban legends 65–66, 95
vagina dentata 156
Vallee, Rudy 62
Vallee Varieties (radio program) 86
Vampira (television host) 26, 82, 165
The Vampyre (novel) 75
van Horne, Harriet 5, 59
The Vanishing (film) 15
The Vanishing Point (radio program) 167
van Itallie, Jean-Claude 93–94
van Sloan, Edward 26
vaudeville 69, 162
"The Venus of Ille" (short story) 75–76
Verne, Jules 152
Volume One (television program) 157, 161

Waiting for Lefty (stage play) 90
Walters, Mike 167
Wanamaker, Sam 31
Webber, Peggy 57
Weigl, Charles 10
The Weird Circle (radio program) 4, 26, 57, 77, 125, 136; "The Horla" 57; "The Tell-Tale Heart" 125; "The Wooden Ghost" 136
Weird Tales (magazine) 132, 133
Welles, Orson 1, 6–9, 13, 13–14, 32, 35, 37, 41, *47*, 65, 69, 77, 84, 101, 119, 127, 146, 161, 164
Wells, H.G. 1, 6–9, 25, 53, 89, 100, 125, 134, 135, 153
West, Mae 86
Whalen, Geoff 98–99
"Where Their Fire Is Not Quenched" (short story) 149
The Whistler (radio program) 54, 106, 159
White, Lew 122
Whitehall 1212 (radio program) 157
Whitney, Steven 63
Widmark, Richard 125

Wieringa, Cindy 14, 32, 33
Wilson, Michael 65–66, 112
Wise, Robert 38
Witches Tales (comic) 81
The Witch's Tale (radio program) 4, 9, 11, 24, 27, 61, 69–82, 106, 107, 140, 166; "The Altar" 77–79; "The Altar of Hate" 77–79; "The Bronze Venus" 75–76; "Clarimonde" 75; "The Deserter" 75; "Doctor Jekyll and Mister Hyde" 75; "The Entomologist" 74–75; 89; "The Evil Eye" 75; "The Flying Dutchman" 75; "Frankenstein" 75, 76; "The Golem" 75; "Hangman's Roost" 79–81, 91; "The Happy Ending" 90; "The House of the Gargoyles" 81; "The Image" 73–74; "The Jettatore" 75; "The Lord of the Jungle" 72–73, 74; "Mrs. Hawker's Will" 71; "The Physician to the Dead" 77; "The Queer House" 69; "The Vampyre" 75; "Zanoni" 75
The Witch's Tale (television program) 81
The Wizard of Oz (film) 44, 71
Wolfe, Miriam 39–41, *43*, 70, 78, 107
Wonder Stories (magazine) 131
Woods, Lesley 35
Woolf, Virginia 89
Woolrich, Cornell 166
Wylie, Max 123, 124

X— The Man with X-Ray Eyes (film) 140
X-Minus One (radio program) 18; "Hallucination Orbit" 18

The Yellow Wallpaper (novel) 32, 108, 128
Yellowjacket (comic) 81
Youngkin, Steven D. 55, 56, 59

Zanoni (novel) 75
Zerbe, Lawson 139
The Zero Hour (radio program) 167
Zicree, Marc Scott 61

www.ingramcontent.com/pod-product-compliance
Ingram Content Group UK Ltd.
Pitfield, Milton Keynes, MK11 3LW, UK
UKHW050523150426
5217IPUK00026B/1776